THE FALL OF THE RUSSIAN EMPIRE

By the Same Author

(*In preparation*)

THE SOVIET STATE

THE BIOGRAPHY OF AN IDEA

RASPUTIN

" *Then I saw his eyes, deeply set, of a steely gray color; there was something heavy about them; when they looked at you, you felt a material pressure and it was impossible to look into them for any length of time. . . . A Russian peasant with long hair and uncouth beard, but what a face, all cut up with lines and ridges, full of bumps and hollows. He plays with the hairs of the beard in his accustomed manner. The hand is gnarled, full of savage force, and the fingers could be talons.*"

AUGUR (V. POLIAKOFF)

THE FALL OF
THE RUSSIAN EMPIRE

THE STORY OF THE
LAST OF THE ROMANOVS AND THE
COMING OF THE BOLSHEVIKI

BY

EDMUND A. WALSH, S.J., Ph.D.

Vice President, Georgetown University
Regent, School of Foreign Service

FOREWORD

THIS is not a formal history of Russia; it is the story of the triumph of folly in Russia and the penalty she paid for that historic madness. Neither is this narrative an apotheosis of the Russian Revolution after the manner of Thomas Carlyle. Least of all should it be interpreted as a smug indictment of Bolshevist theory and practice; the patent excesses in both, though not intelligent, are intelligible. In such a tempestuous riot of unchained passions, the worst that human nature can produce rose to the surface — "red scum, white scum." But this retrospect does seek to portray, without retouching, certain outstanding personalities and major events in the hope of supplying the perspective and understanding which becomes indispensable if one hopes to avoid the common errors fostered by propagandists, paid or unpaid, and correct the fallacies of loose thinking and still looser talking indulged in by the pamphleteers.

For the man in the street, the basic and intensely human issues, as well as the serious international problems arising out of that tremendous upheaval, have been systematically obscured or hidden entirely from view. On these momentous times, men, and events, later ages alone can pronounce the final verdict. But contemporary observers can contribute something useful to their day and generation by recording faithfully what they saw, heard, and learned.

The author is aware that no man who sets his name to opinions on Russia can expect to escape the censure which Madelin foresaw for himself in the preface to his study of the French Revolution — to be flayed by every hand, a Ghibelline to the Guelphs, a Guelph to the Ghibellines. But no

man can reasonably expect to escape that fate who owes
allegiance to those two exacting masters, Truth and Justice.
Wherever possible I have let the leading characters tell
their story in their own words, in the belief that we shall
come thereby to a surer understanding of the secret prejudices, the controlling emotions, and predominant passions
that so often displace pure reason as mainsprings of action.
The last Tzar of All the Russias, far from being exempt
from the psychological idiosyncrasies that influence men's
judgments, was notoriously subject to them. The shadow
of a domestic tragedy lay across his latter years and clouded
his reasoning powers. A baby's fingers had been tugging
at his heartstrings for a decade, and the image of the
Empress, battling for her boy's dynastic rights, held first
place at every Council of the Empire.

There usually comes a moment in the conscious development of every human soul when some serious choice, or
important decision, or difficult renunciation must be made,
and made irrevocably. On that decision frequently depend
the lives and fortunes of numerous other human beings —
as happens in the case of the engineer of a fast express who
discerns, dimly, but not surely, some danger signal set against
him; or in the case of the navigator of an ocean liner adrift
in a dangerous sea with a broken rudder. Such a moment
came to Russia's supreme ruler in the Spring of 1917. His
decision affected 180,000,000 people.

Now, the instinctive, instantaneous reaction of the alert
engineer as he reaches for the emergency brake, or the
motions of a seasoned pilot as he endeavors to head his ship
into the teeth of the storm instead of exposing his craft
broadside to the fury of the waves, are not isolated, unrelated
facts bearing no reference to previous training and habitual
modes of action. Such coördination of sense perception,
judgment, and manual execution is not the child of chance
nor the unfailing perquisite of genius. It is the hard-won

achievement of mental discipline. Men wise in the ways of human nature tell us, too, that there are few real accidents in the moral order, though there are many tragedies.

It was no stern necessity of war, nor gigantic despair, nor sudden conjunction of overpowering circumstances that drove Nicholas II into the course of action that wrecked his Empire and provoked the Revolution. His every decision and blunder was a palpable, traceable resultant of previous habits acquired with fatal facility. He lived in the grip of a hidden fear which, because it met him every morning at breakfast, dogged him through his hours of domestic privacy, and slept nearby in the nursery at night, had become inescapable and tyrannous. The elimination of Romanov rule, though inevitable in the long run and a political necessity if the Russian people were to survive, was measurably hastened by a little prince's inherited weakness of physique and his tendency to bleed at the nose or fall into painful convulsions at the slightest bruising of his sensitive skin. Had her son not been a chronic hæmophilic, had she not been an abnormal hypochondriac, the Empress Alexandra might not have been the innocent tool for Rasputin's machinations, Russia might have been spared the scourges that came upon her, and the world might not have known the challenge of Bolshevism — at least not so soon. What men too frequently overlook in chronicling the causes of stirring historic events is the essential humanity of kings and queens and the influence exerted by relatively petty factors on the destiny of states and peoples. Had Anne Boleyn been less comely, Henry VIII might never have repudiated Katherine of Aragon ; there might have been no Spanish Armada, no schism, nor religious wars in England. A diamond necklace and a woman's vanity can never be disassociated from the inner history of the French Revolution and the hecatombs of heads that fell into its baskets. Neither can a withered arm be considered irrelevant by investigators of the rôle played by the German Kaiser in modern times.

That physical deformity, giving rise, during boyhood, to an inferiority complex in the last of the Hohenzollerns, stimulated a conscious — and legitimate — passion to overcome the handicap. The paralyzed hand was trained to rest in a natural way on the sword-hilt hanging at the Kaiser's left side; the feel and rattle of the ever-present sabre became part of its wearer's nature and was a necessary adjunct of every photograph depicting Wilhelm in his favorite histrionic attitude. The fixed idea of personal majesty triumphing over physical limitations became a permanent obsession which transformed itself, eventually, into a political nervosity that unsettled Middle Europe from Berlin to Bagdad and would be satisfied with nothing short of a prominent place somewhere in the sun.

The notes, personal experiences, inquiries, and subsequent research upon which this book is based began on the night when the author first crossed the Russian frontier at Sebesh, between Latvia and Soviet Russia, March 21, 1922. The Russian people, at that moment, were passing through the well-nigh mortal travail of the most appalling famine in their long and stormy history. Twenty-three million human beings were threatened with extermination by inevitable starvation, and their cry for help had been answered generously by Europe and America. Six millions succumbed, — despite the heroic efforts of combined relief agencies, — making the valley of the Volga a huge graveyard, and turning the river itself into a charnel house with thousands upon thousands of skeletonized corpses congealed beneath the ice.

Men spoke of "going in" and "coming out" of that mystery-laden land as they might speak of entering a first-line trench or a sick chamber. For three days the train rumbled and lurched eastward from Riga, crawling laboriously onward in the teeth of freezing cold that cut the cheeks like a razor. The engine, through lack of coal, burned only wood, showering weird geysers of sparks and flaming splinters on to the snow fields that stretched like visible, tangible desolation on all sides. There were no lights in the compartments, save the sputtering flicker of tallow candles, carefully husbanded. As no food was available on board, each man brought his own rations and water, which he prepared over an alcohol flame or on a miniature gasoline stove. *Primus inter pares* was what we called that valuable instrument known to every traveler in Russia. Stops were long and frequent, at one place for exactly twenty-four hours, until a Soviet engine arrived from Moscow to replace the Latvian locomotive. In those days the Lettish Government risked no rolling stock on Soviet territory.

Evening of March 24 found us at the Windau station, in Moscow. There, for the first time, we looked upon the emaciated face of Russia and caught the first reflection of her soul mirrored in the tired eyes of the ragged, jostling, milling mob that thronged this, as every other, railway station. Suffering, self-laceration, and the immemorial sadness which Dostoievsky and her poets have exalted into a religious destiny! *Podvig* is what the Russians name it — meaning, generically, some great act of self-abnegation, expiation, or sacrifice. Nesterov made it the subject of the famous war poster that thrilled Russia during the dark days of 1916. That is why the bread we brought them was often salted from their own eyes.

One year and eight months later, in the company of a diplomatic courier and a Reuter correspondent who was quitting Russia forever because his wife had recently been burned to death, the writer of these lines crossed the Polish border, at Stolpce. It was late November 1923. Like every other man who saw the result of that revolutionary upheaval and the ghastly fruits of civil war and famine, he left Russia with a fuller understanding of the unbelievable capacity for suffering inherent in the human frame as it responds to the indomitable will of man battling to continue in existence.

The intervening period was passed, not in Moscow and Petrograd alone, but off the beaten path — in the Crimea and the Ukraine, in the Caucasus and Black Sea districts, along the Volga and the Sea of Azov, in the Don Cossack country and among the Tatars, in peasant huts and ruined palaces, as well as under the shadow of the Kremlin. The territory covered stretched from the Gulf of Finland to the Kuban, and from the Carpathians to the foothills of the Ural Mountains.

During the course of the succeeding years, from 1924 to 1928, visits were made to practically all the Western countries bordering on Soviet Russia or affected by the Revolution, especially to those crowded European centres where Russians of the dispersion most do congregate — Poland, East Prussia, Danzig, Czechoslovakia, Rumania, Syria, Palestine, Egypt, Greece, Vienna, London, Rome, Paris, Brussels, Louvain, Namur, Lyons, Geneva, Constantinople, and Berlin.

As the Russian Revolution marked the fall of an empire vaster far than Troy, so its human flotsam and jetsam have been cast up on every shore of the known world. The Russian émigré — that tragic and, be it truthfully said, that most amiable personage — can fairly claim kinship with Virgil's Æneas when he says: "*Quae regio in terra nostri non plena laboris?*" And the victorious Russian Communist, preacher of a new Utopia in politics and economics, followed close on the heels of his dispossessed countryman, circling the globe from Chicago to Cathay.

Twenty months, consequently, I spent in Russia during the period of transition and beheld her people

> Wandering between two worlds — one dead,
> The other powerless to be born.

And for four years more I sought the opinions of many men in many lands, always asking, "What think ye of Russia?" But the historian who would track the Russian Revolution to its last ramification must embark on an Odyssean search which will lead to many a hidden byway, as well as to legislative chambers, academic halls, and altar rails — wherever, in a word, men foregather to discuss the age-old problems of the race.

One man's life will not suffice to see the end.

E. A. WALSH

WASHINGTON, D. C.
March 1, 1928

ACKNOWLEDGMENT

For permission to reprint the quotations beginning on page 66 from the *Memoirs of Count Witte* (Copyright, 1921, by Doubleday, Page and Company) and beginning on page 285 from *Recollections of a Foreign Minister* by Alexander Isvolsky (Copyright, 1921, by Doubleday, Page and Company) thanks are due to the publishers of these volumes.

CONTENTS

ILLUSTRATIONS

I

THE STORM CLOUD

" By union the smallest states thrive, by discord the greatest
are destroyed."

SALLUST, *Jugurtha,* x

CHAPTER I

THE FACTS IN THE CASE

"WE are the oldest government in Europe," remarked Chicherin in 1923, during the residence of the present writer in Moscow. This droll comment of the Bolshevist Commissar for Foreign Affairs was historically correct then, — more so to-day, — if by government that astute diplomat understood a given cabinet or a *sovnarkom* exercising supreme power and performing the customary administrative functions. The parliamentary system which requires sporadically a vote of confidence in support of the dominant political party, failing which the cabinet is expected to resign, has indeed occasioned a bewildering succession of ministries upon the stage of European politics since November 7, 1917. The Moscow system, on the contrary, provides, antecedently, for the liquidation of any menacing opposition by the simple device of eliminating the opposers. Those who attempted serious political resistance found themselves either in the execution chamber of the Loubyanka or on their way to freezing exile in the convict camps on Solovetsky Island in the White Sea.

To be sure, during the decade just ended, there have been notable losses and substitutions in the higher ranks of the Soviet hierarchy. Sverdlov, Volodarsky, and Uritsky, all active leaders, were assassinated in the early days of the Revolution. Lenin, the flaming torch that fired the Russian masses and sought to fire the world, the creator of the Soviet State and founder of the Third International, died the thousand living deaths of a deranged paralytic before his actual demise in 1924. Vorovsky, able propagandist and first Soviet representative to Italy, was murdered in Switzerland in 1923 and lies buried outside the Kremlin walls, close to the grave of John Reed. On the afternoon of Vorovsky's funeral the author of this work wandered through Red Square and meditated on the significance of the strange fellowship that could so unite in common burial a Russian revolutionist and the brilliant but erratic Harvard graduate.

Krassin, easily distinguishable among the other commissars as brains temporizing with victorious passions, recently succumbed to a mortal illness while Soviet Ambassador to France. Dzherzhinsky, chief of the dreaded secret police, the Cheka, executioner of 1,800,000 victims, the man with the eyes of a gazelle and the soul of a Fouquier-Tinville, expired suddenly and mysteriously in 1926 after an impassioned speech of protest against certain heterodox tendencies of his colleagues. Voikov, who signed the death warrant of Tzar Nicholas II and the imperial family, was himself murdered in Warsaw on June 7, 1927, falling victim to the vengeance of an exiled Russian youth not twenty years of age. Joffe, veteran revolutionist and pioneer coworker with Karakhan in the Far East, committed suicide in December 1927.

But after each casualty the ranks closed tighter. Internal dissension is met by stern domestic discipline. Trotsky, Zinoviev, and Kamenev dispute the supremacy of Stalin, Bukharin, and Rykov. They pay the penalty of schism by relegation to obscure posts within the Party; then, when it is safe to do so, they are expelled entirely. Thus the essential dictatorship of ten men, the Political Bureau of the Communist Party, persists unchallenged over 146,000,000 Russians.[1] With unshaken confidence, Moscow is cele-

[1] The present population of Soviet Russia, taking into account the losses occasioned by wars, famine, disease, executions, and by the surrender of territories now included in Poland, Lithuania, Latvia, Finland, Esthonia, and Bessarabia. The population of Imperial Russia was estimated at something upward

brating its tenth year in continuous control of approximately one seventh of the habitable surface of the earth.

If history may be conceived as philosophy teaching by example, may it not be time, even as early as the tenth year after the event, to seek a helpful interpretation of the Russian experiment?

For Russia not only presents a story that will engage the best historians of the world for generations to come; it is an actual, insistent fact of the present, too. Bolshevism is an international reality which only the hopelessly intransigent can ignore. If the World War did not entirely destroy modern organized society, it assuredly did bring civilization to the crossroads. The victors of the second Russian revolution, that of November 1917, frankly and brutally took the road to the extreme left, driving a weakened, demoralized Russia before them, calling on stronger nations to follow. That way madness lies, as they have now learned and reluctantly admitted, taught by the inexorable laws of nature operating through economic pressure. *Naturam furca expellas, tamen usque recurret.*[1] But it is my deliberate judgment, based on six years' close observation of European and Russian affairs, that no lasting peace is possible in Europe or Asia until the breach between Russia and the West is securely bridged. For that difference, that breach, is not a chasm dug by national hatred, by historic feud or racial antipathy. One or other of such specific motives made Greeks the natural enemies of Turks, made France distrust Germany, and set Celt against Saxon. But the issue created by the second Russian revolution strikes at the very concept

of 180,000,000; exact census-taking was not possible under conditions existing in the heterogeneous admixture of nationalities. Similarly the land surface here referred to means the extent of present-day Russia; later in this book another figure is used which describes Russia before the Treaties of Brest-Litovsk and Versailles, when her territories covered approximately one sixth of the land surface of the earth.

[1] "Drive out Nature with a pitchfork, she will come back every time." — *Horace*

of human society as now organized and proposes an entirely new civilization.

It was not merely a revolution in the accepted sense as historically understood, — that is, a re-allocation of sovereignty, — but revolution in the domain of economics, religion, art, literature, science, education, and all other human activities. It sought to create a new archetype of humanity, the "collective man," and a new culture adapted to the impersonal "mass man" who should displace forever "the soul-encumbered individual man." It was meant, and so proclaimed by its protagonists, to be a challenge to the modern State as constituted, not merely in Imperial Russia, but throughout the entire civilized world. It was philosophic materialism in arms, the most radical school of thought that has ever come upon the stage of human affairs.

The leaders of Bolshevism deliberately identified and confused, in the estimation of the masses, all civilization with the particular Russian form detested by the peasants because of their economic serfdom under it and hated by the liberals because of the savage repression of all their efforts for the enlargement of human liberty through constitutional reform. Interpreting all life, therefore, in terms of their own memories of Siberia, the Bolsheviki generalized savagely, and, of course, erroneously. Lenin registered his bitter oath of universal revenge on the day his brother Alexander Ulianov was executed by the Tzarist Government in 1887 for attempted regicide. Lenin was wrong. But the Tzars were equally wrong in obstinately refusing to modify an insupportable autocracy that drove men to such desperation.

Revolution in the land of the Tzars swept to inevitable catastrophe with an almost mathematical compulsion. By all the laws of nature and human progress, the disappearance of the Muscovite Empire became a political necessity, and was achieved with a ruination of physical and moral values on a scale to challenge the combined creative genius of an

Æschylus, a Sophocles, a Euripides, and a Shakespeare adequately to depict. If the individual and, what is more, the imaginary sufferings of an Electra, an Œdipus, or an ill-starred Prince of Denmark still move, and probably will continue to stir, the collective heart of humanity because of their universal appeal, what should be the reaction of a properly informed posterity to a recital of the woes through which an entire Christian nation has recently passed? Every conceivable scourge which flesh is heir to came upon them, not singly, but in legions. Few Western nations that I know of could have survived what the Russian people have passed through in the last fourteen years.

For half a century public opinion, like a Greek chorus, waited breathless for the axe to fall, as fall men knew it must; and all the while the press, both within and without Russia, like an unheeded Cassandra, kept uttering prophecy after prophecy.

For the student of political variations, the World War spelled the end of national complacencies based on national isolation and ignorance of international organization. That devastating conflict was fought in vain if it has not left men convinced that the nations of the earth constitute a huge, international family whose basic interests are common, and whose members are far more interdependent, acting and reacting on one another far more seriously and directly, than we imagined prior to 1914. No mortal sickness, be it physical, spiritual, or intellectual, that attacks one member of this social organism can ever again be regarded with indifference even by the healthiest member of human society.

Experienced rulers needed no World War to teach them that. The Tzar of All the Russias, Nicholas I, on hearing of the European revolutions of 1848, is reported to have said to his courtiers: —

"Saddle your horses, gentlemen — a Republic is proclaimed in France."

Russia provides still another *caveat* to give us pause. Once again has it been demonstrated that nations, like individuals and trees, fall to their ruin on their leaning side.

I know, under penalty of being considered unscientific, that history does not moralize; neither does it prophesy. But the facts of history may do both. I am unscientific enough to believe that facts are largely useless unless they result in something more lasting than mere entertainment. If history be a science, — which modern scholarship would seem to demand, — then it must, by its charter, set forth the ultimate causes of things. And causes are vastly more important than effects, at least among free agents capable of penetrating to the hidden sources of transient phenomena.

I am more interested in finding out why Persia fell and Babylon passed than in possessing the exact date of their exit; more concerned to know why modern Greece is not the Hellas of Aristotle and Socrates and Plato, and why her groves and market place are no longer crowded with eager seekers after wisdom, than to determine the exact hour when the well of Hellenic culture ran dry. Rome, I know, was once the seat of a world empire, and *"Civis Romanus sum"* was the proudest boast of antiquity. But Rome became "the lone mother of dead empires" and her Forum the playing ground for barbarians because she fell into the dry rot of an effete civilization. The First Empire of the French perished at Waterloo, through ambition; the Third crumbled at Sedan, through inefficiency, to be followed by a new Teutonic Federation proclaimed in the very Hall of Versailles where nearly half a century later the whirligig of time reversed the scenes and reassigned the leading parts. Victor became victim and the vanquished conquered. Why did Imperial Russia, greater than all of these, perish before our very eyes in fire and internecine strife and woeful famine?

Traveling on Alpine heights in the Austrian Tyrol, I have heard native guides warn careless climbers that the loosening of a single stone may send an avalanche down into the peaceful valley beneath. The reverberations of a pistol shot among those silent peaks have been known to dislodge some stray rock or fragment of ice, which, by accumulating snow and dirt and other débris in its mad rush downward, increases in size and speed until it becomes a roaring monster, uprooting trees, sweeping men to destruction, and grinding those artistic Swiss chalets into splinters. Thirteen years ago the gunfire of an irresponsible youth at Sarajevo, directed primarily against the heir to the Austrian throne, unloosened an avalanche that had been brooding over Europe for a generation. As a result of the forces then set in motion, eighteen rulers — kings, princes, and other potentates — were swept from their thrones, some into exile, some, like the last of the Romanovs, to absolute physical annihilation.

And not so long before his death Blasco Ibáñez was calling upon the Spanish people to unchain the Four Horsemen of the Apocalypse and hurl the nineteenth king into the discard!

These effects were appalling; they blasted the ears and seared the eyeballs of humanity — because the causes had not penetrated its brain.

If, on the contrary, history be literature, as I am inclined to believe it is, and hence one of the fine arts, it must, somehow, hold the mirror up to Nature and show mankind his unchanging, recurrent characteristics. Nature is not all rocks and fauna; her chief concern is man. And it is immeasurably more important to know where he is going than where he came from. All the pother about evolution has obscured the only thing that counts — his destiny.

If history be a looking-glass, it is intended for seeing men; a mirror is useless to a blind man. It is ruinous conceit and stupid chauvinism to imagine that the perpetuity of any state, be it monarchy or republic, can be assured solely by industrial preëminence, superior armament, mastery in the

technique of foreign and domestic commerce, or shrewdness
in the conduct of international relations.   Valuable assets,
these, but edged tools and engines of destruction, unless
controlled by minds liberalized by habits of self-analysis,
comparison, and reflection.   Nor have we on the American
continent any divine guaranty that these material excellen-
cies — too often and too grossly proclaimed as irresistible —
will insure indefinitely our institutions against the cycle of
degeneration through which sister nations have already passed.
Some see signs of that decline already.   Oswald Spengler
is sure that the process has begun for all Western culture.

It is precisely his attitude toward such considerations
that distinguishes the politician from the statesman.   A
politician is a man who keeps his eyes on the next election ;
a statesman keeps them fixed on the next generation.   Politicians abounded in old Russia.   Statesmen were few.
That is why the Bolshevik sits grinning in the throne room
of the Kremlin, munching sunflower seeds.

It is an easy error to consider the Bolsheviki as simply
barbarians and so dismiss their program with a contemp-
tuous gesture.   Certainly the rank and file of their followers
have been guilty of inhuman excesses and unpardonable
bloodshed.   But the authorities ruling Russia to-day are
not barbarians.   They are the fruits of barbarian practices
in government extending through three centuries.   Russia
survived the barbarians from without, outlived the Mongolian conquerors under Genghis Khan.   It was the barbarian within that destroyed her — those imperious autocrats in high places and petty tyrants in low places, more
concerned with the perpetuation of dynasties and the conquest of new principalities than with the happiness, the
natural rights, and the development of the hordes under their
control.   Human life and human rights were always cheap
in the East and still are in Russia to-day, a relic, doubtless,

THE VACATED THRONE OF THE ROMANOVS IN THE KREMLIN

and a blending of two influences that cut themselves deep into the character of the ruling classes — Asiatic callousness and Byzantine haughtiness.

The Russian problem derives its hugeness and its complexity from the very soil that gave it birth, inheriting these characteristics as legitimately and historically as the Russian peasant does his wise simplicity and his naïve mysticism. To be sure, such of the intelligentsia as escaped the Cheka during the Terror often begged us foreigners to consider Bolshevism, not as Russian in character and origin at all, but as a distinctly foreign invention, imported into Russia by the German High Staff during the war as a purely military manœuvre to destroy the morale of the Russian people and cripple the army. Both objectives were actually achieved with characteristic efficiency, even though the Frankenstein monster thus created almost destroyed its sponsor when Bolshevist revolutionary propaganda nearly triumphed in Germany in 1923.

In substantiation of their protests, it was often pointed out to us by native Russians that the anti-individualistic character of Soviet institutions is as far removed from the dreamy idealism of Slav peasantry as it is from the avowed aspirations of typical revolutionary leaders like Alexander Herzen, Plekhanov, Kropotkin, Tolstoy, Chernov, Martov, Spiridonova, Milyukov, Pitirim Sorokin, and Grandmother Breshkovskaya. This reservation must, however, be interpreted as their criticism of Bolshevism's impracticable, unworkable answer to Russia's century-long struggle for political freedom and economic independence. It does not, I think, invalidate my contention that Russia's present fate was clearly Russia's destiny, self-imposed, foreseen through decades, and inescapable, granted the policy pursued by the Russian Government for the thirty-seven years that elapsed between the assassination of Alexander II and the murder of Nicholas II.

Time, before whose impartial tribunal all men and institutions pass for judgment, is gradually furnishing the perspective indispensable for an objective and unobstructed view of that sinister record of blunder, Asiatic callousness, reaction, and Byzantine haughtiness. The unfolding panorama of Russian history from 1613 — when young Michael Romanov, son of the Patriarch Philaret, mounted the throne — until the last of the Romanovs perished in the hideous massacre of Ekaterinburg reveals a destiny that swept to its finale with the inevitability of a Greek tragedy. A thesis common in monarchist and émigré circles labors to prove that the Bolshevist revolution was an unnatural, un-Russian phenomenon artificially created by two foreign influences, German militarism and Jewish hatred, and then imposed by treachery on a demoralized and exhausted people. But on the strength of the record, and in view of the testimony of representative Russians supported by documentary evidence now becoming increasingly available, I am obliged to reject that theory. Though the instrumental rôle played both by Jews and by Germany was considerable and active, and though I am familiar with the remarkable work of Mrs. Webster tracing the revolutionary movement, through Lenin and Marx, back to Bakunin, Anacharsis Clootz, — " the personal enemy of Jesus Christ," — Gracchus Babeuf, and the Illuminati of Weishaupt, I maintain that Bolshevism is a natural phase in the evolution of a strictly historical process originating in the soil, the culture, and the politics of Russia itself. When one disentangles the matted roots of that gnarled and knotted growth, he will discover many domestic causes: one philosophic, another geographic, some political, economic, and racial, one religious, and the final, psychological and emotional.

The chronicling of the Russian Revolution may safely be left to the scientific historian. The determination of certain practical political consequences, such as the maintenance of diplomatic relations with the Soviet Government, concerns the statesman. Mutual recrimination, hateful charge and countercharge, will occupy politicians and professional prop- agandists, White and Red. Concessions and commercial opportunities are fascinating traders and merchandisers of credit. But the basic issue belongs to mankind.

In the first place: The impetus and direction given to revolutionary thought by the morbid pessimism of so many Russian intellectuals during the latter half of the nineteenth century only served to tighten the noose around their own necks. Thirty-seven years before the storm broke that destroyed and dispersed such an unbelievably large number of Russian intellectuals, Feodor Dostoievsky, one of Russia's most gifted sons, addressed a notable gathering of fellow authors, publicists, and officials at the unveiling of the Pushkin Memorial in Moscow. This statue stands near the site of the old Tverskaya Gate where the Sadovaya Boulevard crosses the Tverskaya. It is one of the busiest corners in Moscow. I have often paused beneath that huge bronze figure and visualized the brilliant scene on that June day, in the year 1880. Where now congregate innumerable non- descripts, mostly ragged children peddling cigarettes and sunflower seeds to the jostling crowds of young Communists who saunter through this popular boulevard on summer evenings, then stood a distinguished audience composed of the élite of Moscow and old St. Petersburg society. With all the liberty and authority of his literary eminence, and with a vision clarified by his four years of imprisonment in Siberia, Dostoievsky flayed them unmercifully. He pic- tured the abyss toward which the cynics, lounging luxuri- ously in gilded salons, were dragging unhappy Russia. Their cosmopolitan education, he said, obtained abroad, had estranged them from their own people; they had formed a little class which despised the common herd for their ignorance, and yet did nothing to remove it, or to develop the sacred ideals that smoulder in the breast of every moujik. He scored the lack of understanding and sympathy shown by the upper classes toward the great peasant masses and accused the Russian intellectuals, as a body, of endeavoring to transform his beloved Russia into a grotesque caricature of Europe. Whereas in Western Europe, he said, he had found that parents strove to evoke patriotism in the hearts of their children and to make them good Englishmen, good Frenchmen, good Italians, Russian parents seemed engaged in awakening in the child a positive hatred of their fatherland as if it were an offense in the nostrils of humanity.

"It is we," writes Dostoievsky's daughter, Aimée, "we, the hapless victims of the Russian Revolution, who now see all his predictions fulfilled and have to expiate the irresponsible chatter of the liberals."

The Viscount de Voguë, in his severe but penetrating analysis of Russian temperament in the "forties," comments on the same blunder : —

The Minister of Education himself sent his own candidates to Berlin or Göttingen. These young men, when properly loaded with moral philosophy and the leaven of Liberalism, — equipped with ideas for which there was no use in their own country, — return to Russia discontented and rebellious. The Minister was eternally bewailing the astonishing sight of a hen hatching ducklings. These suspicious emissaries of the West were recommended to the care of the Police — whilst others continued to be sent to the same school.[1]

Griboyedov, in his comedy, *Misfortune from Intelligence,* satirizes the same superficiality.

Ivan Bunin, perhaps best known for his realistic searching for the roots of evil in *The Village* (1910), had long before seen the gathering storm cloud. After his escape from Russia he wrote : —

[1] *The Russian Novel,* Ch. IV.

What the Russian Revolution turned into very soon none will comprehend who has not seen it. This spectacle was utterly unbearable to anyone who had not ceased to be a man, in the image and likeness of God, and all who had a chance to flee fled from Russia. Flight was sought by the vast majority of the most prominent Russian writers, primarily, because in Russia there awaited them either senseless death at the hands of the first chance miscreant drunk with licentiousness and impunity, with rapine, with wine, with blood, with cocaine; or an ignominious existence as a slave in the darkness, teeming with lice, in rags, amid epidemic diseases, exposed to cold, to hunger, to the primitive torments of the stomach, and absorbed in that single degrading concern, under the eternal threat of being thrown out of his mendicant's den into the street, of being sent to the barracks to clean up the soldiers' filth, of being, without any reason whatever, arrested, beaten, abused, of seeing one's own mother, sister, or wife violated, and yet having to preserve utter silence. . . .

Some critics have called me bitter and gloomy. I do not think that this definition is fair and accurate. But of course I have derived much honey and still more bitterness from my wanderings throughout the world and my observations of human life. I had felt a vague fear for the fate of Russia when I was depicting her. Is it my fault that reality, the reality in which Russia has been living for over five years now, has justified my apprehensions beyond all measure; that those pictures of mine which had once upon a time appeared black and wide of the truth, even in the eyes of Russian people, have become *prophetic*, as some call them now?

But nobody — at least among the autocrats — heeded the rumbling of a distant drum. They could not see Birnam Wood for the trees until each tree moved, with its armed man, on Dunsinane, and the witches' curse was fulfilled.

Secondly: The "land hunger" of the peasants, that perennial thirst of primitive agricultural communities, was but poorly satisfied, nay, was aggravated, by the terms of the political Emancipation of 1861, which still left them, to all intents and purposes, economic serfs. In the latter part of the following chapter we shall examine that phase in greater detail.

Thirdly: The "constitution hunger" of the moderate and truly patriotic liberals and constructive intellectuals was answered by a stupid policy of savage repression and a reassertion of autocracy that drove the revolutionaries underground, thus creating a multiplicity of secret organizations dedicated to the overthrow of Tzardom through ruthless direct action and political assassination. In a succeeding chapter we shall see more of this duel between the government and the secret societies, particularly during the typical reigns of Alexander III and Nicholas II, when governmental reaction reached its apex of folly.

Fourthly: The rapid growth of industrial and factory life in Russia, notably from 1867 to 1897, without a corresponding improvement in the status of labor gave rise to a bitter class consciousness. And class consciousness is the fertile soil where professional agitators sow the bitter seeds of class hatred. Class hatred is the sure herald of revolution.

Fifthly: The bewildering ethnological composition of the population, which was nothing more than a loose agglomeration of over two hundred unassimilated nationalities, will, I think, bear me out in believing that Russia was probably the only land on the face of the earth that could have produced so swiftly and so completely the chaotic enigma she now presents to the civilized world. Walk with me through the streets of Moscow, that mart where East and West meet, but blend not. Let your gaze range from the fair-haired Slav of Aryan Russia and Siberia to the semibarbaric countenances and Asiatic types discernible among the slant-eyed soldiers, worshipers of Buddha, who thronged the streets in 1922. Scrutinize the brutal physiognomy of the Lettish janizaries that guard the Kremlin, worshipers of no God save Nikolai Lenin, whose corpse now lies embalmed before its walls; read the consciousness of an awakened East in the swarthy Mohammedan peddler from Turkestan, in the emancipated Jew already uneasy for his life because of his swift ascent to power and affluence, and in the turbaned rug dealer from Bokhara, squatting idly on his wares and dreaming of the promises of the Prophet.

Then ride southward and eastward to the Cossack villages along the frozen Don, there to study the pitiful remnants of those incomparable horsemen whose wild riding struck terror into the finest troops of Europe; or push farther eastward to the settlements of the Mongoloid Kalmuks, worshipers of Lama; enter the tents of skin that shelter the Kirghiz and the Chuvash; undertake even to catalogue those other seminomadic tribes inhabiting the foothills of the Urals and the mountainous regions between the Black Sea and the Caspian.

Russian ethnologists find in the Caucasus alone, that sieve which caught and deposited so many types from the unceasing migrations surging to and from Europe, something like two hundred distinct races. You will find tribes in the mountains of Daghestan whose speech is absolutely unintelligible to their neighbors in the nearest village! On his return from this region, in March 1923, Dr. Frank Golder, special investigator of famine conditions for the American Relief Administration, regaled us at Moscow headquarters with reports that would have sounded fantastic on the lips of another man. The learned Professor of History at Leland Stanford University described the inquisitive interest shown in this strange American by the primitive mountaineers. Their first curiosity satisfied, they interrogated Professor Golder about America. Was it not on the under side of the earth and so in darkness? Did not men plough the fields with oxen bearing candles on their horns? How did he get to their land, except by a big hole through the earth? They knew the Tzar had a ladder for that. But how could men walk upright in America, being, as it were, upside down? They must crawl about like flies on a ceiling!

Or, traveling westward, take your stand among the sturdy Ukrainian peasants in the "Black Earth" region that was once the richest granary in Europe. Pass through the trim, orderly villages of German colonists in the North Crimea and round about Saratov. In a word, visualize the component human elements of the far-flung empire of the Tzars and you will begin to appreciate what Kipling meant when he wrote that Russia must be considered, not as the most eastern of Western nations, but as the most westerly nation of the East. And you cannot help but agree that this heterogeneous admixture of races, religions, and antagonistic interests contained within itself the fatal germs of domestic discord, the seeds of fratricidal strife and bloody revolution, to end eventually in complete economic and social disintegration.

Russia was an ethnological museum superintended by a vigilant autocrat and policed by the notorious Third Section of Chancery, the Political Police. The origin and activities of this progenitor of the Bolshevist "Cheka" have been minutely described by one who felt its heavy hand, Prince Peter Kropotkin, in his *Memoirs of a Revolutionist*. Founded by Peter the Great as a Secret Department, it was an omnipotent institution, a true "state within a state"; its agents were found in every populous town and at every railway station, spying on functionaries of the Empire as well as on citizens suspected of liberal thought or action. Ignoring law and law courts, the Third Section arrested whom it chose, kept its victims imprisoned as long as it pleased, and transported thousands to Northeast Russia or Siberia at the whim of its all-powerful camarilla. The fortress of St. Peter and St. Paul was its Bastille. There Peter the Great tortured his son Alexis and killed him with his own hand; there Princess Tarakonova was immured in a cell which

A ROMANOV AT BAY
Tzarina Sophia Alexevna

filled with water during an inundation, the rats climbing upon her shoulders to save themselves from drowning; there the relentless Minich tortured his enemies and Catherine II buried alive those who objected to her having murdered her husband. From the days of Peter I, throughout two hundred years, this forbidding pile of stone rising from the Neva directly in front of the Winter Palace of the Tzars received an unending procession of men and women condemned to a living death, or to be murdered outright, or to be driven to insanity in the loneliness of those damp and dismal dungeons below the level of the river.

This central stronghold of the autocracy was plainly visible from the windows of the Winter Palace. When the overseer fell and his policeman was murdered, bedlam broke loose in the Empire. It cannot be too often repeated, therefore, that the Russian fact, as crystallized in Bolshevism, is essentially different from reparations, the evacuation of the Ruhr, immigration, disarmament, the League, or the World Court. Each of these current themes, though of tremendous international importance, is nevertheless a political problem, a military question, or a legal device to promote peace. But the Russian challenge involves all these elements, because it is a human problem, a social challenge directed not only to the 146,000,000 Russians directly involved, but extending its influence to every corner of the globe where men strive for human betterment or gird themselves to die for liberty.

Russia was a pyramid, but an inverted pyramid with a huge, unwieldy, and inert superstructure of discontented, illiterate masses balanced unsteadily on that slender apex furnished by the fraction of the population included in the nobility, the aristocracy, and the bureaucracy. With the crumbling of the demoralized autocracy, upon which practically the whole of organized life was balanced, human society turned turtle. As the area affected was one sixth of the surface of this planet, and as the human element then filled with water during an inundation, the rats climbing upon her shoulders to save themselves from drowning; there the relentless Minich tortured his enemies and Catherine II buried alive those who objected to her having murdered her husband. From the days of Peter I, throughout two hundred years, this forbidding pile of stone rising from the Neva directly in front of the Winter Palace of the Tzars received an unending procession of men and women condemned to a living death, or to be murdered outright, or to be driven to insanity in the loneliness of those damp and dismal dungeons below the level of the river.

This central stronghold of the autocracy was plainly visible from the windows of the Winter Palace. When the overseer fell and his policeman was murdered, bedlam broke loose in the Empire. It cannot be too often repeated, therefore, that the Russian fact, as crystallized in Bolshevism, is essentially different from reparations, the evacuation of the Ruhr, immigration, disarmament, the League, or the World Court. Each of these current themes, though of tremendous international importance, is nevertheless a political problem, a military question, or a legal device to promote peace. But the Russian challenge involves all these elements, because it is a human problem, a social challenge directed not only to the 146,000,000 Russians directly involved, but extending its influence to every corner of the globe where men strive for human betterment or gird themselves to die for liberty.

Russia was a pyramid, but an inverted pyramid with a huge, unwieldy, and inert superstructure of discontented, illiterate masses balanced unsteadily on that slender apex furnished by the fraction of the population included in the nobility, the aristocracy, and the bureaucracy. With the crumbling of the demoralized autocracy, upon which practically the whole of organized life was balanced, human society turned turtle. As the area affected was one sixth of the surface of this planet, and as the human element then involved numbered over 180,000,000 people, the resulting chaos was proportionate to the possibilities for disorder and destruction, which were boundless, inherent in such an unstable system, never far from the surface and only outwardly controlled by the Okhrana, the secret police of the Tzars. Consequently, when the crash came, it marked the most stupendous single political event, I believe, since the break-up of the Roman Empire. Not only did the ensuing human wreckage cover the plains of Muscovy, but the flotsam and the jetsam have been washed up on every shore of the civilized world.

Russia was the last island fortress of absolutism in the rising tide of democracy, the outstanding anachronism of the twentieth century. Ringed round by the bayonets of the Preobrazhensky and Volinsky regiments, its ukases executed by the knouts of Cossacks and the flashing sabres of the Hussars, it defied the elements for three hundred years — until the deluge came.

Then, too, the influence of sectarianism cannot be overlooked in any complete account of the progress of revolution in Russia. Apart from the twelve million Roman Catholics residing within the confines of the Empire, mainly of Polish origin and consequently treated with hostility as tolerated aliens, and the seven millions or more of Lutherans, there existed a bewildering complexity of dissident sects. Tenacious of their old and new beliefs, fanatically opposed to the state religion, the sectarians were prepared to die, as they frequently did, for their religious practices. If we add to the strictly Orthodox communities of Raskolniks (Separatists) and Starovyeri (Old Believers) the rationalist and chiliastic groups, the Adventists and the New Adventists, the Nemoliakhi and Neplatel'schiki (nonpayers of taxes), the Stranniki (pilgrims), the Medal'shchiki (medalists), the Jehovists (universal brothers), the Sviadodukhovsti (adherents of the Holy Ghost), the Dukhobors and Molokani

(Zionists), the Fire Baptists and Morel'shchiki (self-immolators), the Khlysty (scourgers), the Skoptsy (self-mutilators), and the Trudnoviki (cloistral communists), a total is reached which embraced probably a third of the population. And since orthodoxy and autocracy were inseparably linked in the Russian idea of the State, non-conformists were penalized and systematically oppressed. The victims were in moral and intellectual rebellion long before the armed revolt of 1917. They constituted a socio-political factor of truly elemental power, smouldering with resentment and ripe for explosion.

You must revise your standards of measurement when you approach things Russian, at least if you would understand her and judge her aright. Russia always suggested to Occidental minds men and events on a huge scale — physical giants bearded and wrapped in skins of animals, imposing grenadiers, boundless plains called "steppes" that tire the eye with their unending monotony, wildernesses of snow and ice, bitter, cruel cold, hunger, famine, bloody peasant revolts like those of Pugachev and Stenka Razin, and other elemental things.

Four words, *Tzar, Siberia, vodka, pogrom,* exhausted the common ideology. And that mythical band of hard-pressed travelers, galloping madly across snow fields and casting a succulent child into the gleaming fangs of yelping wolves, sufficed as a satisfactory epitome of Russian manners and customs.

The literary, the spiritual, the scientific, and the artistic achievements of Russia were, until comparatively recent times, known only to connoisseurs, students, and occasional pioneers. "Very few people born west of Riga," writes Prince Mirsky in his *Contemporary Russian Literature,* "knew anything at all about the facts that are relevant in this connection." In the United States, particularly, the common judgment was inspired by experience with the streams of Jewish immigrants and husky Slavs making for the Scranton coal fields or Pittsburgh factories; a Moussorgsky, a Tchaikovsky, and a Rimski-Korsakov in music, a Mendeléev in science, and Soloviev, the Newman of Russian philosophy, could with difficulty hope for the popular acclaim accorded to a Mr. Irving Berlin.

It was only the occasional traveler or diplomat and trader who came to appreciate the cosmopolitan refinements of the Nevsky Prospekt that made old St. Petersburg another Paris transplanted to northern snows by the Europeanizing policies of Peter the Great, and made the Petrovka and Kuznetsky Most in Moscow rival the Rue de la Paix of Paris. Even the railroads in Russia are built with a wider gauge than those of Western Europe. This peculiarity was as deliberate as it was symbolic, serving as a physical device to isolate Russia. It caused considerable inconvenience to the American Relief Administration during the famine, as all supplies shipped via the Polish route had to be unloaded at Stolpce and reloaded into Russian wagons. But on the through line from Berlin to Riga via Eydtkunen in East Prussia, and Wirballen in Lithuania, the Germans, during their occupation of the Baltic provinces, had the foresight to Europeanize the tracks. They moved one rail nearer the other and then cut off the superfluous ends of the crossties, so that the Russian gauge could not be restored without rebuilding the entire system.

Geographically, Russia was a Triton among the minnows. Glance at a map of Europe! Politically, Russia was "the bear that walks like a man." Now, the bear is a huge, lumbering animal whose hug means death. Persia, Mongolia, Manchuria, and China experienced that squeeze within our own memory and Constantinople has never been quite out of the shadow of the outstretched paw.

CHAPTER II

"WE ARE YOURS, BUT THE LAND IS OURS"

IT would indeed be a fascinating and a profitable excursion into an almost virgin field of inquiry to trace step by step the origins and colorful vicissitudes of the Russian State from the dim and distant obscurity which enshrouds the first appearance of the Eastern Slavs in historical literature, through the periods of Tatar and Polish domination, down to its final form under the Princes of Moscow. But the limits of this present book do not permit more than a bare recapitulation of the main characteristics. The monumental work of Klyuchevsky, the celebrated historian of the University of Moscow, unfolds a panorama of colossal magnitude and importance. With the entrance of Rurik into Novgorod in the middle of the ninth century (862) began the steady process of expansion and Russification of conquered provinces, notably in the reign of Ivan III, that eventually carried the double-headed eagle from Alexandrovno, on the German border, to Vladivostok on the Pacific, and from the Polar Sea on the north to the "warm waters" of the Black Sea on the south, with Constantinople ever the objective and ultimate goal of Russian foreign policy.

There are two prevailing views regarding the dawn of Russian history. One school of research, represented by Schlözer, Karamzin, Pogodin, and Soloviev, dates Russian chronology from the coming of the Scandinavians, under Rurik, to rule over Novgorod and the neighboring Slavonic tribes in the year 862 of the Christian era. According to this belief, these hardy Vikings, who came in acceptance of an invitation to govern the land extended to them by the natives of North Russia, found the great Russian plain which lay between Novgorod and Kiev, stretching to the right and left of the Dnieper, wholly uncultivated and wild, inhabited by Slavic tribes living in a state of rude, anarchic barbarism. From Novgorod, therefore, as a starting point, the Varangian Princes gravitated southward toward Kiev, and by successive federation and consolidation of scattered trading posts established the nucleus of the future Empire.

Another and later group of Russian scholars, ably represented by the Moscow historian Klyuchevsky, now dead, and Michael Rostovtsev, at present lecturing at an American University, seek their orientation farther south, basing their claims on the archæological discoveries in South Russia and the Crimea, where distinct traces of a flourishing civilization have been unearthed showing evidence of Greek culture and Hellenic influence. They record the finding of palæolithic and neolithic relics in the southern steppes, and adduce the mention of Russia made by Herodotus as early as the fifth century before Christ, when Ionian and Dorian Greeks had established themselves along the coast line of the Black Sea in the colonies of Olbia, Chersonese, Panticapæum, Tanais, and Phanagoria. The place names still preserved at Eupatoria and Theodosia in the Crimea are reminders of Greek settlers. But the hinterland was occupied by other peoples, under the headship, first of the Cimmerians, and then of the Scythians.

It will suffice, however, for our present purpose to take our stand upon the common ground where all schools meet and say that the Russian State, viewed as a political community, and apart from its racial content, evolved from that confederation of trading posts between Novgorod and Kiev, which were founded and protected by Varangian chieftains under Rurik and the Slavonic Princes Oleg and Igor. Both Scandinavians — who probably were of Norman origin —

and Slavs were impelled as much by hopes of gain as by visions of glory. "They were as good business men as they were soldiers. . . . Adventurous trade, therefore, by all accounts seems to have been responsible for the early settlements on the Russian Plain." And the very name of Russia or "Rus," to recall its earliest form, is simply Time's modification of "Rurik," the Swedish freebooter.

The first recorded account of the Russian people, that intensely human and picturesque document, *The Chronicle of Nestor*, does not go farther back than 852 A.D.

Now a word about that Russian plain; not only was it to be the scene of all the events here recorded, but it played a very important part in determining some of them. That climatic conditions and geography do materially influence the development of a people is beyond dispute. In fact, it is an article of faith with one school of historians that climate and geography far outweigh psychic and cultural influences in deciding the direction which a nation's development shall take. This theory is, of course, subject to the same exaggeration and unwarranted application which every materialistic interpretation of history and economics is prone to when investigators minimize the free psychological, social, and spiritual instincts that dominate men in defiance of geography and climate. Climate does encourage certain types of genius and discourages others. Philologists point to the Romance languages, with their open, full-voweled, and musical sounds, as the natural expression of races basking under the limpid skies, the orange groves, and the mellow sunshine of the Mediterranean basin. We expect liquid music from a Tetrazzini, a Calvé, and a Caruso, whereas the sterner rigors of Northern Europe tend rather to produce the Wagnerian thunder of Teutonic basses. Laplanders and Eskimos speak a particularly guttural tongue because long experience taught their ancestors to keep the mouth closed as much as possible in those icy igloos, and speak, when they had to, through clenched teeth. And the Ural-Altaic family speaks a throaty and agglutinative language, measuring their words by the least common denominator of vocal effort. But, to confute and confound any theorist who becomes overdogmatic, Jenny Lind comes tripping across the stage, a Swedish nightingale of the North!

The enormous plateau on which Russia sprawls is described as the largest in the world. But it is landlocked. The only southern egress is blocked by an ancient enemy, the Turk, who makes the Black Sea, to all intents and purposes, an inland sea as long as Islam controls the Dardanelles; of the northern ports, both Petrograd and Archangel are frozen in nearly half the year. Even when open for navigation, these northern outlets lead into the narrow straits dominated by Denmark and Sweden. The only other hope of free exit is by Vladivostok, five thousand miles distant from the heart of the Empire. "Nature has been a stepmother to Russia," wrote Soloviev; "Fate was another stepmother." Hence that historic urge which impelled Russia to press outward in all directions — to break, as it were, the chrysalis of geographic despotism which Nature had imposed on her.

At this point our economic determinist may cry triumph and thank us for having proved his very dearest claim. Not so fast. Human nature is capable of most disconcerting tricks in the very teeth of environment. There are numerous points of similarity between the stages of development that led to the final erection of an autocratic state in Russia and the processes that resulted in the present United States of America. Beginning with relatively small territories, both peoples conquered a vast and virgin continent: the Americans through successive waves of colonization across the Rockies westward to the Pacific, the Russians by similar pioneering eastward across the Urals until they reached the same expanse of water that stopped the Americans at the Golden Gate. Both faced natural obstacles and encountered primitive tribes, yellow and red, who contested every inch of the white man's advance. But no two governments on the face of the earth arrived at more contradictory theories and practices as to the meaning of political freedom.

While freely admitting that the physical configuration of Russia's territory did determine, to a measurable degree, the direction of the stream of events that resulted in autocracy, — just as it directs so many of her rivers northward, — it would be an unjustified conclusion to maintain that this ends the diagnosis. There were subtle human factors at work more powerful than rivers or harbors or steppes; it was the simultaneous concentration of mixed forces that led Russia into the errors that proved the undoing of her political and social unity. To these elements we shall devote a later chapter.

The final scene represented a territorial jurisdiction of 8,648,000 square miles, an area more than twice the rest of Europe combined, considerably more than twice the size of the United States. The population in 1914 was something like 180,000,000. But, as I have intimated, it was an artificial structure, the cohesion of whose parts depended, not on any natural affinity, but on the strength of character and resourcefulness of one central figure, the Tzar, in whom resided supreme legislative, administrative, and ecclesiastical power. He was both civil ruler and virtual head of the Orthodox Church. In the words of Peter the Great, he was "the autocratic monarch, who has to give an account of his acts to no man on earth, but has power to rule his states and lands according to his own will and judgment."

The people, his subjects, were divided into clearly defined classes, whose rights and obligations were set forth with legal precision in the Code. Everybody was ticketed and labeled : —

	PER CENT
Peasants	80
Burghers (burgesses), *i.e.*, merchants and artisans	18
Clergy	.5
Nobility, landowners, and officials . . .	1.5
	100.0

The *prikaz*, imperial edict of the Tzar, was the incontrovertible law of the land. He alone could initiate legislation, as he alone could initiate a conversation. To be sure, there was a Council of State, a Committee of Ministers, a Senate, and a Judiciary. But as these were all either appointees of the Tzar and responsible to him alone, or, if elected, utterly dependent on the administration, they were, in point of fact, nothing but an extension, as it were, of the autocrat's person and an instrumentality for the execution of his will. The imperial decree was interpreted and duly executed by an army of governors, vice governors, resident provincial officials, civil assistants, military aids, and scribes and secretaries beyond imagining. Fourteen categories of officials were included in the vast and complicated bureaucratic machine invented by Peter the Great and under which Russia groaned for two centuries. The fourteen progressive stages in the public service embraced all varieties of rank or *tchin*, and the ruling caste thus created were known as *tchinovniki*. "Russia is ruled, not by me, but by my forty thousand clerks," said Nicholas I.

Historians like to lay their finger on a definite circumstance, a known date, or some single event to mark the beginning of mighty political movements. Hilaire Belloc has written an essay in support of his belief that the French Revolution began on the day and at the moment when the Commons of France, excluded by Louis XVI from entering the Assembly Hall at Versailles, on June 20, 1789, rushed in indignation to the enclosed tennis court on the palace grounds and there defied King, clergy, and nobles by holding a separate convocation. The Boston Massacre, preceding the Declaration of Independence by six years, made the American Revolution inevitable. But it would be extremely difficult to specify and designate a date or a single event as the starting point of the Russian Revolution. That deluge grew from many rivers of tears and streams of blood.

There were frequent bloody conflicts of the palace type in early days centring about the "false" Dimitri. Peasant uprisings frequently disturbed the growing Empire, such as that of Stenka Razin in 1670 and Pugachev in 1773. But the first of these resembled more the guerrilla warfare of a popular brigand, rallying discontented elements in opposition to the domination of Moscow, than organized domestic rebellion. The latter outburst, though more serious both in duration and in character, was a revolt of Don Cossacks in support of a pseudo-Peter III against Catherine II. Its forces are pictured by historians as a tatterdemalion horde of disreputable adventurers organized into an army for predatory purposes. Of all previous rebellions the Pugachev revolt came nearest to social and economic revolution.

Local military revolts were not wanting, such as that of the freebooting Zaparojian Cossacks, suppressed by Potemkin, under Catherine II. The numerous Polish insurrections were national uprisings against the political rule of Russia. But domestic revolt only becomes successful revolution in the complete sense when it effects radical political, social, and economic changes in the community.

A correspondent of the London *Times*, in Petrograd during the War, wrote, in March 1917, "An old woman threw a stone at a baker's shop-window and started the Russian Revolution." He means, of course, that the crash of breaking glass in the bread shop rang up the curtain on the last act. As early as December, 1825, a group of ardent revolutionaries, mostly idealistic young officers of the Imperial Army, lately returned from France and Germany, attempted to end the tyranny of Tzardom by open revolt in St. Petersburg. Ill advised, improperly organized, and too weak to be dangerous, it was easily suppressed — in the usual way. Five of the leaders were executed and great numbers of the participants were exiled for life. This pathetic attempt of the "Decembrists" to effect a refined revolution, an affair of cocked hats and gayly caparisoned chargers, forms the theme of Merejkovsky's historical novel, *December Fourteenth*.

The leaders had imbibed new and electrifying ideas during their campaigning in Western Europe, where they had been employed against Napoleon. They aimed at a complete reformation of the Russian State and even dreamed of a constitutional republic modeled on the United States of America.[1] It failed, through inefficiency, the insurgent troops standing drawn up all day in the Senate Square, their officers debating and arguing as to the next move. By evening the loyal troops had time to bring up cannon and leisurely blew them into the Neva. "The Russian is clever, but always too late," according to their own homely proverb.

The Soviet Government, by its official celebration of the Decembrists' centenary in November 1925, recognized the Decembrists as the first strictly social and political revolutionaries which Russia produced.

But all historians and thoughtful Russians admit that it was the Crimean War of 1853 that finally unloosed elemental social forces that could no longer be denied or restrained. "War searches the joints and harness of every state that challenges its verdict; it appraises, first by a rude and sud-

---

[1] The device used by the conspirators to gain the support of the troops is a classic instance of the Russian soldier's naïve credulity. The candidate whom the Decembrists pretended to support was the Grand Duke Constantine; their followers were encouraged to shout for "Constantine and Constitution," the simple troopers imagining that they were defending the rights of Constantine and his wife "Constitutia."

den shock, and then by a long, slow, dragging tension (just as we test and appraise the worth of steel), the endurance and the capacity for survival of each political community." The defeat of Russia by the combined forces of England and France was a national humiliation, regarded, however, by patriotic Russians as a blessing in disguise.

"Sevastopol fell," said Ivan Aksakov, "that God might reveal all the rottenness of the system of government."

"We have fallen," said Samarin, "not before the forces of the Western Alliance, but as a result of our own internal weakness."

This weakness had been manifested to a scandalous degree in the absence of adequate transportation facilities for men and supplies. At the outbreak of the Crimean War there were but two railroads operating in Russia, aggregating 419 miles; one ran from Petrograd to Moscow, while the second, a short spur of fifteen miles, connected Petrograd with the Summer Palace at Tsarskoe Selo. Obviously, both had been constructed either for the convenience of royalty or for upper-class and bourgeois profit. The rest of Russia floundered about in the mud, on foot, on horseback, or in coaches and wagons, as best they might.

During the preliminary planning of the Moscow–Petrograd line, — which is exceptionally well built, straight as the flight of a crow, and running on a firm, level roadbed, — occurred an incident that reconciles one to certain attributes of tyranny. The officials charged by Nicholas I with laying out the route to be followed were neither better nor worse than our modern "logrollers." When Nicholas called for the plans, he observed that a meandering course had been plotted out in deference to certain landowners and interested persons who, if they could not move their property close to the tracks, would lay the rails in circles, if need be, to bring new value to their holdings. The Tzar took a ruler; laying one end on Petrograd and one on Moscow, he said,

"You will construct the line so." And so it runs to this day, 404 miles without deviating a foot to right or left, following an almost mathematically straight line. As one commentator puts it, the Nicholas Railway remains "to all future ages, like St. Petersburg and the Pyramids, a magnificent monument of autocratic power."

Dangerously discredited by the issue of the war and the revelations of disorganization, incompetency, and official corruption, the Government made haste to be liberal.

As the land hunger of the peasants was the most threatening symptom of basic unrest, the agrarian problem was the natural starting point for the great reform that marked the reign of Alexander II. For upward of three hundred years, since the conquests of Ivan IV, which added Kazan (1552), Astrakhan (1556), and the whole course of the Volga to Russia, the peasant population had been undergoing an insidious process of economic limitation that resulted practically in bondage. The acquisition of new and fertile territories opened up huge tracts of land for cultivation. Scarcity of labor sufficient to till the soil obliged the great landholders to use every device to coax agricultural workers to their respective estates. Once on the ground, the "boyars" — the territorial nobility — held them there, sometimes by fraud, more often by force. Obliged to render service to the Tzar in the shape of military aid, taxes, and produce as recompense for his land grants, these feudal lords found it impossible to discharge their obligations unless labor was made available and permanent. Gradually, therefore, the peasant came to be regarded as *belonging to the land* which he tilled, until, under the regency of Boris Godunov (1597), sentiment crystallized in the form of an imperial decree, a *ukaz*, prohibiting peasants from migrating from one property to another, and confirming the legal right of landlords to enforce the return of fugitives. It was the Russian Dred Scott decision.

Volga Boatmen

Klyuchevsky[1] sums up the process in his famous antin-
omies : —

1. Up till the middle of the eighteenth century the external
territorial extension of the Russian State goes on in inverse proportion to the development of the interior freedom of the people.

2. The political status of the laboring classes establishes itself
in inverse proportion to the economic productivity of their labor;
that is, their labor becomes less free in proportion as it becomes
more productive.

From "fixation" to the land, for purely agricultural and
economic reasons, to practical slavery was not a far cry.
By the middle of the eighteenth century serfdom had become
legalized, the serfs being considered as part of the proprietor's *irremovable property*. A man's wealth was com-
puted, not by his revenue, or his dessiatines (dessiatine
= 2.7 acres), or his gold, but by the number of "souls" on
his property. Gogol, the Russian Dickens, has a celebrated
novel on the subject, called *Dead Souls*, satirizing in a master-
ful way one of the abuses of serfdom. There was a periodic
census of serfs, say, once every ten or twenty years. This
being the case, an owner had to pay a tax on every "soul"
registered at the last census, though some of the serfs might
have died in the meantime. Nevertheless, the system had
its material advantages, inasmuch as an owner might borrow
money from the bank on the "dead souls" no less than on
the living ones. The plan of Chichikov, Gogol's hero-
villain, was, therefore, to make a journey through Russia
and buy up the "dead souls" at reduced rates, saving their
owner the government tax, of course, and acquiring for
himself a list of fictitious serfs which he meant to mortgage
to a bank for a considerable sum. With this money he
would buy an estate and some real live serfs and make the
beginning of a fortune. Gogol read this manuscript to his

[1] Vol. III, p. 4.

friend, the poet Pushkin. At the end Pushkin cried out in anguish: "God! What a sad country Russia is!"

Mackenzie Wallace, in that invaluable record he left of his years of wandering up and down Russia, recounts a story which he read of a similar Chichikov in the reign of Nicholas I.

An officer of rural police, when driving on a country road, finds a dead body by the wayside. Congratulating himself on this bit of good luck, he proceeds to the nearest village and lets the inhabitants know that all manner of legal proceedings will be taken against them so that the supposed murderer may be discovered. The peasants are of course frightened and give him a considerable sum of money in order that he may hush up the affair. An ordinary officer of police would have been quite satisfied with this ransom, but this officer is not an ordinary man and is very much in need of money; he conceives, therefore, the brilliant idea of repeating the experiment. Taking up the dead body, he takes it away in his tarantass and a few hours later declares to the inhabitants of a village some miles off that some of them have been guilty of murder and that he intends to investigate the matter thoroughly. The peasants of course pay liberally to escape the investigation, and the rascally officer, emboldened by success, repeats the trick in several villages until he has gathered a large sum.

On August 22, 1767, a *ukaz* of Catherine II deprived serfs of all legal status and protection of the laws, providing that "if any serf shall dare to present a petition against his master he shall be punished with the knout and transported for life to the mines of Nerchinsk."

An advertisement in the *Moscow Gazette* of 1801 ran as follows: —

To Be Sold: Three coachmen, well trained and handsome, and two girls, the one eighteen and the other fifteen years of age, both of them good-looking and well acquainted with various kinds of handiwork. In the same house there are for sale two hairdressers; the one, twenty-one years of age, can read, write, play on a musical instrument, and act as huntsman; the other can dress ladies' and gentlemen's hair; in the same house are sold pianos and organs.

The same paper also advertised: "a first-rate clerk, a carver, and a lackey are offered for sale." Another announcement read: "In this house one can buy a coachman and a Dutch cow about to calve."

The percentage of the total population which was, in Sir Paul Vinogradoff's phrase, "domesticated animals," or "black people" and "backyard people," as the peasants described themselves, may be seen from the table presented by Sir George Mavor in his thoroughly documented study, *The Rise and Fall of Bondage Right.*

Year of Census	Number of Bonded Peasants on Private Estates	Number of Bonded Peasants on Land of the State, Orthodox Church, and Private Properties of Tzar	Total Population of Russia
1722	3,200,000	2,200,000	14,000,000
1796	9,789,680	7,276,170	36,000,000
1812	10,416,813	7,550,814	41,000,000
1835	10,872,229	10,550,000	60,000,000
1851	10,708,856	12,000,000	69,000,000
1859	10,696,136	12,800,000	74,000,000
1859	Total of Bonded Peasants 23,496,136		

On the eve of the Emancipation, therefore, 34.39 per cent of the total population were serfs. But in Great Russia itself (*i.e.*, North and Central Russia, with the northeast part of the "Black Earth" region) 53 per cent were bondsmen.

There were many ways through which a man became a serf, particularly during the early stages in the development of bondage rights: —

1. By captivity following war.
2. By voluntary consent.

3. By the act of parents through sale of a free person into slavery.

4. By way of punishment for commission of certain crimes.

5. By birth from a *kholop* or bondaged man.

6. By insolvency of a merchant through his own fault.

7. By voluntary entrance on the part of a free person into the service of another without a contract guaranteeing the freedom of the servant.

8. By marriage to a *rob* or bondaged woman, without a similar contract.

The Cossacks — the " free people " — of the Southern steppes alone escaped these encroachments and maintained their local autonomy. Whereas their moujik brothers of the North succumbed to serfdom, these hard-drinking, hard-riding, and hard-fighting clansmen boasted of an independence which the Tzars deemed it prudent to respect and tolerate. In return for political privileges and free land tenure, the Cossack settlements furnished military service in the shape of a volunteer mobile militia, each adult Cossack standing ready with his own horse and equipment to answer the call of the Tzar. Democratic feudalism best describes their status in the Empire. A bulwark of the autocracy in its prime, the Cossacks were among the first to declare for the Revolution in 1917.

This pernicious institution of serfdom, one of those periodic manifestations of man's inhumanity to man, became untenable in the fierce light that beat upon Russia and its throne during and after the Crimean War. On the morrow of the peace, in 1856, Alexander announced the beginnings of Emancipation in an address to the Marshals of the Nobility in Moscow : —

For the removal of certain unfounded reports, I consider it necessary to declare to you that I have not at present the intention of annihilating serfage ; but certainly, as you yourselves know, the existing manner of possessing serfs cannot remain unchanged. It is better to abolish serfage from above than to await the time when it will begin to abolish itself from below. I request you, gentlemen, to consider how this can be put into execution and to submit my words to the Noblesse for their consideration.

But it took the Imperial Commission six years to overcome the opposition of powerful landowners who clung obstinately to their vested interests. This history of the negotiations is a tedious story, and in the final compromise may be seen the same fatal tenacity and unwillingness to surrender caste privileges that later practically wrecked the constitutional reform granting a Duma (parliament) in 1906.

The Tzar Liberator, Alexander II, was faced with a problem very different from that which confronted Abraham Lincoln. The emancipator of the American slaves was able, by a single proclamation, to free from bondage the persons of the blacks without conceding that it violated the immovable property rights of the plantation owner. Slavery, which postulates actual ownership of another human being as a chattel, is indefensible under the Christian dispensation which cannot regard human personality as an object included among the various categories of "property." It was Christian morality that first challenged the pagan concept of the intrinsic dignity of the human soul and raised men above the beasts and the plough and the field, which may be owned in the strictest sense. In freeing slaves, therefore, Abraham Lincoln could maintain that he was but righting the ancient wrong that had reduced a large group of rational human beings to the level of irrational animals. He could afford to hew close to the line and let the chips fall where they would.

But the Russian landholders, and, curiously enough, many educated Russians, who have not seriously investigated the development of serfdom, would indignantly deny that legalized slavery of any kind ever existed on their estates. The serfs, they maintained, belonged to the land,

and *it was the land that belonged to the proprietor.* The peasants, on their part, had a different and franker conception of their relations to the master, expressed in the celebrated proverb: "We are yours, but the land is ours."

The landowners' explanation was a disingenuous evasion, and insistence on it led to an unsatisfactory compromise quite characteristic of Russian autocracy. The long-awaited Law of Emancipation, the cherished dream of every Russian peasant, was signed on March 3, 1861, liberating, all told, something over 23,000,000 serfs. The signing of the law was followed by the "Great Manifesto," which was read in all the churches. But disappointment soon displaced the first jubilation, and distrust began to creep into the hearts of the liberated as they gradually learned to comprehend the terms of the law. Abstract conceptions of civic rights and legalistic assurances of independence left the peasant cold and unmoved, if not reduced to concrete, tangible facts. Land, to the Russian peasant, meant just one thing — it meant the soil so vividly described by Uspensky, that talented portrayer of Russian peasant life: —

It is the same soil which you bring home on your rubbers in the form of mud, it is the earth you see in your flower pots, black, wet earth; it is, in a word, the most ordinary, natural earth.

By the provisions of the law all peasants acquired the civic rights common to free rural classes, but, for the most part, they still found themselves without land. Land was actually assigned to each peasant household, but it did not become their property. They held it in "perpetual possession," but were required to pay yearly dues for the use of it. Where land was held in common, under the mir system,[1]

---

[1] *Mir:* A unique Russian institution, a primitive communal system of landholding (in contradistinction to "homestead-holding") under which title to the fields, meadows, and timber land remained vested in the village commune, which distributed the lots and regulated the tenure. It was presided over by village elders elected for the specific purpose of dividing up the holdings among qualified peasants according to their capacity for cultivating the land and the size of their families.

it was the village commune that distributed the lots and determined in what way they could be cultivated. If a peasant was awarded, let us say, ten dessiatines, in a commune of a thousand dessiatines, he usually found that he received his portion, not as a single unit, but probably in ten narrow strips of land, some situated in the fertile fields in the immediate vicinity of the village, others farther off by the river bank, the rest perhaps half a day's journey away on a barren hillside. That is why travelers in Russia, even in recent times, often marveled at seeing the arable land of a Russian village divided up into ribbonlike strips, sometimes less than two yards wide, separated from each other by dilapidated fences or other crude markings to indicate that the strips were owned by different persons. The results were disheartening. Ivan Ivanovich, with laborious industry, cultivated his strip of land and planted wheat. But Grigor Grigorevich, his neighbor, the village ne'er-do-well, allowed his strip to run to weeds, or let animals loose in it. With infinite difficulty Ivan Ivanovich slaved to wring a bare existence from his strip of land and to meet the taxes imposed upon him by the Government as "redemption fees" to be paid to the previous landholder in compensation for his expropriated property. Then, to confound the confusion, the majority of the 109,000 communes in Russia redistributed the holdings every ten or twelve years, and Grigor Grigorevich, the loafer, moved over on to the improved land of Ivan Ivanovich, the frugal.

Small inducement, therefore, to improve one's property or fertilize the soil, while there hovered over it the constant menace that it was destined to pass into other hands, leaving the previous owner to begin again the weary struggle for existence on another narrow strip! Each successive allotment, moreover, was based on the personal needs of the respective families. Households which had increased in number since the last allotment received additional dessiatines, especially if they had increased in male numbers. It was of considerable importance, consequently, that the expected baby should be a boy and that he should arrive before the day for the distribution of communal land. And, on the other hand, the declining years of the aged, lonely couple frequently saw their only means of livelihood automatically reduced, with the result that the evening of their life's hard working day became filled with shadows.

To these dark forebodings must be added the disturbing contrast which met the peasant's eye as he gazed toward the rich, unified, and prosperous estate of his former landlord, the *pomieschik*. In the distribution, the ruling classes saw to it that the gentry did not suffer overmuch. The actual proportion of land expropriated in each case was not large and by no means the best portion of the estate. It is related by one investigator that a certain noble who possessed 106,500 acres retained 100,000 for himself and sacrificed 6500 for his serfs. For the surrendered portion the Government paid him, as it paid all landholders, four fifths of the actual valuation, requiring the peasant — or the mir, as the case might be — to pay the balance in annual installments spread through a number of years. But this "redemption fee" was usually omitted by the peasant himself and ignored by the mir, with the result that the unpaid accumulations became oppressive and enormous. In 1905 Nicholas II was obliged to remit all outstanding redemption dues.

Though politically freed, great masses of the peasants, under the relentless whip of uncontrollable circumstances, drifted back into economic serfdom. In the first place, they were obliged to pay four different taxes: (1) *imperial*, to the central government; (2) *local*, to the zemstvos — an institution for limited self-government which we shall treat of in our next chapter; (3) *communal*, to the mir, for the commune; (4) *redemption dues* for the land expropriated from the proprietors.

THE EMANCIPATION OF THE SERFS

The Reading of the Great Manifesto, February 1861

These financial obligations, complicated by the unproductivity and rapidly spreading exhaustion of the soil under unscientific farming methods, inevitably drove the newly liberated serfs back to their masters as tenants, renting sections of the still huge proprietary estates bordering on the peasant communes. A vicious circle was thus inaugurated and soon completed. Within two decades the major portion of a bewildered and disappointed peasant population found themselves in a state of impoverishment not far removed from their former serfdom. Nay, more — it was often worse. Under the old régime they were part and parcel of a great organized estate, lived in comparatively respectable quarters, according to the disposition of the master, picked their firewood freely in his forest, and in time of famine were rationed from his well-stocked granary. But with freedom these things were no longer free; and in their place came a burdensome and a fallacious self-sufficiency, and the cessation of all manorial privileges.

Exploitation of tenants recommenced, and within a generation the rentals extorted from the peasant farmers amounted, in twenty-seven provinces of European Russia, to 81 per cent of the total proceeds from the land.

The dark legend soon gathered force and currency that the Tzar, as well as the peasants, had been cruelly tricked by the nobles. The "little white Father," *batiushka tzar*, had truly meant to give them the land; it was the landowners who were holding it back and so frustrating the benevolent design of the Emancipator. Agrarian riots were reported with alarming frequency during this period from different quarters of the Empire. Peasant armies swooped down on unpopular proprietors, looting the manor, the barns, and the fields, sometimes submitting the owners to gross brutality — a thing of which a drunken moujik is eminently capable.

This peasant psychology inevitably invited the attention

of the professional agitators both at home and abroad. From his exile in Switzerland the anarchist leader, Bakunin, preached armed insurrection to the peasants. Riots broke out among university students in Moscow and Petrograd, fomented and directed by the revolutionary intellectuals who had established themselves in Zurich as a headquarters.

Karakósov fired at the Emperor in 1866, and the repression which followed practically closed the period of enlightened reform initiated by Alexander II. Governmental repression generated new terrorism, and the annals of modern Russia from 1866 onward record an ever-increasing series of plots, assassinations of governors, of cabinet ministers, and policemen. Siberia began to receive a new quota of political prisoners. Dostoievsky has immortalized prison life there in his novel, *The House of the Dead*, where he tells us "our life was a constant hell, a perpetual damnation."

The long, long trail to Siberia was worn deep with ruts cut by marching parties of condemned prisoners clad in gray exile costume, three hundred to seven hundred at a time, clanking chains fixed to both legs and caught up at the waist. Thus shackled, they sometimes tramped three thousand miles before reaching their destination. And these convoys were not composed merely of criminals, but of "politicals" and "suspects" condemned to "administrative exile" as a result of their "political unreliability."

An American journalist, George Kennan, studied the exile system in Siberia during the year 1885 and issued his report in two rare volumes. He is discussing police methods and the elasticity of the term "punishment" in the vocabulary of a Russian Government official : —

An official copy of this paper, which I brought back with me from Siberia, lies before me as I write. It is entitled : "Rules Relating to Police Surveillance" (*Polozhēnie o Politseiskom Nadzóre*). The first thing that strikes the reader in a perusal of this document is the fact that it declares exile and police surveillance to be, not *punishmen's* for crimes already committed, but measures of pre-caution to prevent the commission of crimes that evil-minded men may contemplate. The first section reads as follows: "Police surveillance (which includes administrative exile) is a means of preventing crimes against the existing imperial order (the present form of government); and it is applicable to all persons who are prejudicial to public tranquillity." The power to decide when a man is "prejudicial to public tranquillity," and when exile and surveillance shall be resorted to as a means of "preventing crime," is vested in the governors-general, the governors, and the police; and in the exercise of that power they pay quite as much attention to the opinions that a man holds as to the acts that he commits. They can hardly do otherwise. If they should wait in all cases for the commission of criminal acts, they would not be "*preventing* crime," but merely watching and waiting for it, while the object of administrative exile is to *prevent* crime by anticipation. Clearly, then, the only thing to be done is to nip crime in the bud by putting under restraint, or sending to Siberia, every man whose political opinions are such as to raise a presumption that he *will* commit a crime "against the existing imperial order" if he sees a favorable opportunity for so doing. Administrative exile, therefore, is directed against ideas and opinions from which criminal acts may come, rather than against the criminal acts themselves. It is designed to anticipate and prevent the acts by suppressing or dis-couraging the opinions; and, such being the case, the document which lies before me should be called, not "Rules Relating to Police Surveillance," but "Rules for the Better Regulation of Private Opinion." In the spirit of this latter title the "Rules" are inter-preted by most of the Russian police.

The pretense that administrative exile is not a punishment, but only a precaution, is a mere juggle with words. The Government says, "We do not exile a man and put him under police surveillance as a punishment for holding certain opinions, but only as a means of preventing him from giving such opinions outward expression in criminal acts." If the banishment of a man to the province of Yakutsk for five years is not a "punishment," then the word "punishment" must have in Russian jurisprudence a very peculiar and restricted signification. In the case of women and young

girls a sentence of banishment to Eastern Siberia is almost equivalent to a sentence of death, on account of the terrible hardships of
the journey and the bad sanitary conditions of the *étapes* — and
yet the Government says that exile by administrative process is
not a punishment!

The terrorist society, "Land and Liberty," openly directed
the revolutionary movement. In August 1878, General
Mezentsev, head of the notorious Third Section (the progenitor of the Cheka), was murdered in broad daylight in a public
square in Petrograd. The murderer Stepniak escaped and
justified his deed in printed circulars widely distributed.
Prince Kropotkin, Governor of the Province, was murdered
at the door of his residence in Kharkov.

No group contributed more to the awakening and steer-
ing of the popular imagination into disturbed channels than
the famous Tchaikovsky Circles. Organized primarily as a
Petrograd club for self-education and self-improvement, its
members at first confined themselves to academic discussions
and the dissemination of harmless books approved by the
censors of the bureaucracy. But the flaming utterances of
Bakunin speedily transformed its meetings into a centre of
intellectual revolt, then into a G. H. Q. of the revolutionary
underworld. Within a few years it had spread fanlike
through the thirty-eight provinces of the Empire, serving as
an intermediary between the intelligentsia and the peasant
masses. In 1872 contact was established with labor, and
thus all revolutionary elements were united in a common
front.

Five shots were fired at the Emperor himself in 1879 by
a young man named Soloviev, but none reached the royal
mark. A new revolutionary organization of inner-circle
leaders called "The Will of the People" openly proclaimed
its intention to remove the Tzar, as the first step in the
destruction of the throne. They mined the railway over
which the Tzar passed in coming from the Crimea, but it

was another train that was blown up, killing numerous innocent victims. A carpenter named Halturin succeeded in
secreting a charge of dynamite in the Winter Palace, intending to explode it as the imperial family sat down to dinner.
The Emperor was late; the dynamite was exploded at the
appointed hour and ten soldiers were killed and fifty-three
injured. Swinburne, in his ode on "Russia," names the
next step : —

> . . . Life takes death for guide,
> Night hath but one red star — Tyrannicide.

Beside the Catherine Canal in Petrograd stands an
imposing structure, the Church of the Resurrection, richly
adorned with mosaics, more than St. Mark's in Venice,
gleaming with precious Ural stones and malachite and
polished jasper. It shelters some cobblestones in their
original setting and a few bloodstained flagstones which
mark a turning point in Russian history. On that spot was
immolated another despot whose brutal taking-off ushered
in the final period of retaliation by the government that
eventually ruined the Romanov dynasty — and Russia.

Six previous attempts had been made on his life; twenty-
six executions had resulted. But the seventh attempt had
been prepared with more diligence.

One of the conspirators, Vera Figner, has left an animated
account of the months of meticulous preparation for the
deed. The Revolutionary Committee rented a vacant
place on Malaya Sadovaya Street and opened a cheese shop.
One of the comrades, Bogdanovich, with his broad, round
face the color of a burnished samovar and with a spade-
shaped beard, was installed as shopkeeper, and three hundred
rubles were expended for the purchase of their harmless,
necessary stock in trade. Under cover of this occupation,
the technicians of the Committee excavated a tunnel and
undermined the street in two places where the Tzar was
expected to pass, emptying the dirt into empty cheese barrels.

"What is the cause of that dampness?" asked a suspicious constable one day, attracted by moisture that oozed through one of the barrels. Bogdanovich was quick-witted — as revolutionists had to be when plying their perilous profession. "During the Carnival weeks we spilled some sour cream there," he answered glibly.

"If the constable had looked into the barrel he would have seen the kind of sour cream it contained," adds Vera Figner in her *Memoirs*.

But the cheese shop was to be cheated of its prey. Alexander II chose an alternative route. So did the Executive Committee, and stationed four bomb-throwers on the quay of the Ekaterinskaya Canal — Grinevitsky, Rysakov, Mikhailov, and Emelyanov. To make assurance doubly sure, Zhelyabov was hovering near, armed with a dagger, should the bombs fail. Shortly after two o'clock the royal victim passed. Sofia Perovskaya waved her handkerchief and Rysakov hurled his bomb; he missed the Emperor but wounded some members of his equipage. Alexander stopped his sleigh and, in spite of the protests of his driver, hurried back on foot to stoop over his wounded Cossacks, whose life-blood was slowly turning the snow into a horrid crimson slush. As he bent over their bleeding bodies in a generous outburst of compassion, an attendant inquired, anxiously, "Are you hurt, sire?" "No, thank God," replied the Tzar. "Too soon to thank God yet," shouted Grinevitsky, hurling his reserve bomb, which struck its mark and blew both the Emperor and Grinevitsky to pieces.

That very afternoon, before leaving for his drive, Alexander had remarked to the Empress: "I have just signed a paper which will, I hope, make a good impression and show Russia that I grant all that is possible."

Princess Radziwill relates that a few hours later the Princess Catherine Mikhailovna attempted to secure possession of the Imperial Manifesto; it might, she thought, be of great use. She was about to open the drawer where it lay when the huge form of the Grand Duke Vladimir, eldest brother of the new monarch, Alexander III, appeared on the threshold; he required his stepmother to hand over to him the key with which she was on the point of opening the drawer of the Tzar's writing table. That night, while the assembled body of the most enlightened and best-meaning despot Russia ever had was being prepared for burial behind the drawn curtains of the darkened Winter Palace, the new sovereign held a conference with his councilors. Standing beside the remains of his father, Alexander opened the private drawer and took out the bulky paper to read it aloud. But one of his advisers, the most trusted and confidential, snatched the document from the Tzar's hands and tore it to shreds. "Now, Your Majesty," said he, "you can punish me, but at least it cannot be said that you stepped upon the throne of Russia with tied hands."

The scattered fragments of paper, lying like snowflakes on the carpet, contained the Constitution drawn up by Loris Mélikov, which Russians had fought and died for and dreamed of through three centuries. If the councilors walked over the fragments as they left the room, — which they very well might have done, — the answer was complete.

Whether this traditional account of the physical destruction of a signed constitution be accurate or not in all its details, the fact remains that it perished with its signer. Ten days later an Imperial Manifesto of another sort, drafted by that evil genius of two emperors, Konstantine Pobyedonostsev, was promulgated to an expectant nation; it reasserted categorically the principle of unlimited autocratic power and hurled defiance at Revolution.

The pendulum swung far under the reaction of the two succeeding Tzars.

CHAPTER III

THE DUEL

IT was to a perilous eminence that Alexander III mounted in March 1881, ascending a throne stained with the blood of his own father. Although the brutal murder on the Catherine Canal, generally speaking, evoked horror and sympathetic demonstrations in favor of the monarch throughout the land, still the underlying conflict between the masses of the people and the ruling autocracy continued unabated. Resentment smouldered in the apathetic souls of the peasants, unsatisfied as they were by the terms of the Emancipation Act; it was fanned by the guarded utterances of the intellectuals and liberals yearning for a constitution; but it flared openly from the secret press of the Revolutionary Party.

I referred, in the previous chapter, to the Imperial Manifesto, published by Alexander III on March 11, 1881, announcing his irrevocable decision to maintain unchanged the autocratic form of government devolving on him after the murder of his father and predecessor. The very same day brought to life a clear-cut rejoinder and declaration of war from the revolutionists in one of the most extraordinary documents I have yet come across in the annals of modern Russia. Naturally this counter-manifesto was never permitted free publication, but was printed and distributed by the underground agencies of the *Narodnaia Volia*, "The Will of the People." I deem it of sufficient importance to be quoted almost verbatim, as depicting, better than any words of mine can do, this tragic duel between the small band of determined men on one side and the armed might of Imperial Russia on the other.

THE EXECUTIVE COMMITTEE TO THE EMPEROR ALEXANDER III

YOUR MAJESTY : — The Executive Committee thoroughly understands the mental prostration you must now be experiencing. It does not, however, consider that it should, from a feeling of delicacy, defer the following declaration. There is something higher even than legitimate human feeling; it is the duty toward our country, a duty to which every citizen should sacrifice himself, his own feelings, and even those of others. Impelled by this imperious duty, we address ourselves to you without delay, as the course of events which threatens us with terrible convulsions, and rivers of blood in the future, will suffer no delay.

The sanguinary tragedy on the Catherine Canal was no mere chance occurrence, and could have surprised no one. After what has happened during the last ten years, it appeared inevitable; and therein lies its profound significance, which should be thoroughly understood by him whom destiny has placed at the head of a State.

The document continues, in the same restrained and coldly analytic style, to examine the social and political provocations that had driven high-minded men to desperation. They went cheerfully to exile, to the gibbet, to torture, if only injustice could thereby be ended. The Tzars were equally energetic in applying the full force of organized autocracy; they could be accused of no "want of energy." But their rigor would prove as powerless to save the existing order as was the punishment of the Cross inflicted on the Nazarene to save the decaying ancient world from the triumph of reforming Christianity.

A terrible explosion, a sanguinary revolution, a spasmodic convulsion throughout all Russia, will complete the destruction of the old order of things. Your Majesty, this is a sad and frightful prospect. . . . But why the sad necessity for this sanguinary struggle? . . . There are two outlets from such a situation: either a revolution, which will neither be averted nor prevented by condemnations to death, or the spontaneous surrender of supreme authority to the people to assist in the work of government.

In the interest of the country, and to avoid a useless waste of talent and energy, and those terrible disasters by which Revolution is always accompanied, the Executive Committee addresses itself to Your Majesty and counsels you to select the latter course. Be sure of this, that directly the highest power ceases to be arbitrary, directly it shows itself firmly resolved to carry out only what the will and the conscience of the people prescribes, you will be able to get rid of your spies, who dishonor the Government, dismiss your escorts to their barracks, and burn the gibbets, which demoralize the people. . . .

We hope that personal resentment will not suppress in you either the sentiment of duty or the desire of hearing the truth.

We also might feel resentment. You have lost your father; we lost, not only our fathers, but our brothers, wives, sons, and best friends. Nevertheless, we are ready to forget all personal rancor, if the welfare of Russia demands it, and we expect as much from you.

We impose upon you no conditions of any kind. Do not take offense at our proposals. The conditions which are necessary in order that the revolutionary movement should give place to a pacific development have not been created by us, but by events. We simply record them. These conditions, according to our view, should be based upon two principal stipulations: —

First, a general amnesty for all political offenders, since they have committed no crime, but have simply done their duty as citizens.

Second, the convocation of the representatives of the whole of the people, for the examination of the best forms of social and political life, according to the wants and desires of the people.

We, nevertheless, consider it necessary to point out that the legalization of power by the representation of the people can only be arrived at when the elections are perfectly free. The elections should, therefore, take place under the following conditions: —

First, the deputies shall be chosen by all classes without distinction, in proportion to the number of inhabitants.

PAUL I, 1796–1801
The Crowned Madman, Assassinated 1801

NICHOLAS I, 1825–1855

ALEXANDER II, 1855–1881
The Liberator, Assassinated 1881

ALEXANDER III, 1881–1894
Father of Nicholas II

LATER ROMANOVS

Second, there shall be no restrictions of any kind upon electors or deputies.

Third, the elections and the electoral agitation shall be perfectly free. The Government will, therefore, grant as provisional regulations, until the convocation of the popular assemblies : —

(*a*) Complete freedom of the press.

(*b*) Complete freedom of speech.

(*c*) Complete freedom of public meeting.

(*d*) Complete freedom of electoral addresses

These are the only means by which Russia can enter upon the path of peaceful and regular development. We solemnly declare, before the country, and before the whole world, that our party will submit unconditionally to the National Assembly which meets upon the basis of the above conditions, and will offer no opposition to the government which the National Assembly may sanction.

And now, Your Majesty, decide. The choice rests with you. We, on our side, can only express the hope that your judgment and your conscience will suggest to you the only decision which can accord with the welfare of Russia, with your own dignity, and with your duties toward the country.

THE EXECUTIVE COMMITTEE [1]

March 10 (23), 1881

Thus far the opposition. The plea for a recognition of inalienable rights could have been written by Thomas Jefferson, Leo XIII, or Henry Cabot Lodge. The Russian Government had its spokesmen, too, and skilled apologists. It is only just, therefore, that we should hear their defense, and from their own lips. *Audi alteram partem* — always hear the other side. And the other side at this period of Russian history had a most competent mouthpiece in Konstantine Pobyedonostsev, one of the tutors of Alexander III, and later of Nicholas II. With the aid of Dimitry Tol-

---

[1] This same Executive Committee addressed a note of sympathy to the Government of the United States when President Garfield was assassinated. It condemned the use of political assassination in America, pointing out the difference between the autocracy they were fighting in Russia and the satisfying liberty in America. See Appendix I.

stoy, Katkov, and Pazukhin, this brilliant jurist practically determined the policy of Russia during the eighties; and subsequently, during the reign of Nicholas II, he exercised similar influence as Procurator of the Holy Synod for upward of twenty years. In the words of Sir Bernard Pares, that true friend of Russia, and the present learned director of the School of Slavonic Studies of London University, "Pobyedonostsev was a thorough despiser of human nature who had turned reaction into a system of philosophy."

What is a parliament, a congress, or any other form of government in which the governed participate? Pobyedonostsev answers: "The greatest falsehood of our time. . . . One of the falsest political principles is the principle of government by the people, the idea which unfortunately became established after the French Revolution, that all power has its origin in the people and is based on the will of the people. . . . Parliament is an institution, serving to satisfy the personal ambition, personal vanity, and personal interests of the representatives."

What is law? He maintains that it is only an obstacle in the path of a strong executive. "If a person whose duty it is to *act* meets restricting instructions on every step in the law itself, and in its artificial formulations, if he is always exposed to the danger of overstepping a certain line of demarkation, then the administrator loses himself in doubts and is weakened by the very thing that was intended to furnish him with power."

Liberty and equality? "Mere folly! A failure everywhere." Freedom of thought? "A humbug." Trial by a jury? "A foreign importation, absurd and dangerous in Russia." Freedom of the press? "One of the false institutions of our time." Education? "Beyond reading, writing, and arithmetic all else is not only superfluous but dangerous. Fear, not love of God, and devotion to the Tzar, are to be cultivated as aids to government. False superstitions are not to be eradicated, rather fostered, being of the highest importance insomuch as superstition is the natural power of elemental inertia."

In pursuance of this mad policy, a circular was issued by the Government in 1887, signed by Delyanov, the Minister of Education, announcing that "the children of coachmen, servants, cooks, laundresses, small shopkeepers, and such-like people should not be encouraged to rise above the sphere in which they were born."

The universities, too, were rigidly controlled by a suspicious ministry that regarded all students as incipient revolutionists, with the result that freedom of science and the diffusion of knowledge were subjected to police supervision. The *tchinovniki* did not seem to know that the history of humankind is mainly the record of a race between education and catastrophe. Catastrophe won easily in Russia. As Macaulay says somewhere, writing of a certain race horse, "Eclipse first, the rest nowhere."

As early as 1864, and particularly after 1870, a unique form of popular instruction was going on among the peasants and factory workers in spite of the vigilance of the Ministry of Education. It was known as "going in among the people." Scores of students, writers, academicians, and countless other enthusiasts among the intellectuals, voluntarily abandoned their easy city life, assumed peasant and workmen costume, as the case might be, and went to live and work among the lower classes, in order to indoctrinate them with revolutionary principles. Without passports, or with forged documents, living under assumed names, these zealous missionaries were commonly known as "the illegals." Much of this activity was directed by Bakunin and Lavrov, from their exile in Switzerland. Unwilling to submit to the repression of a Russian university, hundreds of students flocked to Zurich. The Government, however, became alarmed at the growth of this hotbed of revolution abroad, and in 1873 summarily recalled something like one hundred students. But, as Macbeth ruefully remarks, "We but teach . . . bloody instructions, which, being taught, return to plague the inventor: this even-handed justice commends the ingredients of our poisoned chalice to our own lips." The returning students, fired with fanatic zeal for propaganda, trooped off to the provinces to "go in among the people" and spread the teachings of Bakunin and Lavrov.

The law courts, the last refuge of freemen, lost seriously of their independence during this period and became practically branches of the Administrative Department. The institution of *zemski nachalniki*, or land captains, by the Minister of the Interior in 1886, to all intents and purposes nullified the courts by creating a centralized guardianship of the peasants which regulated their lives in an oppressive and arbitrary manner, even down to the most intimate details of their family relations. It was based on the theory, as Count Witte puts it, "that they are eternally under age, so to speak." In the opinion of that illustrious statesman, it was a profoundly erroneous step fraught with disastrous consequences for the future.

Under these "land captains," supported by an army of policemen, spies, *agents provocateurs*, and other *tchinovniki*, Russia was ruled with the iron precision of martial law. Reaction, therefore, and pure absolutism reached their climax during this period, the reign of Alexander III. Through the convenient invention known as "administrative procedure" the Government was enabled to transport to Siberia, without the slightest semblance of trial or juridical procedure, any and all persons deemed "politically undesirable." MacKenzie Wallace, in his classic study of Russia, quotes the saying, current during the reign of Nicholas I, that nearly all the best men in Russia had spent a part of their lives in Siberia. Hence, it was proposed to publish a biographical dictionary of remarkable men, a Russian

Who's Who, in which every article was to end as follows: "Banished to . . . in 18—." It was to be the *hic jacet* of popular liberty.[1]

It was a duel to the death between the organized forces of official Russia on the one hand and a guerrilla band of determined volunteers on the other. A roll call of the opposition, if made in the ascending order of their radicalism, would reveal the following categories : —

1. LIBERALS, who strove by legal means — and guardedly — to enlarge the boundaries of human freedom by opposing the centralization of authority and the arbitrary exercise of absolutism. Followers of the Decembrists of 1825, they did not necessarily oppose the monarchy as a form of government; they advocated, rather, a voluntary limitation of its powers by a constitution, and endeavored, as cool-headed patriots, to open the eyes and ears of the ruling caste to the social injustices rampant under the tyranny of the *tchinovniki*. If their enthusiasm became too heated, they were first marked as "politically unreliable," "pernicious to public tranquillity," and invited to proceed by direct route to Siberia. Milyukov, Vinogradoff, Struve, and Korolenko may be cited as typical leaders. In the days of the Duma they spoke through the Constitutional Democrats, the Cadets.[2]

2. SOCIAL REVOLUTIONARIES — that is, Liberals of more determined conviction, prepared for drastic measures and

[1] See Appendix II.

[2] Etymologically, the term "liberal" has obvious relation to freedom of some sort. Up to the close of the eighteenth century it had no political significance, being applied to cultural freedom, "a liberal education," "the liberal arts," and so forth. In the nineteenth century it acquired wide political and social connotation in consequence of the theories of Rousseau, Diderot, and Madame Staël. In the twentieth century it denotes a curious variety of claimants who range from sincere crusaders and unprejudiced thinkers to illiberal bigots, cranks, and intellectual dilettantes. For the latter category it frequently serves as a convenient cloak to mask a mental or moral incapacity to face and take a positive stand on serious issues. These are the straddlers, the dabblers, and the *poseurs*, who applaud the most contradictory theories, however ridiculous, rather than strain their nerves by a too close application of logic or endanger their reputation for broadness and tolerance by a public exhibition of their thought processes.

openly advocating a fundamental reform of the existing social and political order. They aimed principally to create a political consciousness — which in Russia inevitably led to political disorder — among the peasants, employing means that were illegal as well as legal. But armed insurrection was not yet on their programme; they avoided the question of Tzar or no Tzar and based their hopes on the action of duly elected representatives of the Russian people. Ballots, not bullets, were to be the instruments of reform. They had representation in the second Duma.

3. SOCIAL DEMOCRATS, who cultivated town and factory workers in an effort to stimulate opposition to the prevailing industrial system. Their manifestoes instructed workers in the technique of strikes, promulgated demands for an eight-hour day, for freedom of speech, conscience, and assembly. These were the pioneers who laid the foundation for Russian Trade-Unionism. They also had deputies in a Duma when it came.

4. SOCIALISTS — the inheritors of the doctrines of Saint Simon, Robespierre, Owen, Lassalle, and Louis Blanc. By appealing to the primitive communal instincts of the Russian peasant, they proposed to establish pure state socialism which would control all instruments of production. Political autocracy was to be displaced by a dictatorship of labor; religion was to be abolished, and individual men were all to be cut on the same pattern, determined by the generic formulæ: "Each for all and all for each"; "From everyone according to his strength, to each according to his needs." They pictured humankind only in a mass, careless of the individual. They, too, won a large number of seats in the Duma.[1]

5. ANARCHISTS. Whereas Socialism — and Communism, its offshoot — demands a highly centralized control of humankind and tends to degenerate into tyrannous bureau-

[1] See Appendix III.

cracy, the anarchist adopted a platform that is the diametric opposite.[1] He is the individualist run mad, seeking to emancipate men from all restraint whatsoever, political, economic, or religious. Let humans roam in a state of pure and unfettered nature; there shall be no state, no government, no municipal ordinances or other limitations to physical liberty; every individual man shall be at liberty to live where, how, and as long as he deems necessary in vindication of his personal rights, which are the only rights the anarchist acknowledges. Fathered by Proudhon, who first expounded it in 1848, this deification of jungle ethics is admirably adapted to turn civil society into a menagerie. It was widely disseminated in Russia by Bakunin, Pisarev, and Prince Kropotkin. Obviously it must reject divinity and religion in any form. "God," writes Proudhon, "that is folly and cowardice. God is tyranny and misery. God is evil. To me, then, Lucifer, Satan."

6. NIHILISTS. This fearsome word first appears in Turgenev's *Fathers and Sons* as a new name for an old disease. It describes, in one convenient term, a state of mind produced by lack of anchorage during severe intellectual storms occasioned by jaundiced contemplation of social and political inequalities. It would be erroneous to maintain that there ever existed an organized anti-governmental party to which the appellation could be applied. Nihilism, strictly speaking, was a nickname, an opprobrious epithet coined by the conservatives and reactionaries to describe all revolutionary agitators.

"Who is this Bazarov?" asks one of the characters in Turgenev's novel.

"He is a nihilist," replies his son.

---

[1] For that reason he is detested and feared by the Bolsheviki. Not far from the house where the author lived in Moscow stood the ruins of the headquarters of the anarchists, where they made their last stand against the Bolsheviki in the November Revolution. No house in Moscow was more riddled with bullets and artillery fire.

"Nihilist?" repeats the old man. "Oh, yes; that comes from the Latin *nihil* — with us 'nichevo,' nothing, as far as I can judge. That just means a man who admits nothing."

"Say rather, respects nothing," adds another old man.

"One who examines everything from a critical point of view," answers the young man. "That's the same thing."

"No, it's not the same thing. The nihilist is the man who bows to no authority, who admits of no principle as an article of faith, with whatever respect such principle may be enshrouded."

But how does the nihilist differ from the anarchist? Only, I think, in being one shade more bewildered by undigested, factual knowledge. His negation of life is more sterile than the positivism of the anarchist. "Nihilism," explains De Voguë, "is the Nirvana of the Hindu, the self-abnegation of the discouraged primitive man before the force of matter and the occult moral world." Turgenev himself hints at the difference : —

"Look here, your Bazarov is not my sort, and he is none of yours, either."

"Why is that?"

"Well, what shall I say? . . . He is a savage brute, and you and I, we are tamed animals."

"This comparison," adds the Viscount, "enables us to perceive, more than would a volume of discussion, the shade of distinction which differentiates Russian Nihilism from the similar mental maladies from which humanity has suffered since the days of Solomon. This Bazarov, a cynical peasant's son, embittered, who sputters brief sentences in a language at times vulgar, at others scientific, who attacks everything, is otherwise an honorable fellow incapable of a vile action. He represses his better instincts out of mere pride, but is at heart a savage, too rapidly educated, who, having stolen our weapons, uses them against us. Turgenev's hero has many points in common with Fenimore Cooper's Red Indian, but a redskin fuddled with the doctrines of Hegel and Büchner, instead of with 'fire water,' and who stalks the world with a lancet instead of rushing about with a tomahawk."

7. TERRORISTS. By this classification is meant, not a distinct party, but a grouping of individuals who may, philosophically, belong to any one of the previous categories. They differ from their more academic brethren of revolt only in method, not in principle or objective. A terrorist may have been an embittered Liberal who has become drunk on bad ink and decides to fling a bomb, wreck an imperial train, or stab a policeman. Or he may be a calculating criminal caught red-handed while perpetrating an inhuman crime, but without the resources to convince a jury that he was "momentarily unbalanced" or "mentally sick" in the Clarence Darrow sense. In any case, his proposal is to write in blood what he cannot get before the public by printer's ink.

The Bolshevik or Marxian Communist of the Left does not effectively appear in the ranks of Russian revolutionists until a somewhat later date; we shall devote a later volume to a study of that figure, the reincarnation and synthesis of all previous revolutionary characters.

Under the passport system a man could neither move from one town to another without governmental permission nor change his living quarters within a given town without registration. Thus the accumulation of visas and registration stamps on a man's passport furnished the police with a full account of his every movement. Neither could he sleep outside his own house, without the porter, or the house janitor, reporting the suspicious circumstances at the nearest police station. A man could as well hope to live

without a soul as without a passport in Imperial Russia.[1]
The rule of "intensified vigilance," as it was called, permitted the police and the detectives of the Third Department of Chancery to search and arrest individuals, enter
homes, and search private residences without warrant.
Government control of the press required supervision of all
written articles by unsympathetic and, oftentimes, uncultivated censors, who not only suppressed at will news items
or articles even faintly criticizing the administration, but
even articles in the field of history, literature, or geography,
which they might not have liked, or could not understand.

The Liberals and revolutionists replied by the secret
publications described by Stepniak in his remarkable volume,
called *Underground Russia.* Prince Kropotkin narrates
how easily it was done. He was returning from abroad with
a heavy consignment of radical literature.

I returned to St. Petersburg via Vienna and Warsaw. Thousands of Jews lived by smuggling on the Polish frontier; and I
thought that if I could succeed in discovering only one of them,
my books would be carried in safety across the border. . . . . . .

I explained to the man [a Jew who was lounging at the entrance
to the hotel] my desire of smuggling into Russia a rather heavy
bundle of books and newspapers.

"Very easily done, sir," he replied. "I will just bring to you
the representative of the Universal Company for the International
Exchange of (let us say) Rags and Bones. They carry on the largest smuggling business in the world. . . . "

In an hour's time he came back with another young man. This
one took the bundle, put it by the side of the door and said, "It's
all right. If you leave to-morrow you shall have your books at
such a station in Russia."

Next day I left Cracow; and at the designated Russian station
a porter approached my compartment and, speaking loudly, so as

---

[1] All these devices for complete control of the individual still exist in Soviet
Russia.

EXILES TRAMPING TO SIBERIA

AN OFFICIAL AND HIS WIFE

RUSSIAN CONTRASTS

to be heard by the gendarme who was walking along the platform, said to me, "Here is the bag Your Highness left the other day," and handed me my precious parcel.

Perhaps the most important of these secret publications was *Kolokol*, "The Bell," edited by Alexander Herzen from his exile in London. It was a fortnightly journal that passed the frontier in thousands and exercised a measurable influence on the progress of revolutionary thought in Russia. Its brilliant editor seemed to know everything that was going on in his distant fatherland, so that even the Emperor himself was a regular reader of the forbidden journal, which he found every two weeks on his table, laid there by he knew not what hand. In this regard, the following anecdote is recounted by Wallace.

One number of the *Kolokol* contained a violent attack on an important personage of the Court, and the accused, or some one of his friends, considered it advisable to have a copy of the paper specially printed for the Emperor without the objectionable article. The Emperor did not at first discover the trick, but shortly afterward he received from London a polite note containing the article which had been omitted, and informing him how he had been deceived.

About this time, in the year 1887, occurred an incident which, like so many other seemingly trivial circumstances in history, probably exerted a tremendous influence on the future destiny of Russia. An attempt was made on the life of Alexander III by a group of terrorists in March 1887. The plot was unsuccessful, the conspirators having been arrested in the streets of Petrograd with the bombs in their possession. Five of the conspirators were hanged, among them a certain Alexander Ulianov. Now, Ulianov had a younger brother who continued the revolutionary work of his elder and spent part of his life in Siberia, from whence he later escaped to Switzerland. His name was Nicholas Ulianov, better known to the entire world under the assumed name of Nicholas Lenin.

There now occurred, in 1889, a change of tactics on the part of the revolutionists. Direct action had been barren of any practical result beyond periodic horror and growing popular impatience at each successive political assassination. The autocratic power seemed impregnable against frontal attack, and political propaganda, designed to hasten a process of political evolution, was gradually substituted for the method of open insurrection and revolution. The Nihilism of Pisarev and the Anarchism of Bakunin began to give way to the Socialism of Plekhanov. With this change of revolutionary philosophy began the era of combinations of workmen and strikes in industry. And more and more recourse was had to parliamentary methods of redress.

There was but one legal opposition in Russia, but one body authorized to voice with impunity the aspirations and defend the rights of the common people. It was the zemstvo, that interesting institution created in 1864 for the purpose of answering to a limited degree the insistent demand for some form of representative government. Theoretically, at least, the emancipation of the serfs had allayed the land hunger of the peasants. Actually, as we have seen, it complicated the situation and became the fecund source of new dangers. It was a characteristic half-measure. Likewise, in the zemstvo was found a half-answer to the constitution hunger of the liberal and the intellectual.

The infection of compromise and procrastination had seeped from the very top to the foundations of the social organism until it became part and parcel of the national character. *Nichevo* (that word of infinite variety, meaning "No matter," "What's the use?" "I don't care"), *sichas* ("right away"), and *zaftra* ("to-morrow"), were not merely popular terms of resignation or evasion — they expressed a

whole philosophy of life. So does the boulder which Brailsford describes in *The Russian Workers' Republic:* —

One noticed continually things which were sinking into dilap-
idation — a railway carriage, for example, or a bathroom — when
a few minutes' work with a screwdriver would have sufficed to
repair them. I used to watch the drivers on the primitive country
roads with a mixture of annoyance and admiration. One saw some
big obstacle in the way, usually a large stone which some might call
a small rock. Almost any English driver would have got down and
rolled it away. The Russian contrived somehow to circumnavigate
it. Rather than remove it, he would drive through the ditch or
over a ploughed field. With a jolt, at an angle which defied
gravitation, with groaning springs and straining horses, we somehow got past it. I arrived, after many experiences, at the conviction that the boulder always had been there. Generations of
Russian drivers had gone round it. It had defied Ivan the Terrible
and Peter the Great and the odds are that it will survive Lenin.

The zemstvo was an attempt at local self-government
through an assembly which met once a year in each district
and in each province, but with no central or national
assembly. The deputies were elected by the nobles, by the
peasants, and by the communes, the nobles having the right
to 57 per cent of the seats, the peasants to 30 per cent, and
the various communes to the remainder. Its functions
were limited to providing for the material wants of the
respective districts — roads and bridges, crops, sanitary
affairs, vigilance against famine, improvement of live stock,
prevention of fire, primary education, and such local interests. But it was severely prohibited from touching national
affairs.

To the zemstvo, naturally, the inarticulate masses looked
for political salvation, as it alone had the right of petition.
Timidly at first, but with increasing confidence, this right
was exercised. In 1880, after the Turkish War, the Zemstvo
of Tver petitioned the Emperor as follows: —

The Emperor, in his care for welfare of the Bulgarian people, whom he has freed from the yoke of the Turk, has considered it necessary to grant them true self-government, inviolability of person, an independent judicial system, and liberty of the press. The Zemstvo of Tver dares to hope that the Russian people, who have borne with such readiness and love of their ruler all the burdens of the war, will enjoy the same blessings.

Again, in 1894, on the accession of Nicholas II, numerous addresses of loyalty were presented by the local zemstvos, voicing, in various degrees, their hope for a continuation of the reforms initiated by Alexander II, but discontinued by Alexander III.   But the old voice of intransigent autocracy was again heard in the land when the young sovereign shattered all illusions in his reply : —

It has come to my knowledge that of late there have been heard the voices of people lured by senseless dreams of representatives of the zemstvos sharing in the conduct of internal affairs.   Let it be known to all that I, devoting all my strength to the pursuit of the good of my people, will maintain the principle of autocracy as firmly and steadfastly as did my late father.

"He howled the words at us," was the way the leader of the delegation described the Tzar's tone.   The same gentleman was soon informed that he should never again show his face in Petrograd.[1]

Shortly afterward Nicholas II received a letter — one of a long series that continued up to the outbreak of the War — from another autocrat, who was sending a wedding present to the new Tzar.

BERLIN, 7/11/95

DEAREST NICKY : —

Egloffstein will, I hope, be able to bring over the whole heap of porcelain without any breakage.   He is instructed to arrange the table so as it would be if you gave a dinner for fifty ; so that you should have the *coup d'œil* of the whole affair.   I hope that my

---

[1] See Appendix IV.

PEASANT TYPES

manufacturer has done everything to fulfill your wishes and that the present may be useful to you both.

Since the sad weeks you had to go through have passed, much has happened in Europe. You have lost an excellent old servant of your predecessors, old Giers, who was a very good fellow whom I much esteemed. France has changed *par surprise* her head and government and through the amnesty opened the doors to all the worst malefactors the former people with difficulty had managed to imprison. The influence given to the Democrats and the Revolutionary Party is also to be felt here. My Reichstag behaves as badly as it can, swinging backward and forward between the Socialists, egged on by the Jews and the ultramontane Catholics; both parties being soon fit to be hung — all of them, as far as I can see.

In England the Ministry is toddling to its fall amidst universal derision! In short, everywhere the *principe de la Monarchie* is called upon to show itself strong. That is why I am glad at the capital speech you made the other day to the deputations in response to some addresses for reform. It was very much to the point and made a deep impression everywhere. . . .

With my respects to your Mamy and my compliments to Alix, I remain,

Your aff-ate friend,
WILLY

The reply to the Zemstvo of Tver was spoken by Nicholas but the hand that wrote it was the hand of Pobyedonostsev. It meant the revival of terrorism and marked the resumption of the duel that had been interrupted since the eighties. Nicholas II, though possessed of a certain mildness of character and native humanity, early showed himself to be as clay in the hands of energetic potters, moulded to eventual destruction by reactionary ministers of the type of Pobyedonostsev, Sipyagin, and Plehve. The Social Democrats, deprecating terrorism, were displaced as leaders by the Social Revolutionaries, who flung aside the pen to seize torch, revolver, dagger, and hand grenade, recognizing in them the only expression of the popular will to which the Russian Tzar would listen.

In February 1897 occurred a typical demonstration of slumbering discontent, scarcely less revealing than the massacre of Bloody Sunday eight years later. A young woman, Marie Feodorovna Vietrov, a student of the Higher School for Women, had been arrested and imprisoned in the fortress of St. Peter and St. Paul for the crime of secreting illegal literature. Seven weeks after her arrest, she committed suicide in prison by pouring kerosene over herself and setting fire to her clothes. The effect on public opinion was electric; circulars describing the harrowing incident were distributed along the streets — unsigned, of course — and indignation ran high. In spite of repeated warnings by the police, thousands of people knelt in the snow of the Nevsky Prospekt outside the Kazan Cathedral and joined their murmurs and sobbing to the funeral dirge. Such popular manifestations had not occurred since the assassination of Alexander II, and thoughtful Russians detected the undertone of revolt.

In vain enlightened and courageous ministers, like Count Witte and Isvolsky, attempted to heal the widening breach between the throne and the nation at large. Count Witte, in his *Memoirs*, recalls a memorable attempt made by him in 1898, when he was Minister of Finance, to recall the young Emperor to a consciousness of the realities and dangers of the moment. It was in the form of an energetic protest, of the kind that exiled many a true Russian patriot "to his estates" during the Great War, when the same Nicholas II was so often begged to rid Russia of the curse of Rasputin. Count Witte's protest ran, in part, as follows: —

The Crimean War opened the eyes of those who could see. They perceived that Russia could not be strong under a régime based on slavery. Your grandfather cut the Gordian knot with his autocratic sword. He redeemed the soul and body of his people from their owners. The unprecedented act created the colossus who is now in your autocratic hands. Russia was transformed, she increased her power and her knowledge tenfold. And this in spite of the fact that after the emancipation a liberal movement was aroused which threatened to shatter the autocratic power, which is the very basis of the existence of the Russian Empire. . . . The crisis of the eighties was not caused by the emancipation of the serfs. It was brought about by the corrupting influence of the press, the disorganization of the school, the liberal self-governing institutions, and, finally, the fact that the authority of the organs of the autocratic power had been undermined as a result of constant attacks upon the bureaucracy on the part of all manner of people. . . . Emperor Alexander II freed the serfs, but he did not organize the life on the firm basis of law. Emperor Alexander III, absorbed by the task of restoring Russia's international prestige, strengthening our military power, improving our finances, suppressing the unrest, did not have the time to complete the work begun by his most august father. This task has been bequeathed to Your Imperial Majesty. It can be carried out and it must be carried out. Otherwise the growth of Russia's grandeur will be impeded. . . .

The peasant was freed from his landowner. . . . But he is still a slave of his community as represented by the mir meetings and also of the entire hierarchy of petty officials who make up the rural administration. The peasant's rights and obligations are not clearly defined by law. His welfare and his very person are at the mercy of the arbitrary rulings of the local administration. The peasant is still flogged, and that at the decision of such institutions as the volost [rural district] courts. . . . The peasant was given land. But his right to it is not clearly defined by law. Wherever the communal form of landownership prevails, he cannot even know which lot is his. The inheritance rights are regulated by vague customs. So that at present the peasant holds his land not by law, but by custom, and often by arbitrary discretion. The family rights of the peasants have remained almost completely outside of the scope of law. . . .

And what of popular education? It is an open secret that it is in the embryonic stage and that in this respect we are behind not only many European countries, but also many Asian and transatlantic lands. . . .

Thus, the peasantry, while personally free, is still a slave to arbitrariness, lawlessness, and ignorance. Under these circumstances the peasant loses the impulse to seek to improve his condition by lawful means. The vital nerve of progress is paralyzed in him. He becomes passive and spiritless, thus offering a fertile soil for the growth of vices. Single, even though substantial, measures will not remedy the situation. Above all, the peasant's spiritual energies must be aroused. He must be granted the plenitude of civil rights which the other legal sons of Your Majesty enjoy. Given the present condition of the peasantry, the State cannot advance and achieve the world importance to which the nature of things and destiny itself entitle it.

This condition of the peasantry is the fundamental cause of those morbid social phenomena which are always present in the life of our country. . . . A great deal of attention is given to the alleged "land crisis." It is a strange crisis, indeed, seeing that prices of land are everywhere on the increase. Widespread discussion also centres around the comparative merits of the individual classes which go to make the nation. An effort is made to ascertain which of them supports the throne. As if the Russian Autocratic Throne could possibly rest on one class and not on the entire Russian people ! . . . On that unshakable foundation it will rest forever. . . . The root of the evil is not the land crisis, or unorganized migrations, or the growth of the budget, but rather the confusion and disorder which prevail in the daily life of the peasant masses. . . . In a word, Sire, it is my profound conviction that the peasant problem is at present the most vital problem of our existence. It must be dealt with immediately.

This superb letter was never answered, and Witte affirms that the Tzar never referred to it in any shape or form. On the contrary, he almost immediately confirmed the Plehve-Durnovo clique, opposed to the liberal tendencies of Witte, who were thus enabled to thwart Witte's hopes for legislative reform. "Whom Jupiter would destroy he first makes mad."

And the blindness to impending disaster was never more manifest than in the inexplicable indifference manifested by the Russian Government toward the rising menace of Japan. Russia's foreign policy under the cunning stimulus of the German Kaiser had been leading her deeper and deeper into the Far East, nearer and nearer to the growing might of a watchful Japan. Early in January 1904 the Japanese ambassador, Kurino, whispered in Count Witte's ear, during an evening party at the Winter Palace, that the Tokio Government was at the end of its patience because of the seeming contempt and indifference with which the Russian Government was treating Japan's representations regarding Manchuria and Korea. He warned Witte that if no reply was forthcoming within a few days hostilities were inevitable! Witte conveyed the warning to Count Lamsdorff, the Minister of Foreign Affairs. "I can do nothing," replied Lamsdorff. For Lamsdorff, though Minister of Foreign Affairs, had been deliberately and completely superseded in the Far East negotiations by a group of industrialists interested in the exploitation of certain forests in the Yalu River basin. On Lamsdorff's protesting, long before this, that such negotiations must be left to the diplomats, the impossible Plehve had replied that not diplomats, but bayonets, had made Russia, and that the Far East problem must be solved by bayonets, not by diplomatic pens. It was so solved.

A few weeks after the *soirée diplomatique* in the Winter Palace, in the gray dawn of a wintry morning, January 26, 1904, a Japanese fleet under Admiral Togo stole into the harbor of Port Arthur and sank a number of Russian warships lying unsuspectingly at anchor. The rising consciousness of the East had thrown down the gauge of battle to the Russian Giant. Once again Russian autocracy had deliberately exposed itself to the dread arbitrament of war. The result shook the Empire to its foundations and marked the beginning of the final catastrophe of 1917.

Plehve had previously remarked that revolution was inevitable in Russia and what was needed to distract public attention was a "small victorious war." So he let Russia drift into the conflict with Japan. His diagnosis was correct but his treatment of the disease was wrong on two counts: the war was neither small nor victorious.

CHAPTER IV

THE BEGINNINGS OF REVOLUTION

THE particular period upon which we are now entering would well merit not one or two, but a dozen separate chapters, embracing as it does the final act of that most tragic conflict between autocracy and revolution. For with the close of the Russo-Japanese War began the swift succession of reverses, both domestic and external, still fresh in our memories, that definitely sealed the doom of the Romanov dynasty and resulted in the disintegration of the Russian Empire. It will be clear, therefore, that I can but touch briefly on the main events and invite attention to the outstanding personalities in the complex panorama that now unrolled itself with such astonishing rapidity.

If the defeat of Russia in the Crimean War weakened the foundations of autocracy, the humiliating outcome of the Japanese War hastened to a measurable degree the disintegration process. It was left for the World War to bring the worm-eaten structure crashing to the ground.

The revelations of unpreparedness and incompetency in the conduct of military operations, the confusion arising from the division of authority between General Kuropatkin and Admiral Alexeiev, the surrender of Port Arthur (although there were three months' provisions and plenty of ammunition in the town), the succession of shameful land defeats, ending in the rout at Mukden and the final crushing naval disaster at Tsushima, which buried practically the entire Russian fleet in Japanese waters, all conspired to destroy the confidence of the nation in a bureaucracy that had

shown itself inept, piddling, and palsied in all things —
except domestic tyranny. The oppressive rigorism of
Plehve, Minister of the Interior, unmodified by any ele-
mentary wisdom that should have dictated liberal and
conciliatory policies during a foreign war, finally left the
Government without a friend in the country and faced by a
victorious foe abroad. To emphasize this complete isolation
and demoralization of the bureaucrats, the terrorists assassinated Plehve on July 28, 1904. Thus, this exponent of
the absolutism of Pobyedonostsev went the way of his friend
and predecessor, Sipyagin, who had already been assassinated in 1902. Yet there still remained to take their
places such hopeless reactionaries as Durnovo, Stolypin,
Stürmer, Protopopov, and the unspeakable Rasputin. It
would seem as if the furious Eumenides that had been tor-
menting Russia for a century had resolved to scourge and
lash her with scorpions to the end of the chapter.

On February 17, 1905, the Grand Duke Serge, uncle of
the Emperor, and Governor-General of Moscow, was blown
to pieces within the Kremlin walls. The Governor of Ufa
and the Vice Governor of Elizabethpol suffered the same
fate at the hands of the terrorists. Police officials began to
be assassinated in alarming numbers. Riots, strikes, and
disorders increased throughout the land, spreading to Poland
and the Caucasus. In January 1905, official statistics
showed that 700,000 men were on strike, a phenomenon that
emphasized, for the first time, the rôle of labor as a factor
contributing to the progress of the revolutionary movement.

The unprecedented industrial development in Russia
during the thirty years prior to the Japanese War testified
to the awakening of the national consciousness to an appreciation of the immense economic possibilities of the land.
Russia is a vast reservoir of undeveloped natural resources.
Raw materials abound in the shape of oil, minerals, furs,
lumber, water power, ores, flax, hemp, wool, tallow, hides,

and the like. The development of these natural assets was greatly stimulated by the emancipation of the serfs, which threw an unlimited supply of cheap labor on the market and caused an influx of peasants from the countryside to towns and cities. No man did more at this time to foster native industry in Russia than Count Witte, who was a devout admirer of the great German economist Friedrich List, following ardently that scholar's basic doctrine that "each nation should above all things develop harmoniously its natural resources to the highest possible degree of independence, protecting its own industry and preferring the national aim to the pecuniary advantage of individuals."

The result was the creation of a new class, the industrial proletariat. Factories and factory settlements sprang up with amazing rapidity, not only in the great centres of population, but throughout the land, while cottage industry began to wane. Unfortunately, industrial abuses were not far behind industrial developments. Working time was generally more than twelve hours per day, and as many as sixteen in some occupations. Wages were unbelievably low, the average wage in the eighties being less than 200 rubles — that is, approximately $105 — a year. In 1910 it was 244 rubles, or $125, per year, scarcely $2.50 a week. Strikes were criminal acts. Sanitary conditions were such as to recall the Black Hole of Calcutta. In many factories no living accommodations were provided for the workers, who slept in the workroom, on benches, or on the floors. The novels of Gorky, Andreev, Chekhov, Gogol, Tolstoy, and Dostoievsky reproduced these conditions with the stark and harrowing reality that ordinarily characterized the Russian masters. "*I shall laugh my bitter laugh,*" was the inscription placed on Gogol's grave as his farewell comment on life in Russia.

Naturally the revolutionary agitators, following their traditional practice of fishing in troubled waters, were not slow to abandon the peasant campaign and concentrate on the city workers. Politics and economics thus became more closely identified than ever. Workmen's associations, and strikes in industry, were thereafter the obvious tactics. Times of popular unrest, like those of 1905, caused by legitimate grievances, presented rare opportunities for effective mass movements in the large cities. This phase culminated in the tragedy of "Bloody Sunday" or "Red Sunday," as it is variously called, on January 22, 1905.

George Gapon, a priest of the Russian Orthodox Church, was a popular leader of the working classes, among whom he had organized numerous clubs in St. Petersburg, achieving thereby considerable influence with the labor unions and the Social Democrats. During a strike of 45,000 operatives of the Putilov Ironworkers, he conceived the idea of leading 100,000 workmen to the Winter Palace for the purpose of presenting a petition to the Tzar. The text of this petition, which I have before me, is not revolutionary in tone, but appeals to the Tzar, as to a father, to mitigate the cruel sufferings of his children.

Sire! I fear the Ministers have not told you the truth about the situation. The whole people, trusting in you, has resolved to appear at the Winter Palace at two o'clock in the afternoon, in order to inform you of its needs. If you hesitate and do not appear before the people, then you sever the moral bonds between you and them. Trust in you will disappear, because innocent blood will be shed. Appear to-morrow before your people and receive in a courageous spirit our address of devotion! I and the representatives of labor, my brave comrades, guarantee the inviolability of your person.

On the appointed day, Nicholas II, ignoring the invitation, remained in the Summer Palace at Tsarskoe Selo. Tens of thousands of workmen, with their wives and children, paraded in orderly fashion to the Winter Palace, bearing, not red flags, but portraits of the Tzar and the royal family.

There they were met by the Cossacks.   With Gapon at their head, the demonstrators, chanting hymns and exhibiting all outward signs of a religious procession, attempted to push their way to the gates of the Palace.   The Cossacks, without warning, fired into the thickest part of the crowd.   When the smoke cleared away one of the most repulsive scenes in modern Russian history was revealed.   Five hundred men, women, and children lay dead in the snow, before that long, grim structure, and three thousand more were writhing on the ground under their wounds ; the rest were fleeing in panic and dismay !   Boys who had climbed up trees and telegraph poles, the better to view the parade, were picked off like birds.

If Hilaire Belloc contends that the French Revolution began on that day and at the moment, at Versailles, when the representatives of the people, prohibited from entering the Palace, retired instead to the tennis court, I should say that the Russian Revolution became inevitable when the first peaceful petitioner fell that Sunday afternoon before the Winter Palace.

The fate of Gapon is of interest, as illustrating the uncertain fate of a man who fastens on duplicity as a profession. He was among the first to fall, but he evidently only pretended to be killed.   He escaped unhurt to Switzerland, whence he continued his attacks on the Government with great bitterness.   But he evidently made peace with the home authorities and soon returned to St. Petersburg, there to assume the rôle that has remained to this day something of a mystery.   He acted as a go-between or mediator between the Government and the revolutionists, but soon became suspected by the revolutionists of being simply a police informer.   He departed one day from St. Petersburg for Finland, carrying with him a large sum of money, £2500, in order to bribe a certain terrorist to betray a plot then being concocted against the Emperor.   Eventually his dead body was found in a lonely unoccupied cottage, near Ozerki, a small village in Finland, close to the Russian frontier. His hands had been tied behind his back and he had been strangled with a rope. About the same time, an unsigned communication appeared in a St. Petersburg newspaper, stating : —

George Gapon had been tried by a workmen's secret tribunal and had been found guilty of having acted as an *agent provocateur*, of having squandered the money of the workmen, and of having defiled the honor and memory of the comrades who fell on the "Red Sunday." In consequence of these acts, of which he was said to have made a full confession to the tribunal, he was condemned to death, and the sentence had been duly carried out.

The odious profession of *agent provocateur*, or police spy and informer, was perhaps nowhere more highly developed than under the Russian Tzars. To be sure, spies have occupied an admitted place and performed a definite function in all lands and times, both in peace and war. But the Imperial Russian type has a particularly repulsive rôle to play. His was the task of persuading the timid to talk revolution and aiding the daring to execute their plots in order that the police might have specious grounds for ruthless repression. To murder a police official, in order that the higher state police, the Okhrana, might make the arrests necessary to justify their existence, was an ordinary detail imposed on the *agent provocateur*. The most famous of them, or rather infamous, was Evno Azev, whose double activity as secret police agent and terrorist lasted from 1903 to 1909. During this time, acting in his dual rôle, he has more than thirty murders, or attempted murders, to his credit. While in good standing with the Government, he organized the murder of Plehve, of the Grand Duke Serge, Governor of Moscow, and he played an active part in the military mutinies of Moscow, Viborg, and Kronstadt. All these terrorist activities naturally endeared him to the Revolutionary Committee, while the inevitable arrests that followed, the executions and exiling to Siberia, ranked him exceedingly high in the eyes of the police.

The case of Ivan Okladsky was brought anew to the attention of the public in recent times by the following news dispatch : —

[Copyright, 1925, by the New York Times Company. By wireless to the *New York Times*.]

Moscow, Jan. 10. — The Russian Revolution placed in the hands of the Bolsheviki the entire archives of the Tzar's Government, but none probably served a greater purpose to the Communists' scheme than the archives of the late Tzar's political police. This inheritance has permitted them to find out a great number of persons who in pre-revolutionary times acted to destroy them and those who while acting in their midst served as *agents provocateurs* in betraying their brother revolutionists. Since the Revolution many such agents already have suffered the death penalty, while many others are still waiting their turn.

Never, however, was there such great excitement among Communists as is called forth by the approaching trial of Ivan Okladsky, who in the early '80s, as a member of the terrorist organization known as "Narodnaya Volia" or national freedom, took a prominent part in all attempts upon the royal family and was concerned in the plot which ended in the assassination of Tzar Alexander II, in 1881.

The Narodnaya Volia, which the Bolsheviki regard as the forerunner of their own party, was in that period the strongest revolutionary organization believing in forcing the Government to adopt a constitutional régime by means of terrorist acts and assassination. Highest state officials, a number of ministers, generals, and other persons of high rank fell victims to their fanatic ideas. This terrorist organization was broken up after the assassination of Alexander II.

Ivan Okladsky, in his confession at that time, betrayed his accomplices. Many were put to death, while a great number were imprisoned for life. Since that period and until 1917 Okladsky served with the Tzar's political police and is credited with exercising the greatest activity in hunting out revolutionaries. Until his arrest six months ago he was living under an assumed name in Leningrad serving as a clerk in one of the state factories. He is now sixty-five years old. He says he was forced to turn traitor by the inhuman torture he was subjected to at the hands of the police at the time of his arrest.

The biggest hall in Moscow has been converted into a courtroom for this trial and several thousand tickets have been issued to workmen and Communists. Despite the lapse of forty-five years, a number of victims and survivors of the early revolutionary movement will appear at the trial as witnesses against Okladsky. Krylenko, the Soviet's ablest lawyer, who prosecuted Archbishop Zeplak and Savinkov, will conduct the trial for the State, while two prominent lawyers were appointed to defend Okladsky.

It is certain Okladsky will be condemned to death, but it is believed that a commutation of sentence will follow owing to his old age.[1]

The effect of Red Sunday was profound, and its significance could not be escaped by the monarch. The Tzar contributed 50,000 rubles for the widows and orphans of the massacre, but the Government did nothing official or in a constructive way. The Holy Synod issued a proclamation in which the irrepressible Pobyedonostsev announced that the labor movement in Russia was being supported by Japanese money.

When, on May 25, the Japanese fleet under Togo swept the Russian Baltic fleet from the high seas and determined the outcome of the war, patriotic indignation flamed forth in Russia proper, in Lithuania, in Poland, and in the Caucasus. The crew of the battleship Prince Potemkin mutinied at Sevastopol, hoisted the red flag of revolt, and for ten days cruised like pirates about the Black Sea, finally surrendering to the authorities of the Rumanian port, Constanza.

For the first time, the Emperor bent under the storm and consented to receive a delegation from the zemstvos and town

---

[1] He was condemned to imprisonment for ten years.

councils on June 19. The leader, Prince Serge Troubetskoy, had the courage to speak frankly and circumstantially on the vices and negligences of the ruinous bureaucracy : —

"By the criminal negligence and misgovernment of your advisers, Russia has been precipitated into a ruinous war. Our army has not been able to vanquish the enemy, our fleet is annihilated, and even more threatening than the danger from without is the internal conflagration that is blazing up. . . . Your Majesty, while it is not too late, for the salvation of Russia and the establishment of order and peace in the country, command that the representatives of the people . . . be summoned immediately. . . . In your hands are the honor and might of Russia. . . . Do not delay. In this terrible hour of national trial, great is your responsibility before God and Russia."

The Tzar replied: "Cast aside your doubts. My will, the will of your Tzar, to call together the elected representatives of the people, is unshaken. You can tell this to all your friends. . . . I hope that you will coöperate with me."

Two months later, on August 19, 1905, an imperial decree announced and granted what every Russian patriot since the Decembrists had been dreaming of — a Constitution.

But once again hope deferred made their hearts sick. Autocracy, even in its final gesture of generosity and liberalism, even while proclaiming its will to grant a representative government, could not shake off the dead hand of Peter the Great, of Ivan the Terrible, of Alexander III, and of Paul, the Crowned Madman. Again the attempt was made to drive round the boulder !

As the emancipation of the serfs was only a half-answer to the land hunger of the peasants, so the constitution of 1905 was only a half-answer to the constitution hunger of the entire nation. It was the work of Bulygin, and fell deadborn on the expectant ears of a long-suffering people. The decree defined the new Parliament or Duma as follows : —

1. The Duma is a permanently functioning institution similar to Western parliaments.

2. All the laws and regulations, both permanent and provisional, as well as the budget, must be brought before the Duma for discussion.

3. The Duma is an exclusively consultative institution, and it enjoys complete freedom in expressing its opinions on the subjects under discussion.

4. The electoral law is based chiefly on the peasantry, as the element of the population predominant numerically, and most reliable and conservative from the monarchistic standpoint; the electoral law cannot be modified without the consent of the Duma.

5. The franchise does not depend on nationality and religion.

In the words of the most consistent defender of popular rights, Count Witte, "It had all the prerogatives of a parliament except the chief one. It was a parliament, and yet, as a purely consultative institution, it was not a parliament. The law of August the sixth satisfied no one. Nor did it in the least stem the tide of revolution which steadily began to arise."

Popular resentment expressed itself at once in organized protests against the miserably insufficient reform which preserved intact the autocratic power and merely created a debating society. It was toying with the Russian people. A general strike followed, which, beginning from St. Petersburg, paralyzed the whole country, affecting, as it did, the railways, telephone and telegraph services, water and food supply, electricity, the tramways, and even the small shops. By October 29, all Russia was practically in a state of siege. A "soviet" or council of delegates elected from factories was organized by the Socialists, with Khrustalev as president and Leon Trotsky as vice president. Forerunner of the ultimate triumph of the same body in 1917, this soviet boldly challenged the Government. Count Witte, who had just returned with enhanced prestige from the peace negotiations with Japan at Portsmouth, New Hampshire, was deemed the only official competent to ride the storm. Though replying to revolution with martial law, he had, nevertheless, the clearness of vision to demand liberal concessions from the Tzar as the only condition of his remaining in power.

In the face of backstairs advisers who were opposed to Witte, the Emperor published, on October 30, a manifesto of considerable historical importance, as it contains the first Bill of Rights ever granted in Russia. It runs as follows: —

Unrest and disturbances in the capital and in many regions of our Empire fill our heart with a great and heavy grief. The welfare of the Russian Sovereign is inseparable from the welfare of the people, and their sorrow is his sorrow. The unrest now arisen may cause a profound disorder in the masses and become a menace to the integrity and unity of the Russian State. The great vow of imperial service enjoins us to strive with all the might of our reason and authority to put an end within the shortest possible time to this unrest so perilous to the State. Having ordered the proper authorities to take measures for the suppression of the direct manifestations of disorder, rioting, and violence, and for the protection of peaceful people who seek to fulfill in peace the duties incumbent upon them, we, in order to carry out more effectively the measures outlined by us, for the pacification of the country, have found it necessary to unify the activities of the higher government agencies.

We impose upon the Government the obligation to execute our inflexible will: —

1. To grant the population the unshakable foundations of civic freedom on the basis of real personal inviolability, freedom of conscience, of speech, of assemblage, and of association.

2. Without stopping the appointed elections to the Imperial Duma, to admit to participation in the Duma those classes of the population which have hitherto been deprived of the franchise, in so far as this is feasible, in the brief period remaining before the convening of the Duma, leaving the further development of the principle of general suffrage to the new legislative order (*i.e.*, the

Duma and Imperial Council established by the law of August 6, 1905).

3. To establish it as an unshakable rule that no law can become effective without the sanction of the Imperial Duma and that the people's elected representatives should be guaranteed a real participation in the control over the lawfulness of the authorities appointed by us.

We call upon all the faithful sons of Russia to remember their duty to their country, to lend assistance in putting an end to the unprecedented disturbances and, together with us, make every effort to restore quiet and peace in our native land.

By the revolutionaries these concessions were interpreted to mean that autocracy was weakening, that its morale was broken. By the conservatives and reactionaries the manifesto was the signal for counter-demonstration organized throughout the Empire, with the result that in the frequent clashes that ensued the victims are reported to have reached three thousand killed and ten thousand wounded.

In the words of one particularly acute student of Russian affairs : —

During the last decades preceding the Revolution of 1917 it became constantly more evident to attentive observers that Russian autocracy was doomed. It was a dying régime, gradually degenerating and decaying from within, whose days were already numbered, like a person with some deadly disease lingering on under the influence of oxygen.

Unfortunately among the Russian ruling classes there were many men who were stubbornly clinging to power, artificially prolonging the régime by making all sorts of compromises ; some among them were selfishly arguing that every extra day in power was a gain to themselves. The most important historical conclusion that one can draw from these last years of autocracy is that, as a political principle, it was not able to save itself by compromise; as soon as concessions to opposite sides were started, autocracy was doomed, its very backbone being broken by such concessions.

These lines were written by the late, ever-to-be-lamented Baron Serge Korff, a Russian of the Russians, whose friendship and confidence, up to his untimely death just four years ago, the author had the honor to enjoy. Descended from a prominent family in Russia, Korff was professor at the Women's University of Petrograd and at the University of Helsingfors in Finland. His last days, particularly his sudden death, may be taken as a minute but typical cross section of the fate of so many Russian intellectuals driven into exile by the Bolshevist *coup d'état*. Under the Provisional Government, Korff was Lieutenant Governor of Finland, a post which he was obliged to vacate on the fall of the Kerensky Government. On his taking up residence in the United States, he was rapidly forging to the front as an acknowledged authority on international affairs. His lectures were in constant demand in the United States and abroad. It was my privilege to offer him a professorship in the Georgetown School of Foreign Service, a chair which he filled with distinction, to the admiration and with the love of his pupils. While conducting his course in the same lecture room where he had opened it three years previously, Korff dropped to the floor and expired almost immediately.

In his passing the world at large lost a scholar and a gentleman, his fellow members on his faculty a beloved colleague; and the University still mourns in him a distinguished and capable historian. I feel that those of his former students who may read these lines will gladly join with me in this passing tribute to one of the victims of the Russian Revolution.

Pogroms and similar inhuman treatment of Jews became a frequent occurrence, probably organized by the Black Hundreds (a secret monarchist organization connived at by the imperial police), composed of reactionaries and employing terrorism as a weapon against the terrorists. The month of November 1905 witnessed a widespread series of political disorders, ranging from the assassination of high officials and the mutiny of soldiers and sailors to the seizure of landed estates by peasants in the provinces. Courts-martial were established and martial law was proclaimed over a large part of the Empire.

No single act during this period of governmental vengeance stands out more senseless than the punitive expeditions of the Semyonovsky Regiment on the Moscow–Kazan railroad line. Armed with blanket authority to punish the populations of whole districts as a mass, the commanding officer, Colonel Rieman, was instructed to take no prisoners and to act mercilessly. Culpable leaders of the insurrection had time to escape before the arrival of the troops; but the Cossacks struck indiscriminately at groups of peasants who, on the average, were as guiltless of political conspiracy as they were of thought. Executing without trial or provocation, the soldiery left a ghastly trail of burning villages, murdered hostages, and peasants swinging from telegraph poles. One has but to read the official protests made in the Duma by appalled delegates to understand the extent of the terrorism that prevailed in the Caucasus and the Baltic provinces as well as in the heart of Russia during the period 1905–6.

It was under such disturbed conditions that the first Russian Duma was opened on May 10, 1906. Its composition is a cross section of contemporaneous Russia. There were : —

Great Russians	. .	265	Letts	. . . .	6
Little Russians	. .	62	Esthonians	. . .	4
White Russians	. .	12	Germans	. . . .	4
Poles .	. . . .	51	Jews	. . . . .	13
Lithuanians	. . .	10	Tatars .	. . . .	8
	Bashkirs .	. . . .	. . . .	4	

The less important nationalities, such as the Chuvash, the Circassians, the Kalmuks, the Mordva, and the Votiaks, had one or two deputies apiece. The first Duma had a short life of seventy-two days, spent almost exclusively in conflict with the Government. It was dominated by the Constitutional Democrats (Cadets), who devoted their full energy to expounding the indignation and disappointment experienced by the country at large at the inadequate reform and demanding a constitution on the English and the American pattern. The entire session was nothing but a prolonged conflict with the Cabinet of Ministers. The Government replied by dissolving the assembly and convoking a new Duma for March 5, 1907. The Constitutional Democrats retreated to Viborg, in Finland, and there published the famous "Viborg Manifesto," urging the people to passive resistance.

The first Duma has gone down in Russian history with the appellation "The Duma of the National Indignation."

The second became known as "The Duma of the National Ignorance," due to the fact that the newly elected deputies were considered less capable, intellectually, than those of the first Duma. Perhaps the most significant fact was the appearance of a strong group of Social Democrats, who had refused hitherto to coöperate with the Duma and would send no delegate. Now they returned a compact group of more than 60, which raised the total Socialist vote from 26 to 83 — that is, 17 per cent of the whole house. From the outset the second Duma assumed a hostile and frankly revolutionary attitude. It lived one hundred days, without being able to achieve anything in a legislative or parliamentary sense. When, on July 14, Stolypin entered the Chamber and demanded the arrest and trial of sixteen members of the Social Democrat Party for sedition and conspiracy, Tsereteli, leader of the Social Democrats, admitted with pride the indictment brought against his col-

leagues, declaring: "We who are accused of having under-
taken the political education of the masses, declare that this
accusation fills our heart with pride and serves as a proof
that we fulfilled honorably the obligations imposed on us."

On the Duma refusing to consent to the arrest and trial of
its members, the Government again dissolved the assembly
on June 16, 1907. The Duma then not being in session,
certain members of the Social Democrat group were arrested,
tried for treason, and sentenced, some to hard labor and
others to exile in Siberia.

For the second time, representative government was
threatened, and it was seriously debated by the Tzar's
ministers if the whole project should not be definitely
abandoned and the Constitution abolished. Better counsel
prevailed, however, and a third Duma was allowed to be
elected, which Stolypin, by clever manipulation of the new
electoral law of June 3, was practically able to control and
direct. Propertied classes and large landholders were in
the predominance and a majority was maintained favorable
to the Government. Witte calls it "a legislative body, not
elected by the Russian people, but selected by Stolypin."

Stolypin soon paid the usual penalty of reaction and
reckless administration, following so many of his predecessors to a bloody end. The record of the various attempts
made on this man's life reads like some of the most lurid
pages of Edgar Allan Poe, rather than the annals of a civilized nation as late as 1911.[1]

But the end came, on September 14, 1911, during an
elaborate theatrical performance at Kiev. In the royal
box sat the Emperor and his daughters, surrounded by
influential members of his court, while cabinet members and
other high officials were scattered through the audience.
Among the ministers present was Stolypin. A revolutionary terrorist, a youthful Jew, succeeded in penetrating close

[1] See Appendix V.

enough to Stolypin to shoot him fatally before the very eyes of the horrified Emperor. Rumor would have it that the assassin was also a secret agent employed by the police department.

The fourth and last Duma — this was the assembly dissolved on August 22, 1917 — began its sittings in 1912, under the presidency of Michael Rodzianko, who was destined to play an important part in the closing scenes of 1917. The two following years were essentially replicas of the preceding period. The Duma and the Government were openly at odds. Popular discontent was never silent, but grew more and more clamorous and menacing. On May Day, 1914, 130,000 workmen were on a strike in Petrograd alone, a condition that soon developed into open warfare. During July, while the clouds of her last war were gathering over doomed Russia, there were armed conflicts in the streets of the capital. Cossacks were charging barricaded workmen and leaving killed and wounded strewn about, exactly as they had done on Bloody Sunday, in 1905.

Alexander Kerensky, aided by a group of disaffected fellow members of the Duma, was actively organizing revolutionary meetings in Southeastern Russia; they had finished their work at Samara and had boarded a steamer for Saratov, Mr. Kerensky's constituency, when they heard newsboys shouting, "Austria's ultimatum to Serbia!" From the tone of the mass meetings which they had convoked in numerous cities, they were convinced that the Revolution would have come, of itself, not later than the spring of 1915.

Then, with open revolution in her streets, and with class hatred seething in the hearts of so many of her people, Russia was suddenly confronted, on July 24, 1914, with the fatal choice between peace and war, the consequences of which pushed her over the precipice.

II

THE DELUGE

"Senseless desperation provoked by senseless tyranny."
JOSEPH CONRAD

CHAPTER V

THE PART PLAYED BY A WOMAN

THE progress of events during the summer of 1914 is still fresh in our memories, though time is making it possible to arrive at a less passionate evaluation of motives than was possible during the heat of conflict. The perspective of years is enlarging certain happenings and figures and reducing others. Many competent historians are of the opinion that a historically complete and impartial version of the initial quarrel between Austria and Serbia — particularly of the ultimatum presented to Belgrade by Vienna after the assassination of the heir to the Austrian throne — has not yet been written.

It so happened that the summer of 1914 found the author of this book in the Austro-Hungarian Empire, where he had been living for a year. The consequent nearness to the sources of the avalanche that then swept over the face of Europe furnished a unique opportunity to view at first hand, as a neutral, impartial observer, the subsequent course of events. Appreciating full well the ambitious Teutonic programme elaborated during the preceding generation, — a programme clearly underlying the secret Treaty of Björkö between the Tzar and the Kaiser, — and disclaiming any intention of entering the perilous field of controversy now being revived by Professor Barnes and other Revisionists regarding the causes of the war, I still believe that the trail of guilt leads as fairly and directly to the then St. Petersburg as to Vienna or Berlin. The important disclosures resulting from the opening up of Russian, German, Austrian, and Allied archives indicate that Russia's historic folly reached its cul-

mination in the diplomacy of Isvolsky, Sazonov, and Sukhomlinov. Of them may it truly be said, "The true author
of a war is not he who declares it, but he who makes it necessary." Their categoric refusal to permit the Austro-Serbian
conflict to be localized is of capital importance.

The text and context of the demands presented to the
Serbian Government by Austria in her peremptory ultimatum of July 23, 1914, were read to the assembled students
of the Austrian university with which I was then affiliated.
The reply of the Serbian Government was likewise publicly
read in the university courtyard. Exception was instantly
taken by the Austrian press to the interpretation placed on
the paragraph requiring the participation of Austrian officials in running down alleged Serbian conspirators on Serbian
soil. This demand, it was then maintained, had been
grossly misinterpreted, — obviously for political and nationalistic reasons, — and did not in fact imply surrender of
her sovereignty on the part of Serbia. Such coöperation,
Austria claimed, is not infrequent between sovereign states
and has a distinct place in international relations. If that
particular point had been yielded, Austria could not have
invoked the refusal of it as legal pretext for war.

I shall not forget the pain and perplexity on the faces of
intelligent and reasonable Austrians when the press of the
world reported that Vienna was demanding participation in
the judicial proceedings on Serbian soil, a thing clearly
inadmissible. The Austrian Government replied — but
indirectly to the Great Powers — that Serbia was deliberately falsifying and misinterpreting the Austrian demands.
Count Berchtold pointed out that the paragraph in question
meant participation in the *recherches préliminaires* (*i.e.*,
preliminary police investigations), as is frequently done
between nations, and not in the *enquête judiciaire* (*i.e.*, not in
the *judicial process*, not in the *actual trial*). Austria charges
that on this specific point Serbia took her stand and made

her successful bid for the sympathy of the Entente. A careful reading of the Serbian reply reveals no attempt at such evasion or distinction.

Moreover, the Serbian Government had included in its reply of July 25 a conciliatory offer to submit the dispute to the Hague Tribunal; but it was a futile gesture. Greater powers than the two prime belligerents were to play out that game of chess. As early as July 25 — before Austria knew what the official Serbian reply would be — Russia had begun the mobilization of one million, one hundred thousand men. And mobilization, under existing conditions, was tantamount to a declaration of war.

The truth of the matter is that Russia was vitally concerned, and, as the protagonist of Pan-Slavism, felt obliged to support a weaker Slavic State against the obvious Germanic threat. Unprepared in 1908 when Austria violated the Treaty of Berlin by boldly annexing the provinces of Bosnia and Herzegovina, strangely enough, Russia felt prepared in 1914, though the sequel will show how tragically she erred in her estimate of national preparedness. There was open revolution in the streets of her capital, as we saw at the close of the last chapter, while Finland was dangerously disturbed over the curtailment of the constitutional rights of her Diet. But Russian psychology is gloriously independent of realities when recourse can be had to emotions. Political, racial, and religious differences were buried under the tremendous outburst of patriotic sentiment and personal fealty to the Tzar that swept over the entire people. Barricades disappeared from the streets of Petrograd; Finland was placated, autonomy was promised to Poland, while discontented minorities such as the Jews, Catholics, and Lutherans were promised a removal of civic disabilities. The Declaration of War acted as a hot iron, fusing all classes and parties into a unified thunderbolt of war.

In marked contrast to the open hostility manifested at the

outbreak of the Turkish War of 1871 and the Japanese War, the Russian capital now became brilliant with flags and excited, enthusiastic crowds. In front of the Winter Palace where, only nine years before, hundreds had been massacred and thousands wounded on Red Sunday, now knelt frequent thousands, chanting the Imperial Hymn and vowing allegiance to the Throne. The Emperor, in an address to the Duma, said : —

"We are not only defending the dignity and honor of our country, but we are also fighting for our Slavic brothers, the Serbs, our coreligionists and kinsmen, and at this moment I behold with joy how the union of all the Slavs with Russia is being strongly and unremittingly carried to consummation."

Russians amazed themselves in the capacity and will suddenly manifested for efficient service and helpful coöperation, thus duplicating that stiffening of the national will that defeated Napoleon in 1812. Foreigners, like Sir George Buchanan, the English ambassador, and Maurice Paléologue, the ambassador of France, are loud in their praise of Russia's initial effort in the war.

But the military disasters of 1915 followed close on the heels of the first victories over the Austrians in Galicia and the Germans in East Prussia. Hindenburg drove the loosely strung-out Russian army into the Mazurian Swamps of East Prussia, where 30,000 were killed and 90,000 surrendered. Once again Russian bureaucracy showed its utter incapacity to deal with a national crisis. Self-interest and class interest began to prevail over the common good. Now followed periods of economic and military demoralization. Transportation facilities, never abundant, became inadequate and hopelessly tangled; food supplies for the civil population ran dangerously low; and, more ominous still, food, equipment, and essential ammunition for the army were becoming scarcer and scarcer. Owing to reckless conscription of labor from industrial centres, steel, iron, and coal

production fell continuously.   The effects of this decrease in
output were not felt during the first year of the war, as
reserve stocks were substantial.   But the decrease in the
production of coal, for example, affected the production of
metals, and decreased production of metals reacted on the
railroads.   Once these nerves and arteries of transportation
became paralyzed, food supplies were endangered — and
once food supplies are cut off, starvation drives men desperate; riots and disorders ensue, and unless speedy relief
is provided disaster stands brooding on the threshold.

Through incompetency and blindness in high places
Russian soldiers were actually sent to the front without
rifles.   The American ambassador, Mr. Francis, wrote to
friends in the United States, on October 26, 1916 : —

Dr. Hurd . . . an American doctor who had tendered his services
to Russia and is now Surgeon-General of an army corps of 40,000
men . . . told me that he had seen a Russian army advancing in
which only every other man had a gun, and the men without guns
were told to seize the guns of their armed comrades when they fell.

We know, too, that shells were manufactured in Russian
factories that fitted no ordnance.   Ammunition trains were
often sent in a direction opposite the point where they were
actually needed.   Sukhomlinov, Minister of War, was
accused of treason, tried, and found guilty.   Russian representatives abroad played a similar treasonable rôle.   The
writer knows of a certain proving ground in Canada —
where ammunition was being manufactured for the Russian
army — which had to be guarded against the very Russian
officers who came to inspect the work.   The Canadian officer
in charge had reason to believe that they intended to destroy
the stores.

To this breakdown in the physical agencies of war must
be added the far more disastrous demoralization of spirit
that crept like a miasma into the heart of the nation.   While

men were dying by thousands on the battlefronts and freezing for Russia among the snows of the Carpathian Mountains, a misguided clique of fawning sycophants and court flatterers, lounging luxuriously in the gilded salons of Petrograd, was destroying, dissipating, and nullifying the fruits of those sacrifices. The Tzar had assumed personal command of the army on August 23, 1915, relegating the popular Grand Duke Nicholas Nicholaievich to a command in the Caucasus, probably at the instigation of the Empress, who hated the Grand Duke for reasons which shall be set forth hereafter. The departure of the Tzar for the *Stavka* (general headquarters), at Mohilev, practically left Russia to be governed by the Tzarina.[1] *Dux femina facti.*

No evaluation of the immediate causes which precipitated the Revolution would be complete without an analysis of the personal influence of an autocratic woman wielding uncontrolled power at the most critical moment in Russian history. To understand how completely the Tzarina came to hold Russia in the hollow of her hand, we must retrace our steps slightly. The catastrophes that crowd the fifth act of *Hamlet* are unintelligible without cognizance of the conflict of wills running through the first four; neither can the final Russian scene be appreciated without an understanding of the rôle and personality of the principal actors. We must face boldly the famous query of the Austrian ambassador: "Did Russia produce the autocrats, or the autocrats Russia?"

[1] To be strictly accurate, the term should be "Tsaritsa," which would correspond more nearly with the Russian equivalent. But "Tzarina" has become popularized in English-speaking circles and may be accepted as current. In general, the transliteration of Russian names has long been as baffling and elusive to translators as was the spelling of Arab names to Lawrence in that amusing foreword to *Revolt in the Desert*. The distinguished Russian scholar, Sir Paul Vinogradoff, when asked if his name should be made to end in "off" or "ov," replied that it should strictly be "ov," but that the German influences under which he was educated had so popularized the "off" termination that he preferred to let it stand that way. Southey, in his bitingly satirical poem on Napoleon, "The March to Moscow," has a classic stanza on Russian patronymics.

Although the part played by this unhappy woman can hardly be overestimated, it would be altogether unscientific and superficial criticism to lay the whole blame for Russia's downfall on her shoulders. The disintegrating process, as we have already seen, antedated her arrival in Russia, and revolutionary agencies were sapping the foundations of the Empire while she was as yet an unknown and insignificant princess of a little known and insignificant German principality. They would have brought the house of the Romanovs down had she never entered it. But the ruin and the form of the revolt might have been less sweeping, the end less shocking, had she not courted disaster by attempting to belittle it. Scorn is but poor poultice for hurt spirits.

A German princess of the House of Hesse, it would appear that she never completely won the sympathy and confidence of her adopted people, but, like her equally unfortunate prototype, Marie Antoinette, she was vaguely distrusted by the Russian people as a foreigner and a Germanophile. The official investigation instituted by the Provisional Government exonerates the Tzarina of the charge of treason; its conclusions show that she did nothing that a wife and mother might not have done in similar circumstances. The limited contact she preserved with relatives in Germany were of a proper character, mostly of a private nature, and nothing was discovered to substantiate the belief that she exercised a pro-German influence. This vindication is particularly significant, as the new revolutionary government would naturally have been glad to discover additional reasons for their overthrow of the monarchy. This verdict frees the Empress of the capital charge; but history will never clear her name of tendencies, practices, and imprudences that contributed notably to Russia's ruin. The domination which this imperious, proud, aloof, and resolute woman exercised over her irresolute and impressionable husband became such a menace that more than one grand duke, duchess, and general cried out in warning against it. They were usually exiled to their estates, far from Petrograd.

Russia had touched the nadir of misfortune and corrupt administration; defeatists destroyed the morale and confidence of the people and evoked the gaunt spectre of national disaster. The treason of Sukhomlinov, Minister of War, was responsible for the inadequate organization of the rear and the demoralization of the front. General Denikin contributes a graphic picture of the situation in the army: —

I shall never forget the spring of 1915, the great tragedy of the Russian army — the Galician retreat. We had neither cartridges nor shells. From day to day we fought heavy battles and did lengthy marches. We were desperately tired — physically and morally. From hazy hopes we plunged in the depths of gloom. I recall an action near Przemysl in the middle of May. The Fourth Rifle Division fought fiercely for eleven days. For eleven days the German heavy guns were roaring and they literally blew up rows of trenches with all their defenders. We scarcely replied at all — we had nothing to reply with. Utterly exhausted regiments were beating off one attack after another with bayonets, or firing at close range. Blood was flowing, the ranks were being thinned, and graveyards growing. Two regiments were almost entirely annihilated by firing.

I would that our French and British friends, whose technical achievement is wondrous, could note the following grotesque fact which belongs to Russia's history: —

Our only six-inch battery had been silent for three days, when it received *fifty* shells. The fact was immediately telephoned to all regiments and companies and all the riflemen heaved a sigh of relief and joy.[1]

[1] "The shortage of munitions had long since become evident; but the War Minister, Sukhomlinov, refused to be disturbed out of his apathy and even declined offers of help from private factories. An officer in the Intelligence Service, Colonel Myasoyedov, detected in regular espionage before the war but saved from disgrace by personal guarantee from Sukhomlinov, had in the operations of the winter battle in Mazovia sent systematic information by airplane to the Germans, which had largely contributed to the Russian defeat. Myasoyedov's new treachery was discovered, and in spite of Sukhomlinov and even of Court connections he was hanged as a spy." — Pares, *History of Russia*

Intelligent ministers, who realized the gravity of both the internal and the external situation and dared to protest, out of loyalty to Russia, were summarily dismissed at the bidding of "dark forces" and "invisible influences," acting through the Empress. Twenty-one cabinet members followed each other to disgrace during the merry game of "ministerial leapfrog." The head and front of the offending was the unspeakable Rasputin, whose sinister influence over the Tzarina gave rise to a mass of scandalous reports that discredited the monarchy, encouraged the enemies of the throne, and drove patriotic Russians to desperation.

Unsavory as this episode must ever be, it cannot be dismissed as a legend. Gregory Rasputin was one of the contributing causes of the Russian Revolution.

On November 1, 1904, the Tzar made a simple note in his diary; the name he there entered was to be written across the entire history of his reign from that day forward: —

"To-day we made the acquaintance of Grigory, the Man of God, from the Province of Tobolsk."

This coarse and depraved adventurer was born a Siberian peasant. Rasputin was not his family name, but a title of reproach conferred on him by the peasants of his village because of his public immorality and criminal record. It means, in Russian, "depraved" or "debauched." His family name was Novihh. While posing as one inspired of God, a *staretz*, as the type is called in Russia, he was "discovered" by the wife of a wealthy Moscow merchant during a pilgrimage to a Siberian shrine. Under her auspices he was introduced to the most exclusive circles of the capital. It should be noted at this point that Rasputin, though frequently called a monk, was not a priest of the Russian Church, nor was he even in holy orders at any time, but was one of the wandering pilgrims so frequently met in the country districts of Russia. As regards ecclesiastical jurisdiction, he was absolutely a free lance and the authorities found it impossible to control his actions. His chief title to preëminence seems to have been a certain power of healing the sick by the application of personal magnetism.

The possession of occult powers, and the mysticism of charlatans, never failed to exercise a fatal fascination for the intellectuals of Russia. Philippe, the butcher's boy of Lyons, whose vogue at the Russian court ceased as Rasputin came on the scene in 1905, is a case in point.[1] And historians of the Russian Revolution will find a curious confirmation of the same psychic abnormality in the quacks, charlatans, spiritists and mesmerists, "table-rappers" and "table-turners," who overawed French society with their dabbling in the supernatural on the very eve of the French Revolution. "They danced to death along a flowery way."

Isvolsky, in his *Recollections of a Foreign Minister*, recalls the influence of the Comte de Saint-Germain over the Land-grave of Hesse, of the "unknown Philosopher" over the Duchess of Bourbon, and of Cagliostro over Cardinal de Bourbon. Similarly, the influence of Rasputin over the Tzarina was based upon his mysterious but conceded ability to heal the young Tzarevitch by means which still remain an open question.

It is a matter of history that the Tzar and the Tzarina had been long disappointed in the birth of four daughters but of no male heir to the throne. This situation continued until 1904, when a boy was born. The Tzarevitch, Alexis, was, consequently, the child of predilection on whom the affections of father and mother were unsparingly lavished. But the rejoicing at his birth soon turned into bitter grief and desperation, for it was found that the infant son suffered from the strange disease often found among royal chil-

---

[1] The Empress cherished devoutly an ikon given to her by Philippe; it had a bell attached which, she firmly believed, would ring of itself whenever an enemy approached either herself or the Emperor. She refers to this bell in one of her letters to Nicholas while he was at the front.

dren in Europe, known as hæmophilia.[1] Victims of this
malady are known in medicine as hæmophilics, or "bleed-
ers." It shows itself in a certain weakness of the veins and
of the arteries of the skin, so that the sufferer is liable, at the
slightest injury or contusion, to bleed profusely. The slightest scratch, or the bumping of a hand or an ankle against
a projection, will cause either bleeding or a discolored swell-
ing on the afflicted member, accompanied with the most
excruciating pain. This mysterious disease is transmitted
through the mother and only to the males. The sister of the
Tzarina, Princess Henry of Prussia, had transmitted it to
all three of her sons. One of the Tzarina's younger brothers
also suffered from it, likewise her Uncle Leopold, Queen
Victoria's youngest son. The oldest son of the King of
Spain, the Prince of the Asturias, is likewise a sufferer, and
grave doubt is now entertained if he will live to succeed
King Alfonso.

Everything known to medical science was done for the
precious heir to the Russian throne, in whom were concentrated all the hopes of the Romanov dynasty. In fact,
the care lavished on her only son gave rise to the criticism
at court that Alexandra was more of a nurse than an empress.
It is at this point that Rasputin enters on the scene.

I consulted many persons in Moscow and Petrograd,
among them physicians and scholars familiar with the current reports involving the Empress and Rasputin. I likewise discussed this and allied topics in London last July with
Sir Bernard Pares, whose lifelong study of Russia and residence in Russia during the Revolution make him one of the
world's leading scholars in the field of Russian history.
Alexander Kerensky, former Premier of Russia in the Provisional Government, who personally visited and conversed
with the Tzarina in her imprisonment, likewise gave me sev-

[1] The marriage of Nicholas and Alexandra was a consanguineous union; they
were second cousins, having had a common grandfather, Louis II of Hesse.

eral hours on the same subject. The consensus of opinion is that Alexandra was, in point of morality, above reproach and cannot be accused of improper relations with the greasy moujik. She was neither his paramour nor his accomplice; she was his victim. The same cannot be said of other high personages in her entourage.

Gregory Rasputin was simply a clever adventurer, a habitual drunkard, and a licentious roué who utilized for his purposes some hypnotic or mesmeric power not definitely catalogued. Whatever the explanation may be, the outstanding fact upon which all agree is that Rasputin could stop the paroxysms of pain into which the young Tzarevitch was so often thrown by his dread affliction. The maternal love of the Tzarina for her boy and her terror when she realized the danger to his health, complicated by an emotional religious fervor, furnished the foundation for Rasputin's influence at court. On one occasion Rasputin was actually sent away from Petrograd by order of the Emperor. The Tzarevitch fell ill. The doctors tried every known remedy, but the hemorrhage grew steadily worse and death was expected at any moment. The distracted Tzarina had Rasputin recalled to his bedside. Over the blood-soaked bandages Rasputin made the sign of the cross, mumbled some incantations, laid his hand upon the still, white face, and the bleeding stopped. He was never again to leave the court, as he himself had prophesied on receiving the order of expulsion.

The manner and secret of his success are still debated. Out of the welter of hypotheses advanced by his contemporaries I select two as the most probable. The first group attributes his influence to a species of mesmerism or personal magnetism, the application of which soothed and hypnotized the sufferer until nature itself was enabled to exercise its recuperative power. The second group advances a more complicated and more subtle explanation. They suspect

that Madame Viroubova, one of Rasputin's admitted
devotees and close friend of the Tzarina, administered an
irritating Oriental drug to the Tzarevitch at stated intervals.
This drug is supposed to have been supplied by a mysterious
Badmaiev, a doctor of dubious origin, who flits in and out of
the scene.

Maurice Paléologue, the versatile French ambassador in
Petrograd during the Revolution, instituted an inquiry into
the antecedents and character of this shadowy figure in the
tragedy.   He describes Badmaiev as a Siberian adventurer,
a Buriat of Mongolian origin from Transbaikalia.   Though
never graduated from any accredited medical institution,
he practised a sort of therapeutic medicine from an office in
the Liteiny.   Relying on the mystery that always enshrouds
the unknown, however ordinary and prosaic, he established
a reputation as a successful quacksalver able to work
astounding cures by the agency of exotic herbs, medicinal
plants, and magic formulæ communicated secretly to him
by sorcerers of the inaccessible Thibet.   As a matter of fact,
he purchased his drugs from an ordinary apothecary.

These simple elements he transformed into high-sounding
nostrums: "Elixir of Thibet," "Powder of Nirvitti,"
"Nyen-Tchen Balsam," "Essence of Black Lotus,"
"Flowers of Asokas," and so forth.   He did a subterranean
business supplying narcotics, aphrodisiacs, anæsthetics, and
similar dangerous drugs, either stupefying or exhilarating, —
take your choice, — to a clientele composed largely of
gullible neurotics and women suffering from female diseases.   He did everything a soothsayer should do, except
read the entrails of animals and divine the flight of birds.
Badmaiev and Rasputin mutually recognized a brother at
first glance.   *Cato mirari se aiebat, quod non rideret haruspex
haruspicem cum vidisset.*[1]

---

[1] "Cato used to say he wondered why one soothsayer did not laugh when he
saw another." — Cicero, *De Divinatione*

The potion was administered so as to coincide with the appearance of Rasputin, who timed his visits shrewdly. As the effects wore off, the impostor made it appear that the cure was due to the hocus-pocus which he pronounced over the suffering child.

The hypnotic explanation receives added force from the testimony of several Russian statesmen not likely to be influenced by romantic tales. Rodzianko, Speaker of the Duma, — a huge man, physically robust, and of demonstrated will power, — confesses that Rasputin, on one occasion, gave him a disconcerting exhibition of occult power. It was at the Tercentenary Celebration of the Romanov dynasty. Rasputin, uninvited, had wormed his way into the place for honor guests at a service in the Kazan Cathedral in Petrograd. Rodzianko ordered him out : —

"I drew quite close to him and said in an impressive whisper, 'What are you doing here?' He shot an insolent look at me and replied, 'What's that to do with thee?'

"'If you address me as "thou" I will drag you from the Cathedral by the beard. Don't you know I am the President of the Duma?'

"Rasputin faced me and seemed to run me over with his eyes; first my face, then in the region of the heart, then again he stared me in the eyes. This lasted for several moments.

"Personally I had never yielded to hypnotic suggestion, of which I had had frequent experience. Yet here I felt myself confronted by an unknown power of tremendous force. I suddenly became possessed of an almost animal fury, the blood rushed to my heart, and I realized I was working myself into a state of absolute frenzy. I, too, stared straight into Rasputin's eyes and, speaking literally, felt my own starting out of my head. Probably I must have looked rather formidable, for Rasputin suddenly began to squirm. . . ."

On another occasion, as far back as 1911, Stolypin, whom no one ever accused of being a weakling, had a similar encounter with Rasputin. Summoned to the Premier's study to answer to charges of notorious public immorality, the *staretz* attempted to hypnotize the statesman.

"He ran his pale eyes over me," said Stolypin, "mumbled mysterious and inarticulate words from the Scriptures, made strange movements with his hands, and I began to feel an indescribable loathing for this vermin sitting opposite me. Still I did realize that the man possessed great hypnotic power which was beginning to produce a fairly strong moral impression on me, though certainly one of repulsion. I pulled myself together and, addressing him roughly, told him. . . ."

It was said at Petrograd that Rasputin also made use of the Orlov affair to entrench himself. Among the officers of the Lancers of the Guard, the Empress's own regiment, was a clever and handsome young colonel of that name whose sympathetic and chivalrous nature distinguished him from his fellow officers. Alexandra found consolation and refuge in his company, giving rise thereby to much backstairs gossip. But a careful reading of the incident, as related by Count Paul Vassili, fails to reveal the slightest grounds for suspecting improper relations, though indiscretions and secret trysts are not to be denied. Finally, to stop slanderous whispering, the popular Orlov shut himself in his lodgings one day and blew his brains out. Rasputin, with his sensitive nose for discovering skeletons in closets, determined to rattle Orlov's bones — if ever so gently — within hearing of the Empress and observe the effect.

He found an apt accomplice in Manassavitch-Maniulov, another trickster, scarcely less odious than himself. Like Hamlet, Rasputin coached his confederate and laid the trap with consummate craft, though now the victim was not the King but the Queen : —

There is a play to-night. . . .
Even with the very comment of thy soul
Observe mine uncle. If his occulted guilt
Do not itself unkennel in one speech,
It is a damned ghost that we have seen,
And my imaginations are as foul
As Vulcan's stithy. Give him heedful note;
For I mine eyes will rivet to his face,
And after we will both our judgements join
To censure of his seeming.

Alexandra, though born a Lutheran, had become fully converted to the Orthodox faith, had even passed beyond sincerity to abnormality and exaggeration in her religious practices. Mindful of the hold which the pseudo-supernatural had over her, Rasputin imposed a fast of three days to ensure a state of grace and psychic receptivity. When the Empress had been reduced to a condition of nervous hysteria, the mummery began : —

The Empress had scarcely touched any food for three days; she had spent the time in long and almost continual orisons. She was just in a condition when any appeal to her superstition would be sure to meet with response. When she prostrated herself beside the "Prophet," she had reached a state of exhaustion and excitement which made her an easy prey to any imposture practised by the unscrupulous. For about an hour Rasputin kept praying aloud invoking the spirits of Heaven in an impressive voice, every word of which went deep into the heart of Alexandra Feodorovna. Suddenly he seized her by the arm, exclaiming as he did so : " Look! Look! And then believe!"

She raised her eyes, and saw distinctly on the white wall the image of Colonel Orlov, which, by a clever trick, had been flashed on it by a magic lantern held for the purpose by Manassavitch-Maniulov.

The Empress gave one terrible cry and fell in a dead faint on the floor. . . .

This was but the first scene of many of the same character. The

Tzarina recovered her scared senses with the full conviction that she had really seen the spirit of the man she had loved so dearly; she was very soon persuaded that he had been allowed to show himself to her and that he would henceforward watch over her and guide her with advice and encouragement in her future life. She quite believed that Rasputin, whom she sincerely thought to be in total ignorance as to that episode in her life, was a real Prophet of God, and that, thanks to him, she would be able to communicate with the dead.

Under such auspices it is not surprising that Rasputin was enabled to exercise a powerful fascination over a certain group of influential Petrograd literati. He had divined the secret of the Russian soul, and his spatulate fingers played on its every stop. He knew it to be a curious synthesis of contradictions, capable of soaring at one moment to the heights of spirituality, then sweeping, on the same wing, through a morass of lubricity. Those of us who had close contact with representative Russians often marveled at the versatility with which in one conversation they would range the full gamut of inquiry, from metaphysics to nymphomania, with an alert, restless curiosity that betokened something more than mere intellectual frivolity. Their souls seemed forever drifting, rudderless, in an immense sea of speculation, but grasping always at the infinite, searching everywhere for God. That is why their favorite mood was melancholy tempered by resignation. *Bogoiskateli*, "seekers after God," occurs often in their mouths to describe themselves. Their *logos* was *podvig* — some voluntary suffering accepted for its expiatory value. The mood was popularized in the favorite proverb : —

> The darker the night, the clearer the stars;
> The deeper the sorrow, the nearer to God.

Hearken to another of their poets : —

> All earthly perishes, thy mother and thy boyhood.
> Thy wife betrays thee, yea, and friends forsake;

But learn, my friend, to taste a different sweetness.
  Looking to the cold and Arctic seas,
Get in thy ship, set sail for the far Pole,
  And live midst walls of ice. Gently forget
  How there you loved and struggled;
  Forget the passions of the land behind thee;
And to the shudderings of gradual cold
  Accustom thy tired soul,
  So that of all she left behind her here
  She craveth nought whatever,
When thence to thee flood forth the beams of light
  celestial.

"Which is a beautiful poem," writes Stephen Graham, "written for those who have become morbid."

"Oh, poor widowed country of the North," cries Maurice Paléologue, after long living in Petrograd, "who has never known the splendors of the South!"

Nor was this mournful mysticism confined to the intelligentsia alone. If anything, it was deeper and more elemental among the "black people" of the soil. The Russian moujik when steeped in vodka reveals a sordid grossness and a slumbering animality limited only by physical capacity. But, the orgy over, he will weep with you in brotherly understanding, condone thieves (was there not a good thief on the right hand of the dying Saviour?), shield murderers with compassion, and manifest instantaneous sympathy with all suffering fellow pilgrims in this vale of tears. He pities himself and you, and murmurs to the stubborn earth, as he ploughs and hoes it in his unending task of wringing a bare subsistence from the soil, "*Gospodi pomilui! . . . Gospodi pomilui!*"

— "Lord, be merciful!" Erected into a philosophy in the drawing-rooms of Petrograd, podvig runs through Russian psychology like an extra letter in the alphabet. "No nation," explains Dostoievsky, "has ever been founded on science and reason; it has always grown about some central idea."

Rasputin discovered the vulnerable spot and capitalized the emotional morbidity he found in high places and in low. "Repent, repent," he preached. "But there is no repentance without grave matter for regret." Coming out of a public bath one day with two young girls, one not sixteen, the other barely twenty, he was confronted by their distracted mother. "Be comforted," he said; "your daughters have found salvation."

Nekrassov's popular verses, "Who Can Be Happy in Russia?" picture a band of rustics, roving about the country seeking an answer to the title of the poem. They return with the report that only drunkards can be happy in Russia — and they only when they are drunk!

Rasputin was but another link in the chain that has, from time immemorial, riveted the Russian people to some form of evil. In *Under Western Eyes* Joseph Conrad has told, as only Conrad can, how a chain became symbolic of Russia. He narrates the history of Peter Ivanovitch, the gloomy Russian exile, whose story was known not only along the Boulevard de Philosophes of Geneva, but in every capital of Europe. It has been translated into seven languages.

Imprisoned in a fortress by "administrative order," the convict had managed to escape, but could not rid himself of the fetters that had been affixed to his limbs by jailers; winding the loose end around his waist, he led an extraordinary existence in the endless forests of the Okhotsk Province.

He became very fierce. He developed an unsuspected genius for the arts of a wild and hunted existence. He learned to creep into villages without betraying his presence by anything more than an occasional faint jingle. . . . These links, he fancied, made him odious to the rest of mankind. It was a repugnant and suggestive load. Nobody could feel any pity at the disgusting sight of a man escaping with a broken chain. His imagination became affected by his fetters in a precise, matter-of-fact manner. It seemed to him impossible that people could resist the temptation of fastening the loose end to a staple in the wall while they went for the nearest police official. Crouching in holes or hidden in thickets, he had tried to read the faces of unsuspecting free settlers working in the clearings or passing along the paths within a foot or two of his eyes. His feeling was that no man on earth could be trusted with the temptation of the chain. . . . The sensational clink of these fetters is heard all through the chapters describing his escapes — a subject of wonder in two continents.

It is a wholly unnecessary hypothesis, therefore, to attribute Rasputin's power to German gold or Russian defeatism. He allied himself with both, but antedated them all. His influence and victims were public knowledge in 1910, and an official protest was lodged with the Emperor himself by Archbishop Anthony. The Emperor's brow darkened and he remarked coldly that the private affairs of the imperial family did not concern the Metropolitan.

"No, Sire," replied the Archbishop; "this is not merely a family affair, but the affair of all Russia. The Tzarevitch is not only your son, but our future sovereign, and belongs to all Russia." The Emperor silenced him a second time. "Sire, I obey your command," replied the retreating churchman, "but I may be permitted to think that the Tzar of Russia ought to live in a palace of crystal where his subjects can see him."

The daily paper, *Golos Moskvy*, published a sensational series of charges against Rasputin in 1911, based on the confiscated pamphlet of Professor M. Novoselov. "*Quousque tandem*," began the article — and launched into a circumstantial and completely documented exposé of the menace to the throne. An interpellation was made in the Duma and a public debate ensued. At a Masonic Congress, held in Brussels at this time, Rasputin was discussed as a possible instrument for spreading the tenets of the order in Russia; it was thought that under his destructive influence the dynasty could be destroyed in two years.

Bishop Feofan, the Emperor's confessor, sought to open the eyes of his royal penitent. He was relieved of his post and transferred to the Crimea. Bishop Hermogen, once a supporter of the *staretz*, but now become a disillusioned crusader, precipitated a public scandal in the hope of atoning for his previous patronage of the impostor. Inviting Rasputin to his house, Hermogen fulminated in his face: "I adjure you in the name of the living God to depart and to cease from troubling the Russian people by your presence at the Imperial Court."

Instead of obeying, Rasputin flung himself on the prelate and nearly succeeded in murdering him outright; a Cossack officer named Rodionov drew his sword and saved the Bishop. "You wait a bit. I'll pay you back!" shouted Rasputin, as he escaped into the street.

A short time after, Bishop Hermogen was ordered to resign from the Holy Synod and leave Petrograd.

The Tzar's mother, the Dowager Empress Marie, arrived to protest. "Either he goes or I go." Rasputin stayed — and it was Marie who departed for her estates in the Crimea.

The Empress and her intimate coterie had their way; Rasputin was a saint, a prophet, and a healer sent by God! The step from personal favor to political power was not difficult in a system of absolutism where all power emanated from the autocrat. Rasputin, it is claimed, made and unmade ministers of State, generals, and bishops. Heads of state departments received orders in scribbled notes: "Do this; do that; so-and-so is worthy of advancement; so-and-so should be dismissed." His lodgings were besieged by petitioners seeking favors at the court. But by the Russian people at large he was considered the evil genius of the hour, a licentious impostor, whose drunkenness and eroticism were masked under the fair mantle of religion. His hold became so powerful that any man who offended or ignored him ran the risk of being dismissed from office, whether he was a cabinet minister or a doorkeeper. No public official was safe at his hands, nor any woman's honor. Among countless others, Sazonov, Minister of Foreign Affairs, was replaced by Stürmer, the pro-German, on the recommendation of the Rasputin clique. This is believed to have been the fate even of the Grand Duke Nicholas, whose removal from the rank of Commander in Chief of All the Russian Armies followed an incident that has become classic in the writings of that period.

Rasputin telegraphed the Grand Duke Nicholas for permission to come to the front in order to bless the troops. The Grand Duke replied: "Do come, so that I may hang you." Mortally offended by this affront to her favorite, the Empress pursued Nicholas with implacable resentment and finally succeeded in having him transferred from the post of Commander in Chief of the Russian armies to innocuous desuetude in the Caucasus, on the Turkish front.

Why did not the Tzar have the courage to cut this Gordian knot that was slowly strangling Russia? In answer to the protests and the warnings of one old general, Nicholas is reported to have said, "I prefer twenty Rasputins to one hysterical woman."

Nicholas II is also quoted as having said that there were two black-letter days in his life. The first was May 28, 1905, the date of the defeat of the Russian fleet in the Straits of Tsushima, between Japan and Korea. The second was October 17, 1906, marking the establishing of a Duma and the proclamation of a Bill of Rights. Shall not history add a third — August 23, 1915, the day on which he left Petrograd for the front, leaving the Tzarina to rule in his stead?

CHAPTER VI

A CASKET OF LETTERS

THE extent and character of the Tzarina's unhealthy influence over the last of the Romanovs may be judged from the
tone of the letters to her husband while he was at the front.
No serious historian of the Russian Revolution can afford
to neglect the revelations contained in these astounding
documents. For that matter, put your discerning investigator in possession of the intimate correspondence, memoirs,
confidential confessions, and diaries of the chief actors in any
great movement, and he will not need the State archives.
Revolutions are made by men and women determining
events. Men are swayed by powerful human emotions.
Women create them. And the master passion, particularly
in neurotic females, can be as elegantly indifferent to the
realities of life and war as ever Montesquieu was to the
existence of God.

The letters of the Tzarina, four hundred in number, preserved with pathetic fidelity in a small black casket of wood
marked with the Tzar's initials, were carried about by him
in his exile from place to place. Discovered by the Bolsheviki at Ekaterinburg after the official murder of the imperial
family, they have been published, with an introduction by
Sir Bernard Pares. All were written in English.

Perhaps never in recorded literature did a human soul
strip itself so bare to posterity as did this ecstatic queen of
forty-five years and mother of five children. "My well
beloved"; "My only treasure"; "My sun"; "My soul."
"The most tender kisses and caresses from your loving little

wife." "I bless you, I embrace your dear face, your pretty neck, and your dear little hands." "Good-bye, dear Nicky — I embrace you again and again. I have slept poorly. All the time I embraced your cushion [pillow]."

"Good-bye, my angel, spouse of my heart. I envy my flowers that you took away with you. I embrace every dear little place of your body with tender love." And so on, through four hundred epistles. One was sent each day, supplemented by frequent telegrams. Reverence for the inviolability of such personal communications and a decent respect for the sacredness of connubial relations would ordinarily safeguard such a correspondence. If it be permissible to lift the veil at all, it is not to dishonor the dead, but to indicate the subtle approach to political issues which the Tzarina made through the gateway of the Tzar's affections. Hers is a cry of frenzied love for her husband and fear for her child. But the moving finger that was writing Russia's destiny on the wall was that of Rasputin and the defeatists.

Note the finesse of the progressive attack on the Tzar's vacillating will : —

I cannot find words [declares the Empress] to express all I want to : my heart is far too full. I only long to hold you tight in my arms and to whisper words of immense love, courage, strength, and endless blessings. More than hard to let you go alone, so completely alone ! But God is very near to you, more near than ever. You have fought this great fight for your country and throne — alone and with bravery and decision. Never have they seen such firmness in you before, and it cannot remain without good fruit. . . . Lovey, I am here. Don't laugh at silly old wifey ; but she has the " trousers " on unseen. . . . Your faith has been tried and you remained firm as a rock. For that you will be blessed. God anointed you at your coronation. He placed you where you stand and you have done your duty. . . . Our Friend's prayers arise night and day for you to Heaven, and God will hear them. . . . This is the beginning of the glory of your reign. He [Rasputin] said so and I absolutely believe it. . . . All is for the good. As our Friend says, the worst is over. . . . When you leave [I] shall wire to Friend to-night through Ania [the Tzarina's lady in waiting, one of Rasputin's devotees] and he will particularly think of you. Only get Nikolasha's nomination [his transference to the Caucasus] quicker done. No dawdling! It is bad for the cause and for Alexeiev [the Head of the General Staff] too. . . . I know what you feel; the meeting with N. [Nikolasha] won't be agreeable. You did trust him, and now you know what months ago our Friend said, that he was acting wrongly toward you and your country and wife. It 's not the people who would do harm to your people, but Nikolasha and his set, Gutchkov [a popular member of the Duma], Rodzianko [the Speaker of the Duma], Samarin [the Procurator of the Holy Synod who was responsible for the second dismissal of Rasputin]. . . . You see they are afraid of me. . . . They know I have a will of my own when I feel I am in the right. . . . You make them tremble before your courage and will. God is with you and our Friend for you. All is well; and later all will thank you for having saved the country. Don't doubt! Believe and all will be well; and the Army is everything. A few strikes are nothing in comparison; as they can and shall be suppressed. . . .

In another letter she repeats this counsel : —

Our Friend [Rasputin] entreats you to be firm, to be master, and not always give in to Trepov. You know much better than that man; and still you let him lead you. Why not our Friend, who leads through God ? Only believe more in our Friend instead of Trepov. He lives for you and Russia.

Would I write thus [she says in a letter dated December 13] did I not know you so very easily waver and change your mind, and what it costs me to keep you to stick to your opinions ?

[To make him firm she strikes the note to duty toward his son.] We must give a strong country to baby; we dare not be weak for his sake. Else he will have a yet harder reign, setting our faults right, and drawing the reins in tightly which you let loose. You have to suffer for faults in the reigns of your predecessors. And God knows what hardships are yours. Let our legacy be a lighter one for Alexei ! He has a strong will and mind of his own. Don't let things slip through your fingers and make him have to build up all again. Be firm. I, your wall, am behind you and won't give way. I know He [Rasputin] leads us right; and you listen to a false man like Trepov.

Only not a responsible Cabinet, which all are mad about. It's all getting calmer and better; only one wants to feel your hand. How long years people have told me the same: "Russia loves to feel the whip." It's their nature — tender love and then the iron hand to punish and guide. How I wish I could pour my will into your veins. The Virgin above you, with you. Remember the miracle, our Friend's vision.[1]

Darling, remember that it does not lie in the man Protopopov or X. Y. Z.; but it's the question of monarchy and your prestige now, which must not be shattered in the time of the Duma. Don't think they will stop at him. But they will make all others leave who are devoted to you, one by one. And then ourselves! Remember last year your leaving for the Army, when also you were alone, with us two against everybody, who promised Revolution if you went. You stood up against all and God blessed your decision. . . . The Tzar rules and not the Duma. . . . Show to all that you are the master and that your will must be obeyed. The time of great indulgence and gentleness is over; now comes your reign of will and power. And they shall be made to bow down before you, to listen to your orders.

On December fourteenth she beseeches the Tzar: —

Disperse the Duma at once — when you told Trepov the 17th you did not know what they were up to. I should have quietly and with a clear conscience before the whole of Russia have sent Lvov to Siberia (one did so for far less grave acts), taken Samarin's rank away (he signed that paper from Moscow), Miliukov, Gutchkov and Polivanov also to Siberia . . . I am but a woman but my soul and brain tell me it would be the saving of Russia — they sin far worse than anything the Sukhomlinovs ever did. Forbid Brusilov etc. when they come to touch any political subject, fool, who wants responsible cabinet, as Georgi writes.

[1] See Appendix VI.

Remember even Mr. Philippe said one dare not give constitution as it would be your and Russia's ruin and all true Russians say the same . . . I know I worry you — ah! would I not far, far rather only write letters of love, tenderness and caresses of which my heart is so full — but my duty as wife and mother and Russia's mother oblige me to say all to you — blessed by our Friend. Sweetheart, Sunshine of my life, if in battle you had to meet the enemy, you would never waver and go forth like a lion — be it now in the battle against the small handfull of brutes and republicans — be the Master and all will bow down to you.

Two letters are particularly significant. Pobyedonostsev could not have counseled the Emperor worse.

Play the Emperor! Remember you are the Autocrat. Speak to your Ministers as their Master. Do not be too good. Do not tell all the world that you bring disaster. Your angelic goodness, your forbearance, your patience, are well known, and everyone takes advantage of you. Make haste, my own darling; your little wife must always be behind you to spur you on.

Be like Peter the Great, John the Dread, the Emperor Paul. Crush them all. No, do not laugh, you naughty child. I so long to see you treat in this way those who try to govern you, when it is you who should govern them.

The answer of the Emperor to these Amazonian commands speaks volumes; the unsexing process is well-nigh complete as the Tzar inverts the order of Nature.

My Darling,
Tender thanks for the severe reprimand in writing. I read it with a smile because you talk to me as to a child. It is disgusting to have to do with a man whom I do not like and whom I do not trust like Trepov. . . . God bless you, my soul, my Sunny. I kiss you tenderly, as well as the girls, and remain your "poor, little, weak husband"
Nicky

Could human folly have proposed a more destructive trio of tyrants as models to guide the feet of a monarch already stumbling to his ruin? Peter the Great, John the Dread, and the Emperor Paul!

Peter the Great — who first started the Russian State on the wrong path, the typical despot who forced men to wear their clothes and shave their beards in a certain style because he so preferred it; the scorner of religion and the Church; regarded as Antichrist by his own people; the murderer who slew his own son Alexis because that unfortunate prince dared to defend the rights of his oppressed countrymen! Dimitri Merejkovsky, in his remarkable psychological novel, *Peter and Alexis*, has left a vivid picture of this incident.

Lenin regarded Peter the Great as the first Bolshevik and declared that he was his political ancestor. Constantine Aksakov, brilliant Russian idealist, ardent lover of his people, and dreamer of a golden age for Russia, has left a characteristic indictment of the compulsory enlightenment inaugurated by Peter: —

A man of genius and of bloodstained fame, you stand far off in the halo of terrible glory and armed with your axe. In the name of usefulness and science you have often dyed your hand in the blood of your people, and your swift thought told you that the seed of knowledge would swiftly grow when watered with blood. But wait! The spirit of the people has drawn back in the time of trouble, but it keeps its eternal right. It is waiting for the hour when a national voice will again call forth the waves of the people. You have despised all Russian life and in return a curse lies on your great work. You have discarded Moscow and, far from the people, you have built a solitary city which bears your name in a foreign tongue. But your feat is a wrong and the nation will rise again some day for ancient Moscow.

Prophetic words! To-day, two generations after Aksakov's death, Petrograd is a decaying, half-deserted city. Its very name has been changed to Leningrad, and the sceptre has returned to Moscow.

Ivan the Terrible — the Russian Nero, who instituted

THE LAST PRAYER OF ARCHBISHOP PHILIP
Murdered by Ivan the Terrible

a reign of terror against his own subjects that has passed into a proverb! "He abandoned the palace in the Kremlin," writes one historian, "and built himself and his satellites a whole new quarter in Moscow, summarily evicting the actual tenants; but he did not live much in the capital, preferring to direct his reign of terror from the forest of Alexandrov, which village he made his residence. Here he led the life of a lunatic, and forced his two sons, Ivan and Theodore, to do the same. The mornings were spent in bell-ringing and prostration, during dinner he read aloud the lives of the saints, in the afternoon he watched his victims being tortured, and in the evening he listened to soothsayers or got drunk. Everybody whom he suspected, he had murdered, tortured, or imprisoned; these included his cousin and all his family, and many of the boyars and their families. The Metropolitan of Moscow was outraged, imprisoned, and finally put to death for remonstrating with him. Not content with this, Ivan toured his unfortunate country, dealing death and destruction wherever he went. He literally devastated the prosperous city of Novgorod, and decimated its inhabitants, because it had dared to oppose his grandfather, and had rendered itself suspect of treachery. Finally, his suspicions fell on his own followers, and some of the chief *oprichniki* were executed. He made the people of Russia realize what it meant to invite a sovereign to come and rule upon his own terms. He did infinitely more material and moral harm to his country and to his subjects in twenty years than the Tatars had done in two hundred, and the irony of it was that he completely failed in his object."

Among his victims was his own son, Ivan, whom he killed in a fit of rage in the presence of the victim's young wife, crushing his head with the heavy iron staff studded with iron points which the father was in the habit of carrying.[1]

"Be like the Emperor Paul!" Now the Emperor Paul

[1] See Appendix VII.

was known throughout Europe as the "crowned madman," whose despotism knew no bounds.   So savage was his persecution, even of his own family, that a band of noblemen penetrated to his sleeping room on March 23, 1801, and murdered him.   The Emperor had leaped from his bed at the sound of the approaching officers and hid behind some friendly curtain, but the leader of the band, touching the bedclothes, said, "The nest is warm — the bird cannot be far away."   The members of the avenging group held the terrified despot, while one of them calmly strangled him with the sash of his uniform.   Among the murderers was the great-great-grandfather of Isvolsky, who served as Minister of Foreign Affairs under Nicholas II, a descendant of the murdered emperor.[1]

On November first the Grand Duke Nicholas Michailovich read a personal petition to the Tzar in which he begged the monarch to listen to the voice of his people: —

". . .   If you could succeed in removing this perpetual interference, the renaissance of Russia would begin at once and you would recover the confidence of the vast majority of your subjects, which is now lost.   When the time is ripe — and it is at hand — you can yourself grant from the throne the desired responsibility [of government] to yourself and the legislature.   This will come about naturally, easily, without any pressure from without and not in the same way as with the memorable act of October 17, 1905. I hesitated for a long time to tell you the truth, but made up my mind when your mother and your sisters persuaded me to do so. You are on the eve of new disturbances and, if I may say so, new attempts.   Believe me, if I so strongly emphasize the necessity of your liberation from the existing fetters, I am doing so, not from personal motives, but only in the hopes of saving you, your crown, and our beloved country from the irretrievable consequences of the gravest nature."

[1] It was on the occasion of the murder of Paul I that a Russian nobleman wrote to a foreign friend, explaining that the Russian Magna Charta was "despotism tempered by assassination."

All in vain. Equally futile were the guarded diplomatic warnings conveyed by Sir George Buchanan, the British ambassador, and Maurice Paléologue, ambassador of France.

In early December 1916, the Grand Duke Alexander, a favorite of the royal couple, was delegated by a group of near relatives of the Tzar to present to the Autocrat a final petition begging him to grant a Constitution — or at least a cabinet responsible to the people — before it should be too late. The Grand Duke, on his return from the interview, reported the conversation : —

"There is a superb chance now at hand. In three days we shall celebrate the sixth of December, Saint Nicholas's Day. Announce a constitution for that day ; dismiss Stürmer and Protopopov, and you will see with what enthusiasm and love your people will acclaim you."

The Emperor sat in pensive silence. He flicked the ashes from his cigarette with a bored gesture. The Empress shook her head, negatively. Nicholas answered : —

"What you ask is impossible. On the day of my coronation I swore to preserve the autocracy. I must keep that oath intact for my son."

Even the thunderbolt which Professor Milyukov exploded in the Duma during November had not shaken the inert mass of bureaucracy and corruption. It was a classic example of oratory, suggestive, as one observer writes, "of the old Hebrew Prophets or of Cicero's attacks on Catiline."

"Gentlemen : We have all heard of funeral orations — sad affairs, yet they serve some purpose. Let us analyze these purposes. First, we see such orations remind the relatives and friends of the deceased of some of his good qualities. Secondly, they may inspire a listener to imitation ; and thirdly, they give the orator an opportunity to relieve his feelings, or, better still, practise his oratorical power.

"But have you noticed, gentlemen, that, whatever the aim of the oration, it leaves the dead dead ? What would you, I wonder, think of an individual who should attempt an oration to resurrect the dead — to revive the spirit which has passed, and bring it back amongst the living? Mad? Yes, I agree; yet there are such occasions when such an endeavor would be permissible. Gentlemen, I am standing on this tribune with this mad desire upon me. Like a fire this desire has burned in my soul. I want to deliver an oration over the dead, to resurrect it, because we, the mighty Russian Empire, cannot think of leaving dead the most precious entity in the nation's possession. . . . This highest inheritance of a nation, its honor, must not be buried. Tarry with me, have patience with me. I am a sorrowful mourner. Honor has died in Russia, and before the world at large becomes aware of our dead we must bring it to life again."

Milyukov then launched upon an astounding revelation of the treason and defeatism of Premier Stürmer, whose appointment he qualified as madness. He charged him with negotiating for separate peace, betraying Russia, disarranging supplies for their sons and brothers in the trenches, and doing it all "for German money."

"I have here a document which shows every mark which he received from Germany from July 1901 to July 1916. Let him come and deny it, and if I am allowed to live after this (though I will gladly die if honor lives) I will bring witnesses to prove the truth. . . . Rise, up, dead Honor! Arise from thy coffin and let us see thee live! Come, face thy high position! Accuse him in front of this Assembly! Let thy voice thunder! . . . Do you know who is crying? Russia! The gallant Russia! The mother of us all, bad and good, is crying. . . . No, Berlin does not pay money for nothing! Stürmer had to earn it, and he did. He paved the way for revolution as the means of separate peace."

Driven finally to desperation by the futility of their efforts to curb the invisible influences and the dark forces surrounding the Empress, a small band of men of high birth, some related to the royal family, resolved to take the law of life and death into their own hands. The first victim marked for death was Rasputin. An intercepted letter revealed the fact that the Empress herself would have been the next to be removed.

The versions of Rasputin's death differ somewhat in details, but substantially they all agree that the "prophet," on the night of December 30, 1916, was enticed to the house of Prince Felix Yousoupov on the Moika, in Petrograd, and there assassinated in cold blood. Besides the Prince, the conspirators included the Grand Duke Dimitri Pavlovich and Pourishkevich, leader of the right wing of the Duma. The body was bundled into a blanket; a dog was killed to explain the pistol shot and account for the blood; the body finally was conveyed to the Neva in the automobile of a very high personage, and pushed under the ice.

When the news spread through Russia that Rasputin was no more, men breathed freely, and hope mounted in their breasts. *Morta la bestia morto il veneno.* ("The beast dead, the poison dies.") But the hope was short-lived. The domineering will of the Empress was unbroken, and a period of depression ensued. The Prince and the other nobles implicated in the taking off of Rasputin were banished, some to their estates in Russia and one to distant Persia. Practically all the members, near and distant, of the royal family united in beseeching the Emperor and the Empress to profit by the manifestations of popular unrest. Seventeen members of the royal family signed this protest. But the Tzarina was unmoved and the Tzar was obliged to request his own mother, the Dowager Empress, to leave the city and retire to her estates in the Crimea. The Romanovs, like the Bourbons, learned nothing and forgot nothing. The Tzarina became more resentful, more bitter, more autocratic than ever.

Three weeks before the final debacle, in February 1917, a faint ray of hope flickered through the thickening gloom.

But once more the invisible forces — or was it the Tzarina ? — intervened.   Rodzianko narrates the incident : —

The Duma was in session for nearly a week.   I learned casually that the Emperor had summoned several of the ministers, including Golitsyn, and expressed his desire to discuss the question of a responsible ministry.   The conference ended in the Emperor's decision to go to the Duma next day and proclaim his will to grant a responsible ministry.   Prince Golitsyn was overjoyed and came home in high spirits.   That same evening he was again summoned to the Palace, where the Emperor announced to him his intention to leave for the Stavka.

"How is that, Your Majesty?" asked Golitsyn, amazed. "What about a responsible ministry?   You intended to go to the Duma to-morrow."

"I have changed my mind. . . .   I am leaving for the Stavka to-night."

Russia was doomed.   And the mainstay of her national existence, the army in the field, was melting away in demoralized despondency.   One million, two hundred thousand embittered deserters had straggled back to their homes by January 1917, and the number was mounting daily.   The casualties in battle had already reached four millions.

CHAPTER VII

THE FALL OF THE MONARCHY

THE insane Protopopov, Minister of the Interior, seized upon the death of Rasputin to increase his influence and consolidate his position with the Tzarina. He announced that the spirit of the martyred prophet had descended upon him; he had visions and went into ecstasy in public; at times, when conversing with the Empress, he would suddenly pause and point dramatically to the empty space behind her, saying that Rasputin was there hovering over them. At other times he would see Christ blessing the Empress and confirming her political wisdom.

But this riot of fantasy, this coinage of a disordered brain, did not impair the exercise of a shrewd wit. It is said that he had his agents compose letters of a flattering nature and mail them from different parts of Russia to the Empress. In these forged epistles the writers, simulating the style and the common errors of peasants, praised the Empress for her devotion to a holy cause and exhorted her to stand fast in her policy.

The die was cast. In the Duma, Milyukov and his colleagues continued to denounce the impossible régime. Within three months from the death of Rasputin the red flag of revolt was seen in the streets of Petrograd. More ominous still, rioting began before the food shops. "An empty stomach has no ears," runs an ancient Russian proverb. An epidemic of madness descended upon the Government. Protopopov, in the final frenzy of reactionary bureaucracy, retaliated with all the apparatus of governmental suppression.   Machine guns were mounted on the roofs and at the street corners of Petrograd.   On March 8 there was a monster demonstration in the streets, and Protopopov's soldiers fired into the crowd.   The mobs, in reprisal, murdered every police official that fell into their hands.   On March 11 the Emperor, absent at the General Headquarters of the army at Mohilev, attempted to dissolve the Duma.   But the Duma refused to be dissolved.   By this time the situation in Petrograd was so out of hand that Rodzianko, President of the Duma, wired the Emperor as follows : —

The position is serious.   There is anarchy in the capital.   The Government is paralyzed.   The transportation of fuel and food is completely disorganized.   The general dissatisfaction grows.   Disorderly firing takes place in the streets.   A person trusted by the country must be charged immediately to form a ministry.

No answer from Mohilev.   The letters of the Tzarina, with their scorn of the growing popular outcry against a corrupt and inefficient government, had blinded the judgment and paralyzed the will of her uxorious consort.   One generous gesture might have saved Russia and changed the course of history.

On March 12, Rodzianko sent a second telegram : —

The position is getting worse.   Measures must be taken at once, because to-morrow will be too late.   The last hour has struck, and the fate of the fatherland and of the dynasty is being decided.

The same day, toward noon, the Tzar's only brother, the Grand Duke Michael Alexandrovich, telephoned from Petrograd that the formation of a new government meriting the confidence of the country was imperative and should be granted at once.   By way of reply the Tzar instructed General Alexeiev to thank the Grand Duke for his advice, but to say that he himself was quite capable of deciding what was to be done.   On the heels of this fraternal warning a telegram arrived from Prince Golitsyn, President of the

Council of Ministers, identical in tone with the message of the Grand Duke. The Emperor's reply took the form of an order to send fresh troops to Petrograd to stop the rioting.

Immediately after these significant events, and before definitely answering Prince Golitsyn, the Emperor spoke for more than one hour with someone over a private telephone. Now, there were two direct lines from General Headquarters, one connecting with Petrograd, the other with the Tzarina at Tsarskoe Selo. On finishing the protracted conversation with his unseen confidential counselor, Nicholas prepared a peremptory telegram in answer to Prince Golitsyn in which he informed the President of the Council that absolutely no modification could be made in the existing government. The telegram ended by ordering the immediate suppression — in the usual way — of all revolutionary movements and revolts among the soldiers of the Petrograd garrison. As this answer was sent by telegram to Petrograd, it is reasonably clear that the Emperor had not been speaking, just before, on the direct line to the capital. Otherwise the telegram was superfluous. The generals surrounding the Emperor concluded — and so must posterity — that Nicholas held that most important conversation, his last state council, with the Tzarina.

But Nicholas soon began to show apprehension, which was aggravated by a telegram from the Empress, at Tsarskoe Selo. She now wired that concessions were inevitable. For the first time she, too, began to see the end. Too late! The Tzar, on March 13, attempted to reach Tsarskoe Selo by train, but revolting troops sidetracked the imperial car and diverted it across country to Pskov. Late in the night, March 14, Nicholas established telephonic communication with Rodzianko and began to speak of concessions. But Rodzianko at the other end of the line, with tumultuous shouts from the streets proclaiming the revolt of each successive regiment as it went over to the Revolution, replied:

"It is too late to talk concessions; it is time to abdicate." By evening of the following day, March 15, two delegates of the Duma, Gutchkov and Shulgin, arrived at Pskov, and in the Emperor's private car announced to him the irrevocable will of the people. The Emperor, bowing his head, murmured, "I have been deceived," and signed the abdication.

The historic document was signed by the Tzar in pencil, between eleven and twelve o'clock on the night of March 15, 1917.

When we had read and approved the formula [Shulgin testifies] it seems to me that we shook hands . . . but at that moment I was undoubtedly very much moved and I may be wrong. I remember that when I looked at my watch for the last time it was ten minutes before midnight. This scene of supreme importance, therefore, took place between eleven and twelve o'clock in the night of the 2/15 to the 3/16 March.[1]

We then took leave. It seemed to me that on neither side was there any ill feeling. For my part, I felt an immense pity for that man who had just bought back, with a single act, his past faults. The Tzar was in full control of himself, friendly rather than cold.

We had agreed with General Russky that there should be two copies of the Act signed by the Emperor, for we feared lest, in the troublous times through which we were passing, the document we bore should be lost. One copy was kept by the General; we kept the other. As I have said, the signature of the Tzar was in pencil, while the Lord Chamberlain [Count Frederiks] countersigned in ink.

[1] The double date was frequent in old Russian writings and represents the difference between the Gregorian calendar in use in Western Europe and the Julian calendar which Russia tenaciously observed. Russia was, in consequence, thirteen days behind the rest of the world, in a calendar sense. The complete adoption of the Gregorian calendar came in 1923, during our stay in Moscow. The change occasioned many embarrassments. Thirteen days thus disappeared mysteriously from one's life, as the calendar suddenly jumped thirteen days overnight! Some of the employees in our relief stations inquired if they would be paid for the lost working days. Of course their fears were groundless. In point of fact, the next pay day — we paid off every fortnight — came within a day after the previous one. It was a bit complicated for the ordinary moujik and he simply marked it off as another Bolshevist trick.

Shulgin and Gutchkov Receiving the Abdication of Nicholas II in His Private Car Pskov, March 15, 1917

It is of importance to note that Nicholas named as successor to the throne, not his son, the Tzarevitch, but his own brother, Grand Duke Michael Alexandrovich. It was, in point of fact, a double abdication.

That very day, before the arrival of the Duma delegates, he summoned into his presence Professor Feodorov, one of his personal physicians: —

"Tell me frankly, Serge Petrovich, is Alexis's malady incurable?"

Realizing the import of the question, Feodorov answered, "Science teaches us, sire, that it is an incurable disease. Yet those who are afflicted with it sometimes reach an advanced old age. Still, Alexis Nikolaievich is at the mercy of an accident."

The Tzar hung his head and sadly murmured, "That is just what the Tzarina told me. Well, if that is the case and Alexis can never serve his country as I should like him to do, we have the right to keep him ourselves."

He then composed the text, which ran as follows: —

By the Grace of God, We, Nicholas II, Emperor of All the Russias, Tzar of Poland, Grand Duke of Finland, etc., etc., make known to all our loyal subjects: —

In the days of the great struggle with the external enemy who for the last three years has been striving to enslave our country, it has pleased God to send to Russia a new and painful trial. Internal troubles threaten to have a fatal effect on the outcome of this hard-fought war. The destinies of Russia, the honor of our heroic army, the happiness of the people, the whole future of our dear country, demand that at any cost the war should be carried to a victorious close.

Our bitter enemy has shot his bolt and the moment is near when our valiant army, in concert with our glorious allies, will finally crush him.

In these days that mean so much for the life of Russia we have thought our conscience compelled us to make easy for our people a close union and organization of all its forces for the rapid realization of victory.

That is why, in full accord with the Duma of the Empire, we have judged it well to abdicate the Crown and put off the supreme power.

Not wishing to part from our beloved son, we bequeath the heritage to our brother, the Grand Duke Michael Alexandrovich. Blessing him on his accession to the throne, we adjure our brother to rule in affairs of State in full and unbroken harmony with the representatives of the people in the legislative institutions, on principles which they shall determine, and to take an inviolable oath to this effect, in the name of our dearly beloved country.

We call upon all faithful sons of the fatherland to fulfill their sacred duty to it by obeying the Tzar in this grave time of national trial, and to help him, along with the representatives of the people, to lead the Russian State on to the path of victory, prosperity, and glory.

May the Lord God help Russia.

(Signed) Nicholas

"The document was a fine and noble composition," says Shulgin, who received it from the Emperor's hand. " I was ashamed of the draft we had scribbled hastily on our way."

Milyukov had already announced the forthcoming abdication to throngs collected in the Tauride Palace. "The power will pass to the Regent. The despot who has brought Russia to complete ruin will either abdicate or be deposed. The power will be transferred to the Grand Duke Michael Alexandrovich. Alexis will be the heir to the throne."

A shout went up: "It is the old dynasty!"

Sensing the popular mind, the leaders of the Revolution took steps to prevent the news of the Tzar's abdication in favor of Michael from reaching the public. An all-night session was held, Milyukov alone defending the succession of the Grand Duke; all others opposed. Shortly before dawn, Alexander Kerensky rang up the apartment of the Grand Duke on the telephone and begged him to make no decision or announcement until a deputation should wait on him.

At ten next morning Kerensky, Prince Lvov, Milyukov, and Rodzianko waited on the Grand Duke to convey to him the opinion of the majority.   Milyukov again dissented and delivered a lecture lasting over one hour.   During his peroration, Shulgin and Gutchkov arrived from Pskov with full details of the abdication.   Gutchkov supported Milyukov, and the cause of monarchy revived.   But after a wearisome debate and signs of frayed nerves, the Grand Duke decided to decline the dangerous dignity.   On March 16 he issued his manifesto : —

A heavy burden has been laid on me by the will of my brother, who, in a time of unexampled strife and popular tumult, has transferred to me the imperial throne of Russia.   Sharing with the people the thought that the good of the country should stand before everything else, I have firmly decided that I will accept power only if that is the will of our great people, who must by universal suffrage elect their representatives to a Constituent Assembly, in order to determine the form of government and draw up new fundamental laws for Russia.   Therefore, calling for the blessing of God, I ask all citizens of Russia to obey the Provisional Government, which has arisen and been endowed with full authority on the initiative of the Imperial Duma, until such time as the Constituent Assembly, called at the earliest possible date and elected on the basis of universal, direct, equal, and secret suffrage, shall, by its decision as to the form of government, give expression to the will of the people.

It was the last official act of the Romanovs.   The Grand Duke, imprisoned by the Bolsheviki, disappeared in June 1918, and it is generally supposed that he was murdered, somewhere in the vicinity of Perm.

What Mr. Kerensky calls the first act in the drama of the Revolution — meaning the period covering the disappearance of the old régime and the advent of the Provisional Government — lasted exactly one hundred hours.

The Tzar attempted to recall his abdication in favor of

Michael almost as soon as he had issued the document. Probably repenting of the juridical injury done his son in thus depriving him of the succession, and perhaps apprehensive of the Tzarina's reaction, he made an ineffectual attempt to set the Tzarevitch on the throne. General Denikin, in his account of the incident, furnishes the following information : —

Late at night the imperial train left for Mohilev. Dead silence, lowered blinds, and heavy, heavy thoughts. No one will ever know what feelings wrestled in the breast of Nicholas II, of the monarch, the father, and the man, when on meeting Alexeiev at Mohilev, and looking straight at the latter with kindly, tired eyes, he said, irresolutely, "I have changed my mind. Please send this telegram to Petrograd." On a small sheet of paper, in a clear hand, the Tzar had himself traced his consent to the immediate succession to the throne of his son Alexis.

Alexeiev took the telegram — and did not send it. It was too late; both manifestoes had already been made public to the army and to the country. For fear of "unsettling public opinion," Alexeiev made no mention of the telegram and kept it in his portfolio until he passed it on to me toward the end of May, when he resigned his post of Supreme Commander in Chief. The document, of vast importance to future biographers of the Tzar, was afterward kept under seal at the Operations Department of General Headquarters.

Before signing the original abdication on small sheets of paper, which had as headings the word "Stavka" (General Headquarters) on the left, and "Chief of Staff" on the right, Nicholas bore proud and sonorous titles: "Nicholas II, by God's grace, Emperor and Autocrat of All the Russias, King of Poland, Grand Duke of Finland, Tzar of Moscow, Kiev, Vladimir, Novgorod, Kazan, Astrakhan, Siberia, the Tauric Chersonese, Georgia, Lord of Pskov, Grand Duke of Smolensk, Lithuania, Volhynia, Podolia, Prince of Esthonia, Livonia, Courland, and Semigallia, Samogitia, Bielostok, Karelia, Tver, Yougoria, Perm, Viatka . . . Lord and Grand

Duke of Lower Novgorod, Chernigov, Riazan, Polotsk, Rostov, Yaroslav . . . Lord and Sovereign of the lands of Iberia . . . and the Provinces of Armenia . . . Sovereign of the Circassian and Mountaineer Princes . . . Lord of Turkestan, Heir of Norway, Duke of Schleswig-Holstein . . . of Oldenburg, etc. etc."

When Shulgin and Gutchkov stepped down from the royal car and entered their own to hurry back to expectant Petrograd, they left him plain "Colonel Nicholas Alexandrovich Romanov."

The Provisional Government was unusually meticulous in the matter of the Tzar's titles and saw to it that letters and newspapers reaching him in his prison should bear only the title "Colonel." The Tzarina's name on her mail and newspapers was likewise corrected; the appellation "Her Majesty" was always scratched out and replaced by "Alexandra Feodorovna Romanov."

So, Louis XVI was called "Citizen Capet" by his jailers. One of the Tzarina's ladies in waiting, Marfa Mouchanow, who shared her imprisonment at Tsarskoe Selo, tells us in her memoirs that this particular detail — the refusal of the Provisional Government to permit the Empress to retain her title — was of all her misfortunes that one that seemed most to have embittered her.

On March 16, the day following his abdication, Nicholas started, not to rejoin the Empress at Tsarskoe Selo, but for Mohilev, General Headquarters of the Russian army, to take leave of his troops. He remained there until the twenty-first, the day on which four representatives of the Provisional Government reached the camp and informed General Alexeiev that the ex-Tzar was under arrest and should be transported to Tsarskoe Selo. Nicholas had previously expressed his desire to retire to the Crimea, there to end his days on his estate at Livadia. The Provisional Government was unable to acquiesce. The Emperor obeyed, asking only one final privilege, to take leave of his army in a last "Order of the Day," which he composed as follows: —

8(21) *March*, 1917. No. 371

I address my soldiers, who are dear to my heart, for the last time. Since I have renounced the throne of Russia for myself and my son, power has been taken over by the Provisional Government, which has been formed on the initiative of the Duma of the Empire.

May God help it to lead Russia into the path of glory and prosperity. May God help you, my glorious soldiers, to defend the Fatherland against a cruel enemy. For two and a half years you have endured the strain of hard service; much blood has been shed, great efforts have been made, and now the hour is at hand in which Russia and her glorious allies will break the enemy's last resistance in one common, mightier effort.

The unprecedented war must be carried through to final victory. Anyone who thinks of peace or desires it at this moment is a traitor to his country and would deliver her over to the foe. I know that every soldier worthy of the name thinks as I do.

Do your duty, protect our dear and glorious country, submit to the Provisional Government, obey your leaders, and remember that any failure in duty can only profit the enemy.

I am firmly convinced that the boundless love you bear our great country is not dead within you.

God bless you and may Saint George, the great martyr, lead you to victory.

NICHOLAS

The inexplicable mentality of the Provisional Government, its confused indecision which finally lost itself in the maze of oratory and hesitation that accelerated Bolshevism, forbade the publication of this touching farewell to the army. It was suppressed, despite the fact that it was obviously a sincere appeal to support the new authorities and probably would have strengthened their hand to a notable degree. Whether the decision to pigeonhole it was motivated by fear or exaggerated prudence or old resentments, it was the first injudicious step of a most injudicious régime.

A passing flash of pathos comes slanting across the sombre scene at this juncture. As the clouds gathered over the head of the doomed monarch, while friends and erstwhile supporters were dropping away like banqueters from a Timon of Athens, as regiment after regiment went over to the revolutionists, — one of them led by the Tzar's own kinsman, the Grand Duke Cyril, — there arrived from Kiev one whose loyalty never faltered and on whose bosom the weary, uncrowned head might rest as it had reposed there in complete confidence when an infant. The first of his family to take her place by Nicholas's side after his fall was his mother, the Dowager Empress Maria. She remained with him until the twenty-first, when he was conducted under arrest to Tsarskoe Selo.

They were never to meet again. The broken-hearted queen-mother found refuge in Denmark, her native land, whence she had departed as the lovely Princess Dagmar to wed Alexander III in 1866. During that half century she saw the political face of Europe transformed; saw dynasties flourish and fall; saw a resurgent Poland outlive the three mighty empires that had sinned the sin of the ages in partitioning that land and people among themselves as the spoils of war; finally, she saw that country over which she had ruled as joint sovereign descend into the very Valley of the Shadow. But, with the indomitable faith which seems to seize upon and sway the imagination of all who fall under the spell of Russia's mysticism, she clings imperiously to the vanished sceptre, refuses to believe that her royal son is dead, and so forbids the customary prayers for his soul.

Though the name of Nicholas Romanov has been deleted from the *Almanach de Gotha*, the social register of nobility, to his exiled mother he is still Tzar of All the Russias and will one day return to resume the great Russian crown which the Bolsheviki keep in the Gochrana, within the Kremlin, and exhibit on occasions to privileged visitors. With the other crown jewels this dazzling accumulation of diamonds, pearls, and precious metals is preserved in a massive steel box. On its domelike top rests the blazing Peking ruby, big as a pigeon's egg, surmounted by a cross of rarest diamonds, aggregating in all twenty-eight hundred carats. The head that last wore it was desecrated by a fiendish executioner, who poured sulphuric acid over it, then smashed it into an unrecognizable pulp and burned the bones to ashes.

Beside this may be seen the Tzarina's crown, described by one who saw it recently as 'an exquisite flowerlike creation, all a-shimmer with perfectly matched diamonds and pearls — a mass of iridescent fire. It was fashioned for Catherine the Great by Pauzier of Geneva, who was the Cellini of his day.' The last head that wore this sign of royalty was, as we shall shortly see, likewise beaten into fragments at Eka-terinburg. The aged Dowager Empress, brooding now over the mysteries of life in her retreat outside Copenhagen, had also worn it in the days of pomp and glory. It has been replaced on her brow by that other diadem which mothers so often inherit : —

. . . A sorrow's crown of sorrow is remembering happier things.

March 22 was a dark and dreary day, as March days can be in Russia. At eleven in the morning the Emperor, accompanied by Prince Dolgorúky, Marshal of the Court, arrived at Tsarskoe Selo and went straight to the Tzarina, who was waiting in strained suspense. He was never to be separated from his family again, except for the brief moment at Tiumen during the transfer from Tobolsk to Ekaterinburg.

In the meantime, before the arrival of Nicholas, General Kornilov, Commander of the Military District of Petrograd, had waited on the distracted Tzarina to inform her that she was under arrest. Witnesses of that extraordinary scene record that the silence which followed the General's laconic announcement was that of the tomb. It was revolution in

its starkest reality. The Empress, having entered the audience chamber and seated herself with her accustomed formality and air of royalty, was stunned to hear Kornilov say,
"I must request you, madame, to stand up and listen with
attention to the commands I am about to impose on you."

"Commands!" It was the first time in three hundred
years that mortal had addressed this word to a Romanov.

But commands came with military directness. She was to
consider herself under arrest; she was forbidden to send or
receive letters without the permission of the officer in charge
of the Palace; she was not to walk alone in the park or about
the grounds; she was to execute immediately any further
orders signified to her. Count Benckendorff, Master of the
Palace, who was in attendance, showed by his countenance
that he felt there was nothing left but for the earth to open
and swallow them all. Little did he or the Empress seem
to realize that in Petrograd, not more than fifteen miles
away, an infuriated mob was parading through the streets of
the capital bearing placards that called for the immediate
trial and execution of the Empress as one guilty of high
treason.

Three weeks later she learned how deep the resentment
lay. During the night of Thursday, April 5, a company
of soldiers exhumed the body of Rasputin from its resting
place of honor in the garden of the Summer Palace and
transported it to the forest of Pargolovo, fifteen versts
north of Petrograd. A scaffolding of pine wood had been
erected in a clearing; prying the body out of the elaborate
coffin with sticks and rods, — no one dared to touch the
oozy mass, as putrefaction was far advanced, — they hoisted
it high on the barrow, drenched it with gasoline, and set
fire to the pile.

The flames roared for six hours before the carrion was
wholly consumed. Dawn found the soldiers burying the
ashes beneath a blanket of snow.

In April 1922, the writer of these lines made a trip to Petrograd and was permitted by the Soviet authorities to visit the spots where these revolutionary episodes were enacted.[1] If my memory and notes do not deceive me, on the wall of the Tzarina's room in the Alexander Palace, in a corner near a window, hung a large tapestry, depicting in life-size proportions Marie Antoinette and her children. It is said to be after Madame Vigée Lebrun's famous painting and was presented by the French Government. The ill-fated queen of France, in all the classic beauty that Burke perpetuates in his vivid word-portrayal of her charms, sits in regal splendor with her children grouped around her, one on her knees. The Empress of all the Russias, herself a foreign princess, as was the Austrian consort of Louis XVI, passed the latter years of her private life under the shadow of that mute warning. The fate of Marie Antoinette, though longer deferred and immeasurably more brutal when it came, was never far away from Alexandra Feodorovna.

Their careers were cast in almost identical moulds.

The daughter of Maria Theresa came as a young girl to France from a Teutonic court. Vienna of the latter eighteenth century was more a stronghold of the Hapsburg dynasty than the capital city of a distinct nationality. The Empress of Russia came from a German principality, too, though a far less brilliant one — that of Hesse. Marie Antoinette journeyed to Versailles to be bride to a Dauphin destined to rule a kingdom already in the throes of incipient revolution. His ancestors had made themselves absolute personal monarchs — and passed the final reckoning on to

[1] Among other rooms, we visited the study of the Tzar, which has been preserved unchanged by the Soviets. Another American, Mr. Newman, who is at present giving entertaining travelogues on Russia, enjoyed a similar privilege within the past few months. Someone must have been "spoofing" Mr. Newman, as his remarks and photographs, published in a New York newspaper, depict "the desk at which the Tzar signed his abdication" and show the actual pen he used. This should not be mistaken for authentic history. The Tzar signed his abdication in a railway car at Pskov, some one hundred and fifty miles distant, and used a pencil.

him. Alexandra came to Russia to assume a rôle particularly congenial to her character in the most autocratic court of Europe. Marie Antoinette never fully lost her foreign bearing and accent. Neither did Alexandra — French and English were her preferred tongues. It is said she never spoke Russian except when obliged to — and quaintly at that. Marie Antoinette was destined to follow her husband to the death of a common criminal. So was Alexandra.

Enmity and jealousy pursued the *Autrichienne*. She began her reign under a cloud; scores of Parisians were trampled to death during the coronation fêtes. Alexandra, from the first day of her arrival, moved through a deepening atmosphere of suspicion and distrust. Her first official appearance in Russia had been at the obsequies of Alexander III and the nuptials followed a few days later. Wedding bells mingling with a dirge! In consequence she was to be known as the "funeral bride." The day of her coronation was marred by the tragic accident at the Khodinka field where thousands of innocent citizens were trodden to death in a sudden panic that ensued when the crowds of waiting spectators broke through the police lines. Foreign diplomats driving out to the field passed truckloads of mangled bodies being conveyed to the city. Within a few yards of the reviewing stand from which the pale and trembling monarch spoke his words of appreciation lay a heap of corpses, the arms and legs bulging grotesquely through the canvas coverings that had been thrown hastily over them. The customary state ball went on as usual that night, though there were death and mourning throughout Moscow. It was regarded as an evil omen.

Marie Antoinette cherished a passionate yearning for a son, but was long denied the bliss of motherhood and was bitterly disappointed when the first child was a girl. Alexandra lived in morbid anxiety until, after four daughters, a son and heir was born who proved to be at once her joy and her undoing. Marie Antoinette was publicly accused of treasonable traffic with the enemies of France. Alexandra's name was placarded in the streets of Petrograd as a traitor and accursed Germanophile. Marie Antoinette was the victim of domestic calumny and legends of debauchery circulated in the Paris coffee shops. Alexandra had Rasputin and a similar undeserved stigma. Marie Antoinette never fully understood — in fact, mildly disdained — her adopted people. Alexandra never quite fathomed the Russian masses or sympathized with them. She was paid back in like coin.

Marie Antoinette exercised a disastrous political influence during the five years that preceded the fall of the Bourbons. In her salon gathered the forces of intrigue and reactionary opposition to Parliament. The States-General she contemned. Her "New Order" was regarded as a despotic invasion of popular rights. The Tzarina lent aid, comfort, and counsel to the invisible influences and fell victim to the dark forces that ruined the Romanovs. Marie Antoinette put Necker in power: the court rose and chased him out. Alexandra sponsored Stürmer and Protopopov: Petrograd hoisted the red flag. Marie Antoinette was held hostage in the Tower. Alexandra passed sixteen months in an imprisonment that was mild and dignified at first, but which swept with furious crescendo to its hideous termination. Marie Antoinette worshiped her son, the Dauphin, with the entire devotion of her being. The Tzarina would not permit herself to be separated from the Hope of the Throne even in their common death.

As Marie Antoinette mounted the steps of the guillotine shortly before noon on October 16, 1793, the advance of the rescuing counter-revolution was halted and routed at Maubeuge. As the émigrés and Bourbon nobles retreated with the banners of monarchy, her head fell into the basket. Kolchak's White Army and the Czechoslovak troops were on the point of taking Ekaterinburg, as Alexandra Feodo-rovna sank to the floor of a cellar, riddled by the murderous fire of Lettish executioners.

There now followed five months of a relatively easy and mild imprisonment in the Summer Palace. The Tzar spent his time mostly in physical exercise, digging in the garden, clearing away the snow, walking in the park, or sawing wood in the fields. The Tzarina occupied herself in the care of her children. Three of the Grand Duchesses were ill and the Tzarevitch was stricken with measles, complicated by a re-currence of his hereditary disease. In her free moments she worked unceasingly making garments and bandages for the Red Cross. The two ex-rulers were not allowed to meet or converse together, even at meals, without an officer of the guard at their elbow.

The Palace was guarded as a beleaguered fortress. On one occasion a sentry caused a wave of excitement by firing a shot to summon the Commandant in order to inform him that signals, with red and green lights, were being made from the Tzar's apartments. Visions of secret code and possible rescue rose before the Commandant's mind. He rushed into the house and ordered an investigation. The mystery was soon explained. The Grand Duchess Anastasia and the Tzar were sitting in the same room, the Emperor reading while his daughter, ensconced on the window ledge, was doing needlework. Her workbasket was on a table near by. As she stooped to pick up the things she needed she was alter-nately covering and uncovering two different lamps, one with a green shade, the other with a red, by the light of which the Tzar was reading.

The young Tzarevitch, Alexis, played in the garden and received regular instruction from his private tutor, Pierre Gilliard, a Swiss professor who was permitted to remain with the family until very near the end. His testimony, extending through thirteen years and reaching to Ekaterinburg, furnishes source material of prime historical importance. No place else is it more clearly demonstrated how fatally the destiny of Russia was determined by such a pathetically human consideration as the health of the only son. In the person of that frail, winsome — but spoiled and over-petted — child you have the explanation of the Empress; you have the reason for Rasputin; you have the key for the abdication in favor of Michael and the subsequent attempted withdrawal by the Tzar; you have one of the redeeming traits in both Tzar and Tzarina. They jeopardized an empire to save one delicate boy from the clutches of a congenital disease which she, all unwittingly, had transmitted to him. The Tzarevitch in turn dominated not only his parents and sisters, but all Russia in them.

Mr. Kerensky, Procurator-General in the Provisional Government, visited the Palace frequently. On April 3, his first visit, after shaking hands with the royal family, he said to the Tzarina, "The Queen of England asks for news of the ex-Tzarina." Pierre Gilliard records that the Empress blushed violently. It was the first time that she had been addressed as "ex-Tzarina."

The British Government from the outset manifested a desire to assure the physical safety of the dethroned monarchs. An offer of asylum in England was made through Sir George Buchanan, British ambassador at Petrograd, and it was understood that the German Government had agreed to permit one English ship to pass through the submarine zone without attack to meet the imperial family at Port Romanov. The benevolent design proved abortive, and around the failure has grown up an acrimonious controversy. Princess Paley, widow of the murdered Grand Duke Paul Alexandrovich, accuses the British ambassador of having deliberately foiled the plan of King George to rescue his cousin. Sir George Buchanan defends himself vigorously in

THE EMPRESS ALEXANDRA AND THE TZAREVITCH ALEXIS

" This son is the apple of the eye of the parents. They watch over him with unceasing anxiety for they know that at any moment a fatal accident may deprive them of their treasure. The boy is . . . an extremely handsome child. The long, finely-chiseled face, the delicate features, and the auburn hair, with a copper glint in it, are like those of the mother. But where the likeness becomes positively uncanny is in the large, blue-gray eyes, at the moments especially when, during an attack of bleeding, there comes into them a look of tragic surprise. A solid spiritual link exists between mother and son; they do not need words to understand one another."

AUGUR (V. POLIAKOFF)

his published memoirs and blames the Provisional Government, who "were not masters in their own house."

This version is probably correct. In an interview with the author, Mr. Kerensky confirmed the report that such an offer had been made by the British Government, but so strong and hostile was the Soviet of Workmen at Petrograd that the Provisional Government did not dare to take the necessary steps. The Bolsheviki threatened to tear up the rails before the train should the Government attempt to move the imperial family. It might have been possible at a later date, but Mr. Kerensky left me under the impression that the ardor of the British Government seemed to cool. He intimated that Lloyd George's policy had changed.

In the course of the interview in question Mr. Kerensky was asked if he cared to comment on the following incident as currently reported in Russia.

During one of his visits to the Summer Palace on a tour of inspection, Mr. Kerensky was accosted by the young Tzarevitch : —

"Are you Mr. Kerensky ?"

"Yes."

"You are Minister of Justice. Will you answer me a question ?"

"Yes."

"Did my father have the right to abdicate for himself and for me too ?"

Kerensky paused, then replied, "As your father, he probably did not; as Emperor, I think he had the right."

The boy seemed satisfied with the hairsplitting and returned to his play.

On hearing my story, Mr. Kerensky laughingly tossed it off as a monarchist fabrication.

During the captivity day followed day with monotonous similarity. Nicholas adapted himself to the new conditions with an amazing ease and with an air of indifference that was in marked contrast to the sullen resentment of the Tzarina. Her bitterness was directed as much against the Tzar as against her fate. She could not soon forget that double abdication. "There must be a mistake!" she had cried out on first hearing the news. "It is impossible that Nicky has sacrificed our boy's claim!" Her rage became uncontrolled when at last the truth was inescapable, and she exclaimed, "He might at least in his fright have remembered his son."

Her intuition, always sharper than that of Nicholas, seemed to realize the danger to their lives. "They will put us in the fortress," she confided one day to Marfa Mouchanow, "and then kill us as they did Louis XVI." To her youngest daughter, the Grand Duchess Anastasia, who was stunned and thrown into tears by the sudden reversal of fortune, Alexandra said, "It is too early to cry yet. Keep your sorrow for another occasion." In the words of an eye-witness, the reprimand was given "in a hard voice." It was only the lapse of time and the growing hardship of their common misfortune that softened her animosity toward the husband whom she considered a weakling.

The Tzar, for his part, seems to have abdicated in spirit and in truth. Though following with keenest and intelligent interest the progress of the war and the movements of the Russian army, he never attempted to exercise political influence or indulge in critical comment. He accepted obscurity with the same fatalistic confidence he had shown in clinging obstinately to his waning autocracy.

CHAPTER VIII

A REVERY IN THE SUMMER PALACE

NICHOLAS is teaching his son Russian history. To while away the snail-like hours, the last of the Romanovs devotes much time to pedagogy, instructing Alexis, the Tzarevitch, in topics of fundamental importance for one born to be the future ruler of a vast empire. The three hundred and four years of Romanov rule which had come to such an anti-climactic end would yield for his speculations an unfolding panorama of bewildering complexity, unending political tumult, and vast geographic expansion.

This king should make an excellent teacher. The sinister voice of his own tutor, Pobyedonostsev, was stilled, hence no warning finger could be raised to suppress the truth or skillfully guide his prison thoughts; there are no military reviews to hold, no state balls to inaugurate; there are no frivolous courtiers about to distract, nor wassail to inebriate, only the measured tread of sentries outside his door and occasional noises at the changing of guards under his window.

One wonders if his lesson ever touched on certain reasons why Alexis was now surrounded by jailers, why his sisters wept so often, why his mother clasped him so strangely to her breast, or why Mr. Kerensky slept in the great bed of the emperors in the Winter Palace? I suppose not; the boy was too young for a philosophy of history.

But did Nicholas himself ever fall into revery that was something more than vain regret? Did he ever seek to determine in his heart of hearts the historical responsibility for the processes that had culminated in this almost solitary confinement? But yesterday the word of a Romanov might have stood against the world; to-day there are only a handful of servants and a few aged courtiers to do him reverence. The ease with which the monarchy fell, and the swift, utter, and callous abandonment of their monarch by friends and people alike, should have furnished grounds for salutary meditation. Solitude divests flattery of its sham and unction. Truths which in the warm glow of prosperity and security one is apt to consider as unpleasant annoyances, mere jeremiads of the hypercritical, become sombre revelations in the cold, pitiless light of adversity. Did Nicholas come to comprehend at last the inexorable realities which so many ardent patriots had sought in vain to make him understand?

If he did not, — which is the probable case, — I can conceive of no more ironic figure, in the Greek sense, than this dethroned master of Tsarskoe Selo, already marked to atone in blood for the sins and imbecilities of three hundred years of misrule.

The capital error committed by his ancestors who controlled Russia's destiny and moulded the forms of her political life lay in their failure to create in the minds of the people a consciousness of common destiny. Historically, Russia evolved into two entities, distinct, antagonistic, and perpetually at odds with each other. Government was not conceived as a delegation of power to be exercised for the common good by a responsible trustee, but as a vested dynastic right to be jealously safeguarded and exploited for the aggrandizement of a small, privileged minority. Rulers and ruled, consequently, were never fused into a single unified community.

For a brief space following the period of anarchy, *smutnoye vremia*, the recognition by the Romanovs of a national assembly, *zemsky sobor*, and a boyars' Duma reveals a hesitating tendency to return to the primitive democratic traditions of ancient Slav civilization, which historians picture as gay, boisterous, full of color, individualistic, and vociferously independent. The autonomous republics of Pskov and Novgorod are outstanding types of municipal organization that gave free expression to popular sovereignty. Novgorod, best type of old free Russia, was a city-state as jealous of its freedom as was ever Ghent or Florence. Its "Court of Jaroslav" held popular assemblies, *Veche*, summoned for legislative deliberation by the clanging of the great bell in its tower, six hundred years before the Mayflower set sail; its Declaration of Independence was drawn up seven centuries before the Philadelphia document and was much shorter too: "If the prince is bad, into the mud with him." And the people acted on it frequently, so frequently, in fact, that in the course of a single century the chronicles record how the free men of Novgorod drove out as many as thirty princes whose rule did not please them, an average of one every forty months. Thus, in 1136, Prince Vsevolod Mstislavich was summarily deposed and expelled by the hard-headed burghers because he was "too fond of sport and too neglectful of his duty."

But "Lord Novgorod the Great," *Gospodin Veliki Novgorod*, succumbed ignominiously in 1471 to the growing might of the near-by Principality of Moscow, when Ivan the First, called Great, advancing upon the republican stronghold, slaughtered the freemen right and left, transported whole families in chains to Moscow, and brought the last free city under the yoke of Moscovite autocracy. Finally, in 1570, Ivan the Fourth, known as the Terrible, repeated the chastisement of his grandfather and again devastated Novgorod with fire and sword, butchering sixty thousand inhabitants.[1] The great bell which had summoned Novgorodians to the councils had already been dismantled, brought to Moscow, and there erected to mingle its tones with the victorious

[1] See Appendix VII.

clamor from Ivan's towers. Cast for liberty, it ended in slavery, symbol of Russia's own eventual destiny. "An eagle, many-winged, with lion's claws, has fallen upon me," laments the Chronicler of Pskov, which had suffered the same fate; "he has robbed me of three Cedars of Lebanon — my beauty, my wealth, my children. Our country is deserted, our city is in ruins, our markets are destroyed. My brothers have been carried to a place where neither our fathers nor our grandfathers nor our forefathers have dwelt. . . ."

By the close of the sixteenth century, the democracy that flourished in that then unknown corner of Europe was obsolete and a haunting memory. It must have been the ghost of that far-off, golden age of Russian freedom that President Wilson evoked when he said from the floor of Congress, on April 2, 1917: "Russia was known by those who know it best to have been always in fact democratic at heart, in all the vital habits of her thought, in all the intimate relationships of her people that spoke their natural instinct, their habitual attitude toward life. Autocracy that crowned the summit of her political structure, long as it had stood and terrible as was the reality of its power, was not, in fact, Russian in origin, in character, or purpose; and now it has been shaken off and the great, generous Russian people have been added, in all their native majesty and might, to the forces that are fighting for freedom in the world, for justice and for peace. Here is a fit partner for a League of Honor."

These native tendencies crop out sporadically in later generations, but were consistently suppressed during the reign of the Romanovs, particularly during the reforms of Peter the Great, as each succeeding Tzar reverted to the belief that the Russian land and people were the private asset of the sovereign, his *votchina*.

The destruction of the primitive political and social forms

TROIKA RACING IN A RUSSIAN VILLAGE

which had characterized the first Russian republics may be attributed to definite causes.

In the first place, that great Russian plain to which we have already referred, stretching, as it did, without mountains or other natural barriers from the Danube and Dniester to the Yenisei, and from the Arctic Ocean to the Hindu Kush Mountains, encouraged the Princes of Moscow to embark upon that adventuresome enlargement of their domain which resulted, as imperialism always does, in the necessary creation of a ponderous administrative machinery and required a huge personnel. Faced in each successive advance by fierce Asiatic nomads, the Russian Tzars from Ivan the First, the "Coagulator of Russia," regarded each completed wave of emigration as just so many outposts — military spearheads, as it were — to be utilized for supplying the sinews of war to the expanding state. Step by step with the double-headed eagle, as it advanced into the northern forests, the southern steppes, and the Siberian wastes, went the tax collector and the recruiting sergeant. Under Yermak, conqueror of Siberia, vanguards of Cossacks pushed ever forward, founding their fortified villages, *stanitsas*, until, in 1775, they had reached the Pacific and crossed Behring Straits to Alaska and the American continent.

Large grants of land were freely made to a favored caste on the sole condition of supplying men and money for Moscow. As the size of the domain depended on the number of recruits the *pomieschik* could muster, each emigrant was viewed in the light of a potential soldier. By a natural evolution, consequently, the military class became rulers of the newly conquered territories, absorbing not only all fiscal functions, but full civil and judicial powers as well, while the colonizers and peasant population were gradually reduced to economic serfdom and loaded with military obligations to their feudal overlords. The consciousness of political right was smothered by the hosts of officialdom and the vision of common interest was dispelled by the tyrannous exaction of landholders, petty clerks, and military governors responding with tribal solidarity to the pressure from Moscow.   Thus the Russification and expansion policy operated, to a measurable degree, as an obstacle in the formation of a self-conscious, national state.

Had not Nicholas himself plunged Russia into a disastrous war with Japan in order to safeguard certain timber concessions on the Yalu River?

At the very epoch when Western Europe was experiencing the renaissance of political theory and the rise of parliaments, Russia was crystallizing and hardening into a palace state, wherein the only political philosophy tolerated was that of the *oprichniki*, riding unchecked through the land, broom and dead dog's head at the saddle bow, sword and knout in hand, massacring every man, woman, and child who presumed to question, much less to oppose, the *prikaz* of the Tzar.   And, with slight modification, Imperial Russia remained a palace state until her fall, political progress frozen, like her mighty rivers, into icy immobility.   It took the dynamite of universal indignation to split the glacier.

"Scratch a Russian and find a Tatar," has been attributed to Napoleon.   As a qualified observer of Russian military prowess, he does assuredly command respect; still it was not so much Alexander I and his generals, as General Winter and his ally, Cold, that brought Bonaparte to grief, transformed the Grand Army into a demoralized mob, and sent it limping and freezing back to the Dniester and the eventual disasters at Leipzig and Waterloo.

Like most generalizations, the saying is a fallacious admixture of truth and falsehood.   *Fraus latet in generalibus.* The falsity in this case lies in the assumption that there ever existed a single, all-inclusive type, a sort of universal Russian to be scratched, and his inner self thus easily catalogued.

The raw materials of the Russian people were as varied ethnically and composite as were the geographic and racial sources from whence they came. Napoleon's scratching instrument might at one time have laid bare pure Slavic stock, at another brought Græco-Byzantine blood, or revealed Swedish, Teutonic, Finnish, or Livonian as well as a true Tatar strain, depending entirely on the region and particular subject of his experiment. He would have needed a sizable collection of test tubes for his blood analysis of the races in the Caucasus. But the truth of the jibe is not inconsiderable and has undeniable historical justification.

The Russian steppes, sprawling monotonously eastward and unrelieved by mountain chains, invited invasion westward from Asia as openly as later they tempted Russian adventurers to expand their frontiers eastward. In the year 1224 these plains were suddenly alive with an Asiatic host from the great unknown regions beyond. As the Russian chronicler tells us, "There came upon us for our sins unknown nations. No one could tell their origin, whence they came, what religion they professed. God alone knows who they were, or where they came from — God, and perhaps wise men learned in books." Like an avalanche, hordes of Tatars and Mongolians from the neighborhood of Lake Baikal and the Gobi Desert swept down on the scattered and disunited Russian principalities. Taken by surprise and rent by internal discord, the Russian princes were enveloped and vanquished one after another by the unending swarms of Genghis Khan's cavalry. Russia of the thirteenth century resembled France of the early fifteenth. Whereas modern France is a synonym for glowing patriotism and pride of nationality, five centuries ago there was, strictly speaking, no France, but an agglomeration of rival feudal chiefs and independent strongholds; there were no Frenchmen, but plenty of Parisians, Royalists, Burgundians, Armagnacs, Bretons, and Provençaux. But France merited a Joan of Arc and salvation. Russia had neither. Instead came the Ivans, both great and terrible, Boris Godunov, anarchy, the Romanovs, Rasputin, and last of all, closing her strange, eventful history, the Bolsheviki.

The Russian annalist of the period records with consternation the appearance of those wild horsemen, sweeping like hawks upon the unsuspecting land, armed with long, steel-tipped arrows, huge scimitars, pikes with villainous hooks, and supported by battering rams never before seen or heard of. Fired with a dream of universal domination as a result of his success in mobilizing the Mongols and Tatars of Asia for the conquest of Europe, Genghis Khan rallied about him another formidable array of nomads and shepherd tribes inured to wandering and long marches, masters in the saddle, pitiless in warfare, perfectly at ease on uncultivated plains or in the depths of uninhabited forests. Warfare for those barbarians was not an incident or an isolated event; it was the breath of their nostrils. They could ride continuously for two days and sleep in the saddle while the horses grazed. Marco Polo, who lived seventeen years in Tatary, is authority for the statement that when other food was lacking they drank blood from their chargers' veins.

The surprised Russians fled to their cities before the irresistible manœuvring of the mobile Tatar cavalry. With the exception of one pitched battle, and some trivial skirmishes, the war was one of sieges. As with all plundering barbarians, fixed city ramparts were the chief obstacles in the way of their roving empire. Hence they made war on walls. *Hannibal ad portas* became "The Tatars are at the gates." The walls of Kiev, strongest of Russian fortresses, were breached in one day under the terrific pounding of the Mongol battering rams. Vladimir was infested and destroyed. Moscow was burned; Riazan, Tver, Suzdal, Chernigov, all went down before the invincible horde. The great tent of the conqueror, mounted on wheels and drawn by oxen, moved steadily westward as far as Poland and Hungary. The Pope called for a united Europe. The advance was stopped only by the Czechs and Bohemians. Six hundred thousand Tatar warriors were seen at one time by Plano Carpini, the Minorite friar, sent as legate to the Tatar Khan Batu by Innocent III.

All Russia, except Novgorod the Great, bent its neck and bore the yoke for two hundred and fifty years.

But the galled jade will wince. Two centuries and a half of vassalage under Eastern despots of the school of Genghis Khan and Tamerlane could not fail to modify enormously the social and political structure of the Slavic communities. The Tatar master left his mark on Russia's soul and his seed in Russia's blood as definitely as the Norman invader left his imprint on Anglo-Saxon civilization. The taint spread from the head downward, from prince to common folk.

It might have been different had the conquerors set themselves to absorb the conquered and transform Russia into a huge khanate. The national will might have been stiffened under persecution, as was that of Poland, Ireland, and Belgium during foreign occupation. A cause would have been created and a battle cry for freedom. But the Khans were neither colonizers nor permanent governors. They sent no Verres, no Pontius Pilate, no Cromwell, Pizarro, or Clyde, as vicegerent to govern judicially the subjugated provinces or incorporate them into the Tatar empire. To be sure, they installed local representatives, *baskaks*, in the subject territories. But tribute, not government, was their mission. Provided, therefore, that the princes of Russia paid promptly the annual taxes and tithes, and sent envoys to the Horde to perform acts of submission, such as holding the stirrup, or bending low to permit the Tatar horses to feed off their backs, they might rule, or misrule, their own people as they chose. It was the easiest way for the Tatars, but ended in demoralization for the Russians.

Disunited before the advent of the Tatars, the Russian princes resorted to trickery and servility to conciliate the Khans and strengthen their individual positions. It was *Sauve qui peut* — and the Tatar devil take the hindmost. They accepted the odious function of tax collectors for their absentee landlords, conspired against each other, and oppressed their groaning subjects in order to retain Tatar favor. The Khans, on their part, displayed an Oriental cunning, playing one prince against another. No Russian could be invested with princely authority in his own patrimony unless by consent of the Khan. Before his gorgeous throne in Mongolia bowed prince after prince of Russia, after journeyings that took a year to complete, suing shamelessly for favor, or whispering damning insinuations against some rival countryman. All Russia learned to crook the hinges of the knee. Gifts, bribes, intrigue, and domestic terror became the accepted instrumentality for retaining power, with the common folk and peasants always the pawn, played by prince against prince, and by the slant-eyed Mongolian against the entire board.

Out of this slough of national humiliation rose Moscow to the ascendancy she has since maintained. By virtue of his authority as principal tax collector for the Tatars, Ivan I, Grand Prince of Moscow, called *Kalita*, or "Money Bag," first oppressed his own subjects and then attacked his most formidable domestic rivals, Tver, Novgorod, and Yaroslavl; he marched himself with the avenging Tatars against revolting cities, and by slow degrees, partly by his wealth, and largely by sycophantic subservience to the Khan, achieved for Moscow undisputed hegemony over the smaller principalities. Novgorod, in particular, felt his fury. Because of the northern latitude in which it lay, the old republic escaped the Tatar yoke; so Ivan Tatarized it himself. And as it was Moscow that dominated Russia thereafter and determined her likeness, to this period must be attributed the beginning of the autocratic tradition that characterized the rule of the Tzars long after the foreign yoke had been lifted. Modes of thought, traits, and propensities accumulated through two and a half centuries cannot be easily shed. The habits of sire become instincts in son and ingrained character in the son's posterity. A spirit of submissiveness and passivity was engendered in a cowed and semi-Orientalized people, rendered more and more fatalistic and accustomed by this time to frequent change of masters but not of treatment. Here you have the answer to that oft-repeated question put in later days by critics of the present Bolshevist régime: How is it possible that a small communist minority, probably less than a million persons, can hold a hundred and forty-six million people in such complete subjection?

The Tatar suzerainty ceased on the fall of the Golden Horde in 1502. Slavery ended, but the slave-driver remained. It is not an accident that the Russian term *naigaka*, the knout, is one of the purely Tataric words still remaining in the Russian vocabulary. Both the symbol and the thing symbolized persist in Russia to this day.

What the Tatars began, the Ivans continued. Peter the Great completed the transformation.

Around no ruler of Russia — until perhaps Nicholas Lenin — have such controversial currents raged. One historical school, the Westernizers, will exalt this physical giant — Peter was six feet seven inches high — to a corresponding apotheosis of merit above all preceding and succeeding emperors. Was it not the First Peter who picked up Russia bodily, carried her to the Finnish marsh, and set her down in a new, shining capital there, though he had to wade knee-deep in water and drive down a wilderness of piles into the mud to do it? Did he not build St. Petersburg to serve as an "open window to Europe" and thus bring the Russian people within the orbit of Western European influence? He created a Russian navy, organized an efficient army, introduced German, French, English, and Italian culture and industrial methods, reformed the laws, improved civil administration, the Church, and the alphabet; he broke the power of the Turks, conquered the Ukraine, as well as Livonia, Esthonia, Ingria, and Karelia; he beat the Swedes, — though by a slight margin, — enlarged all boundaries, and increased the general prosperity of the State.

He issued the first textbook of social behavior, instructing Russians "to be amiable, modest, and respectful, to learn language, to look people in the face, take off their hats, not to dance in boots, or to spit on the floor, or sing too loud, put the finger in the nose, rub the lips with the hand, lean on the table, swing the legs, lick the fingers, gnaw a bone at dinner, scratch one's head, talk with one's mouth full; and his assemblies or social gatherings, at which he made attendance compulsory, were the first crude school of European conventions.

"It was further ordained that every transgressor of the rules should be obliged instantly to empty the 'great eagle,' a large bottle full of brandy, a grotesque punishment, which exists also among the Chinese. This was not a very likely way to preserve the decencies of social intercourse; but these were little regarded by Peter. He beat Metchnikov in a ballroom for dancing without having taken off his sword." [1]

He bestrode Northern Europe like a Colossus and left Russia in a position to speak with authority in the family of nations. He made a new, a mighty, a modern Russia. Tzar for forty-three years, he displayed an inexhaustible energy, and paused only to die.

But the rest of Russia, the Slavophils, regarded Peter from the beginning as half demon, Antichrist, and usurper. Was he not driving Russia, under the knout, to new and

[1] See Appendix VIII.

PETER THE GREAT AND HIS SON, THE TZAREVITCH ALEXIS

Alexis was murdered by his father

strange paths, unsuited to her historic traditions? He had forsaken holy Moscow, than which there was nothing higher save God, to build himself an abomination, named in vain-glorious egotism "Peter's city," among the bogs and fogs and marshes of an alien territory at the mouth of the Neva. Did not a hundred thousand workmen perish in that fetid swamp? He spent his time abroad, among Turks and Germans, who were very much of the same kidney for a Russian. He let loose swarms of officials, clerks, and other *tchinovniki* to batten on the substance of the people, rushed them into foreign wars and intrigues, drove his subjects to domestic rebellion by extravagant taxation, ordered men to defile the image of God by shaving off their beards, and even ordained the particular cut of their clothes. He per-secuted the Church of Christ by abolishing the Patriarchate, and convoked a farcical conclave during which an inveterate drunkard, Sotov, was proclaimed patriarch and made to ride through the streets astride a keg of brandy and followed by a hierarchy of buffoons.

Of a truth, he had opened a window to Europe, but opened it on to a swamp, exuding miasmic effluvia. He exposed the pure soul of Orthodoxy to the blighting infection of the atheism and deism of France, and made poor Russia's brain reel with the dizzying wisdom of Prussia. It was a spurious civilization!

What, in the last analysis, was the influence of Peter's reform on the final destiny of Russia? The Colossus was tumbling to pieces at that very moment in Petrograd, a scant fifteen miles away.

"Ruinous," reply the Slavophils. "Necessary and glorious," maintain the Westernizers.

The truth lies somewhere between, but probably nearer the Slavophils. We have Lenin's authority for that, and he should know a destructive agency when he sees one. In the first place, Peter hated Moscow and all it stood for;

he never denied the charge. Moscow meant stagnation, backwardness, and the stifling atmosphere of static Orientalism. Flushed with his victory over the Swedes, and in possession of a new seaport opening into the Gulf of Finland, he ordered the great transfer. The capitol was moved from the heart of ancient Muscovy — an act that was sure to offend — and not another stone house was to be built until the new buildings were well under way. Thousands of peasants, and even the nobles, were compelled to slave in the unhealthy swamp, driving down the piles and transporting stones for the structures. Over them towered Peter himself, his tremendous will power shirking neither personal labor nor the application of the lash to the shoulders of the others.[1]

It is not difficult to imagine the estrangement that ensued. "With Peter the Great," writes the Viscount de Vogüé, "the moment arrived when commenced perhaps the most singular and unquestionably the most abnormal attempts for experimenting with the historic development of a people. Continuing the above figure, imagine a ship in which the captain and his officers steer for the west and the crew set their sails for a wind that would carry them to the east. . . . A few, carried away by the uplifting movement, detached themselves from the masses, but the bedrock of the nation remained rebellious, immovable, with minds firmly set toward the east like the naves of their churches, and the praying Tatars, their former masters.

"Forty years have passed, yet only the summits have caught the Western light; the vast valleys still lie plunged in the shadows of the past — with difficulty will they arise therefrom."

In the Church, too, a correspondingly violent reform was effected. In 1721 Peter abolished the supreme spiritual office of Patriarch and subjected the administration of ecclesiastical affairs to a Holy Synod composed of bishops

[1] See Appendix IX.

acceptable to the Government, but presided over by a layman, the *Ober-Procuror*, intended by Peter to be the "Tzar's eye." This secularization of the Church and its subordination to the civil power marked the beginning of that unfortunate decrease of popular confidence which the Orthodox Church has admittedly suffered.

But such was and must ever be the fate of every church that forfeits, either by force or by voluntary surrender, the liberty of its spirit and subordinates its divine mission to political threat or human expedience. The Orthodox Church of Peter's day would have done better to perish fighting. It is more probable that not the Church but Peter's assault would have been ended. The Church was the one institution that might have tempered domestic tyranny then — and afterward; but, instead, it fell victim to the environment and just missed a glorious destiny.

Russian Christianity, like all Christianity that came from Constantinople, seemed enervated in its origin by an oppressive Cæsarism and Erastianism that paralyzed initiative and encouraged obsequiousness. The finer spirits of the Orthodox Church often longed for an opportunity to exercise the spiritual leadership and championship of the rights of the people so often manifested by the Western Church in its frequent conflicts with kings, emperors, robber-barons, and miscellaneous oppressors of the common folk. But the Crown, working through the Holy Synod, had a genius for transferring to Siberia any Russian priest or bishop suspected of an inclination, or even a capacity, to assume the rôle of an Ambrose of Milan before a Theodosius, the royal murderer of Thessalonica, or the part of a Gregory before a Charles IV of Germany. Had there been an occasional Canossa in Russian history, there might have been no Red Terror, there might have been no imprisonment in a Summer Palace. But the dead hand of the Emperors of Byzantium ruled the Orthodox Church long after their bones had mouldered into dust in the imperial tombs on the Bosphorus or had been desecrated by the Moslem masters of Santa Sophia.

The bureaucracy which Peter established, and which every succeeding Tzar preserved, completed the social cleavage and made internal cohesion impossible. Under his imperious will, Russia for the first time assumed international importance, but it was achieved at the expense of internal stability. He created a Colossus, yes — but its feet were of clay; the Allies learned that in 1917.[1]

If atavistic memories should arise to disturb the history lessons, Nicholas might well doubt if he was really a Romanov at all. Versed in the family record of his line, he must have been familiar with the controversy regarding the paternity of his ancestor, Paul I. Romanov blood had been transmitted undiluted and unchanged as far as Peter the Great, but there the stream was mingled with German substitutes. By marrying the buxom, illiterate, peasant campfollower Catherine Skavronsky, Peter had become a logical Westernizer of Russia's reigning family as well as its social institutions. The Empress Anna Petrova, daughter of that union, swung farther away from Romanov stock by espousing Charles Frederick, Duke of Holstein-Gottorp. Their son, Peter III, took to wife Catherine, Princess of Anhalt-Zerbst, and the confusion becomes hopelessly confounded. Even before the death of her first husband, Peter III, whom she herself had deposed and then permitted to be killed in a drunken brawl by her lover Orlov, Catherine had embarked on a long list of lovers and amours. If, as was commonly believed, Paul I, though her true son (and a lunatic), was not the child of her legitimate husband, Peter III, but of Serge Saltikov, then the Romanov succession thereafter was a dynastic fiction.

[1] See Appendix X.

MICHAEL FEDOROVITCH
1613–1645
First of the Romanov line

PETER I, 1689–1725
Greatest Romanov

THE EMPRESS ANNA, 1730–
1740

CATHERINE THE GREAT, 1762–
1796

EARLY ROMANOVS

Not only was the succession of a line of true Romanovs to the throne extremely doubtful from that day onward, but every succeeding emperor introduced a foreign princess to Russia as his bride. The poet Pushkin, in his sarcastic moments, was accustomed to entertain St. Petersburg society with an ocular demonstration to show how far his country's rulers had been de-Russianized. He would place a row of six empty wine glasses before him, then call for a bottle of red wine and a carafe of water. The first glass he would fill to the brim with wine: "There is our glorious Peter the Great — Russian blood, pure, undiluted. See how it sparkles with rubies." The second glass he would fill half with water and half with wine; the third would receive but one fourth wine to three fourths water; the fourth glass but one eighth of wine and seven eighths of water, and so to the end, the wine decreasing in inverse proportion to the water. The last glass in Pushkin's day would stand for Alexander II, then Tzarevitch. The liquid was barely rose-colored, consisting of one part of wine to thirty-two parts of water.

If Nicholas II ever amused himself in the same fashion, his last glass, representing his own son, the future Tzar Alexis, would show one drop of Russian blood to two hundred and fifty-six drops of foreign infiltration. Imperceptible! Rhine wine to Burgundy.[1] And there on his stationery before him and emblazoned over his throne, as well as at every corner of the royal apartments, his eyes would rest on the emblem of Romanov dynasty, a double-headed eagle holding crown and sceptre, surmounting a shield representing Saint George and the dragon. This heraldic sign symbolized a double fact and another dubious legacy.

[1] "Who would take this miserable record as the history of a people? Not any serious historian. Of the six immediate successors of Peter I, three are women, one a boy of twelve, one a babe of one, and one an idiot. Through the barrack capital of St. Petersburg, situated outside Russian soil and cut off from the life of the Russian people, brainless or squalid adventurers succeeded each other." — Sir Bernard Pares, *History of Russia*

The earliest scutcheon of the princes of Moscow had borne Saint George alone, slaying his dragon. But on the fall of Constantinople in 1453 and the death of the last Christian ruler, Constantine Palæologus, who died on its walls in ineffectual combat with the victorious armies of Mohammed, Byzantium bequeathed its political supremacy to Moscow as it had already imposed on Russia its Oriental Christianity. Zoë, daughter of the last Byzantine emperor, found refuge, first in Rome, then in Moscow, where in 1472 she became wife to Ivan III, assuming the name of Sophia. She brought as dowry not only the double-headed eagle, and set it above Saint George on the Russian coat of arms, but transplanted the proud customs and the ancient traditions of haughtiness, pomp, and ceremony which had exalted the court of her fathers. More portentous still, she furnished inspiration and pretext for Ivan to assume titles never heard before in the mouth of Slavic princes — Tzar, Sovereign of All the Russias, *Samoderzhets*, Autocrat. He proclaimed Holy Moscow the "Third Rome." The first had perished; the second, Constantinople, had now fallen; "the third, Moscow, now stands, and a fourth there will not be."

And here sat the inheritor of Byzantium's splendor and Moscow's might an actual prisoner in his favorite retreat, this well-intentioned and urbane, but woefully weak and indecisive monarch. Retribution was beginning in the very palace which popular imagination made a symbol of isolation and estrangement. It was to Tsarskoe Selo that Nicholas and the imperial family fled in 1905 when the thousands of petitioners, led by Gapon, marched to the Winter Palace to seek redress of wrongs from the "little Father" — and were massacred by his waiting Cossacks. Only once in eight years did the royal family reside in Petrograd, and then for four days only, on the occasion of the Tercentenary. They

NICHOLAS II

The Last of the Romanovs

lived in virtual seclusion at Tsarskoe Selo, the fifteen miles to the capital constituting a moral chasm between them and their people.

So had the Bourbons deserted Paris for Versailles. Paris hated them for it, and waited a hundred years to welcome them back — to the guillotine.

Harassed and crushed by the weight of an inherited responsibility too heavy for his shoulders, wearily answering "Yes" or "No" to importunate counselors who knew how to play shrewdly on his fears, his prejudices, and his superstitions, Nicholas had lived, as it were, a phantom king in a haunted palace. On the very day of his coronation he had succumbed publicly to exhaustion when entering the Cathedral of the Holy Archangels at Moscow. Fatigued by the weight of the ponderous crown, and staggering under the heavy ceremonial robe of cloth of gold fringed with ermine, he let the sceptre he was carrying slip from his grasp to the ground. In the impressionable minds of those who witnessed the incident, it remained an evil omen. The court gossipers recalled the ill-fated Louis XVI complaining, during his coronation at Rheims, that the crown he wore was too heavy and was hurting his head.

E. J. Dillon, who knows Russians as well as any man alive, recounts an anecdote which may or may not be true, but which reproduces exactly the "paralysis of volition" which reduced Nicholas to clay in the hands of political potters.

One day, the story ran, a nobleman of great experience and progressive tendencies was received in audience by the Tzar. He made the most of his opportunity, and laid before his sovereign the wretched state of the peasantry, the general unrest it was occasioning, and the urgent necessity of removing its proximate causes by modifying the political machinery of government. During this unwelcome exposé the Emperor, whose urbanity and polish left nothing to be desired, nodded from time to time approvingly and repeated often, "I know. Yes, yes. You are right. Quite right." The nobleman, when retiring, felt morally certain that the monarch was at one with him on the subject. Immediately afterward a great landowner, also a member of the nobility, was ushered in, who unfolded a very different tale. According to this authority, things on the whole were progressing satisfactorily, the only drawback being the weakness and indulgence of the authorities. "What is needed, sire, is an iron hand. The peasants must be kept in their place by force, otherwise they will usurp ours. To make way for them and treat them as though they were the masters of the country is a crime." During this discourse also Nicholas II was attentive and appreciative, nodding and uttering the stereotyped phrases, "Yes, I know. You are right. Quite right." And the conservative, like the liberal, departed happy.

Then a side door opened and the Empress entered, looking grave. "You really must not go on like this, Niky," she exclaimed. "It is not dignified. Remember you are an autocrat who should possess a will strong enough to stiffen a nation of a hundred and fifty millions."

"But what is it that you find fault with, darling?"

"Your want of resolution and of courage to express it. I have been listening to the conversations you have just had. Count X., whom you first received, pleaded the cause of the disaffected. You assented to everything he advanced, telling him he was right, quite right. Then M. Y. was introduced, who gave you an account of things as they really are, and you agreed with him in just the same way, saying, 'You are right. Quite right.' Well, now, that attitude does not befit an autocrat. You must learn to have a will of your own and assert it."

"You are right, dear, quite right," was the answer.

Never master of his own will, Nicholas spent his life awaiting the judgments of the Pobyedonostsevs, the Stürmers, and the Protopopovs who surrounded him, and of the Empress who ruled him. Mr. Kerensky was to convey the next decision of Russia's newest master, *Monsieur le peuple*.

On August 10, the Premier of the Provisional Government waited on the ex-Tzar and announced a momentous resolution. The imperial family was to be transferred to Siberia.

CHAPTER IX

SIBERIA

THE reasons for the summary and unexpected transference of all the prisoners to Siberia, entailing, as it did, fatal consequences that are now part of history, were explained by Mr. Kerensky to the ex-Emperor with careful precision, and have been similarly repeated to this day by apologists of the régime responsible for it. It was due, the Premier insisted, to the concern felt by the Provisional Government for the physical safety of the ex-Tzar and his family. The Cabinet had decided to suppress with a firm hand the increasing disorder in the country and come to grips with the growing challenge of Bolshevism. Such a step would very probably lead to popular rioting, which, in turn, would have to be met with armed force; should serious strife ensue, the royal family would be among the first victims demanded by the mob. He had experienced one such manifestation already. At Moscow, as early as March 20, extremists had interrupted Kerensky during his first speech in that city and demanded the execution of the Tzar. Kerensky had shouted in reply: "I will not be the Marat of the Russian Revolution!"

One abortive attempt, moreover, had actually been made to kidnap the Tsar and imprison him in the Russian Bastille, the fortress of St. Peter and St. Paul. A certain Maslovsky, a Social Revolutionary of the Left, had presented himself one day, in the uniform of a colonel, to Khobylinsky, the responsible officer in charge of the Summer Palace, and presented an order requiring the Commandant to deliver up Nicholas Romanov. The document purported to be issued by the Executive Committee of Workmen and Soldiers, bore an authentic seal, and was signed by Tcheidze, a member in good standing of the Duma. Maslovsky declared he was empowered to conduct the Emperor immediately to St. Peter and St. Paul. Khobylinsky refused to acknowledge such authority; Maslovsky lost his head, stormed about, poured abuse on Khobylinsky, and threatened vaguely that blood would flow. But Khobylinsky held his ground and Maslovsky made off in a rage.

Those who have ever seen two Russians of the revolutionary period, each armed with class-consciousness and a "mandate" arguing their respective rights and jurisdiction, will readily visualize this scene at the gate of the Summer Palace.

With a view to averting similar dangers in the uncertain future, Mr. Kerensky had dispatched two confidential agents, Verchinin and Makarov, to Siberia for the purpose of selecting a spot sufficiently remote from Moscow where the prisoners would not be exposed to the threat of mob violence. They chose Tobolsk, a town of twelve thousand inhabitants, on the right bank of the River Irtysh, near the mouth of the Tobol, some two thousand miles from Petrograd. It was a tranquil spot, undisturbed by the revolution: then, too, it boasted a comfortable Governor's Palace which had been prepared for the ex-Tzar and his family.

But why, asks Nicholas Sokolov, the judge who conducted the judicial inquiry into the circumstances of the murder, did not Mr. Kerensky send the family to South Russia — to the Crimea, for example, where so many royalists had found safe refuge? If Mr. Kerensky was sincere in his protestations of concern for the safety of his charges, why did he not send them to the one region from which escape to a foreign land was still possible? All the relatives of the imperial family who reached the Crimea were eventually saved.

Mr. Kerensky replies that a voyage through the heart of

Russia, then in the hands of revolting peasants and Bolshevist workmen, was impossible. But was not a journey by rail and water from Petrograd to Tobolsk equally perilous? counters Judge Sokolov. No, answers Mr. Kerensky: the regions to the east were not aflame with revolution and peasant uprisings as was South Russia. Judge Sokolov is not satisfied, and his final report suggests that there was but one reason for the choice of Siberia — the dethroned Autocrat of All the Russias must be made to taste the bitterness and dreariness of exile in Siberia, must be made to experience the icy blasts of that House of Dead Souls to which he and his ancestors had banished so many Russians!

On August 14, at 6.10 in the morning, the journey was begun, but not until the ex-Tzar had spent a dismal night sitting in a large salon on the ground floor, waiting patiently for the train which had been promised for the previous evening. The Tzarevitch celebrated his thirteenth birthday on the eve of the departure. Forty-six court attendants voluntarily accompanied the family, making, in all, a party of fifty-three persons, exclusive of the military escort. It took two trains to accommodate the voyagers, their baggage, the government representatives, the jailers, and soldiers. By rail to Tiumen, thence by river steamer to Tobolsk, the trip consumed five days and ended at four o'clock in the afternoon of August 19. Pierre Gilliard, who accompanied the exiles, relates an incident that must have awakened memories that stabbed. On the eighteenth the boat passed Pokrovskoie, the birthplace of Rasputin. The house of the *staretz* was plainly visible among the izbas. Did the Tzarina, standing an exile on the deck, recall the prophecy of Rasputin: "My death will be your death"?

Life at Tobolsk during the first month was another idyll of domestic calm and undisturbed tranquillity. The ex-Tzar breakfasted, studied, walked, lunched, exercised, dined, taught history to Alexis, and held family reunions in the evening to an extent never possible before. Special religious services were held for the royal family in the town church and they were permitted to leave the house for that purpose. The children prepared and enacted dramatic pieces in French and English. The townspeople showed themselves courteous and sympathetic, frequently sending gifts, particularly fresh food, and saluting the members of the family respectfully or blessing them with the sign of the cross when they appeared at the windows of the Palace. It was only the unending monotony, the drab Siberian monotony, that oppressed, together with the almost complete absence of news.

The first rift appeared in September 1917. Two new Commissars, Pankratov and Nikolsky, arrived, with authority from the Provisional Government to supersede the humane Khobylinsky, who remained, however, in a subordinate capacity. Had his régime been too mild? In any case, the new Commandants, who were Social Revolutionaries, one of a genial but fanatical and the other of a vulgar mentality, instituted a propaganda which rapidly demoralized the guards and initiated a progressive persecution of the prisoners. Insulting inscriptions began to appear on the walls and fences. The soldiers now refused to return the salute which Nicholas scrupulously accorded each in passing. Permission to attend divine service in the outside church was withdrawn. Nicholas was ordered to remove his epaulettes. The harmless "snow mountain," which the whole family had built as a joint recreation and which gave them much distraction, was demolished.

It is not within the scope of the present chapter to trace, step by step, the declining fortunes of the Kerensky Government and the corresponding rise of the Bolshevist power. Suffice it to say, at this point, that the reasons for the increasing severity in the treatment of the royal hostages became apparent in distant Tobolsk about the middle of November. The Petrograd experimentation in democracy was at an end; Russia's one short summer of freedom had passed and a change of masters was at hand. While the Duma theorized and perorated interminably, Lenin mounted to the balcony of the Kshesinskaia Palace — owned by a ballet dancer once the favorite of Nicholas II — and shouted his political platform in four promises: '*Peace, land, bread, power.*' Magic words, easily understood by all! Under the irresistible appeal of universal formulæ, never intended to be fulfilled, popular imagination, already surfeited with war and hungry for booty, was whipped to easy mutiny. Petrograd seethed again. Constitutional Democracy was swept into the discard and Militant Communism emerged an undisputed victor. It was a second Russian Revolution, which left Nicholas Romanov and his family in the hands of his most relentless personal enemies.[1]

When a Bolshevik draws his sword in class warfare, he throws away the scabbard. *Væ victis!*

The long-postponed liquidation of a three-hundred-years-old account was about to begin. The punishment started in the kitchen. First coffee, cream, milk, butter, and sugar were removed from the table of the prisoners at Tobolsk. News of the signing of the humiliating Treaty of Brest-Litovsk reached Siberia toward the middle of the following March. Nicholas was saddened and embittered. "It is such a disgrace for Russia," he said, "and amounts to suicide. I should never have thought the Emperor William could stoop to shake hands with these miserable traitors. But I 'm sure they will get no good from it; it won't save them from ruin." The ex-Tzar indignantly repudiated the

---

[1] On February 9, 1918, the Bolshevist soldiers expelled the two representatives of the Provisional Government, Pankratov and Nikolsky, but permitted Khoby-linsky, who seems to have been universally liked, to remain in charge, pending the arrival of a new Commandant from Moscow.

suggestion made in the newspapers that Germany had demanded of the Soviets to hand over to them the person of the Tzar unharmed. "That is either a manœuvre to discredit me or an insult." Pierre Gilliard adds that the Tzarina said in a low voice, "After what they have done to the Tzar, I would rather die in Russia than be saved by the Germans." Then follows a most significant entry in Gilliard's journal of the captivity : —

Friday, March 22: At a quarter past nine, after the evening service, everyone went to Confession — children, servants, suite, and finally Their Majesties.

But it was not until April 22 that the real prologue to the tragedy began. On the evening of that day still another figure appears on the scene in the person of Vassili Vassilievich Jakolev, in command of a troop of one hundred and fifty horsemen, including an experienced telegraph operator. It was late and dark when he arrived; nothing could be done then, so the latest arrival from Moscow passed the night in the Kornilov house opposite the Tzar's prison. On the morning of the twenty-third, he introduced himself to Khobylinsky as an "Extraordinary Commissar," producing three documents from the *Tzik*, the Central Executive Committee of the new Soviet Government. The first two papers, addressed to Khobylinsky and the guard, respectively, required entire and immediate submission to any order of Jakolev, who was authorized to shoot them on the spot should they disobey. The third document declared that Jakolev was charged with a mission of "particular importance." These orders were signed by Sverdlov, Chairman of the Central Executive Committee, and by another Soviet official, Ovanessov.

The nature of the particularly important mission was revealed at two o'clock on the afternoon of April 25, when Jakolev appeared before the ex-Tzar; having asked the

Empress to leave the room, which she refused to do, Jakolev began : —

"I have to tell you that I am the special representative of the Moscow Central Executive Committee, and my mission is to take all your family out of Tobolsk, but as your son is ill I have received a second order which says that you alone must leave."

Nicholas replied : "I will not go anywhere."

Jakolev protested : "I beg of you not to refuse. I am compelled to execute the order. In case of your refusal I must take you by force or resign. In the latter case they would probably decide to send a less scrupulous sort of man to take my position. Be calm ; I am responsible with my life for your security. If you do not want to go alone you could take with you the people you desire. Be ready ; we are leaving to-morrow at four o'clock."

No indication was vouchsafed as to the ultimate destination ; but Khobylinsky was able to deduce from certain hints let fall by Jakolev as to time and distance that it was Moscow. He communicated his belief to the royal pair. "Then," said Nicholas, "they are trying to make me sign the Treaty of Brest-Litovsk. I will let them cut off my hand rather than do it." "I shall go with him !" cried the Empress, in a violent agitation. "If I am not with him they will force him to sign something as they did before." She mentioned Rodzianko, evidently referring to the abdication at Pskov.

Alexandra suspected a German intrigue and declared to Gilliard that afternoon, in a tempest of emotion : "They will take him away, alone, in the night. . . . I cannot abandon him at such a moment. . . . I know they are preparing some ignominy. . . . They will make him sign a peace at Moscow. . . . The Germans are behind it, knowing that only a treaty signed by the Tzar has any value. My duty is never to permit that nor abandon him. But how can I leave

Alexis [who was ill again]? What would become of him
without me?"

Torn between love of son and fear for the safety of husband, — or was it apprehension that he might again show a
weakness detrimental to the dynastic rights of Alexis? —
she paced distractedly back and forth, like a caged tigress,
wringing her hands and talking to herself. Gilliard records: —

I remember with precision the next phrase she spoke. "Oh,
God! What a ghastly torture! . . . This is the first time in my
life that I am not sure what I should do." . . .

But she finally found herself and became the old Alexandra Feodorovna of the Rasputin days. . . . "Now I am
determined." . . .

At that moment Nicholas entered, returning from his
walk.

"I will not let thee go alone!" she cried. "I will go with thee!"
"As you will," he replied.

It was agreed that the Empress and the Grand Duchess
Marie should accompany the father, while Alexis and the
three remaining Grand Duchesses were to be entrusted to the
protection of Gilliard. She left the Tzarevitch suffering
from a cruel attack of his hereditary disease and bathed in
tears.

But before their departure another messenger had slipped
out of Tobolsk. It was a spy, of Jewish extraction, Zaslavsky by name, who, after insinuating himself into the favor of
the local guards, had spread poisonous rumors as to the intentions of Jakolev and had, moreover, sent reports by wire
to Sverdlov in Moscow. Now that the transfer was about
to take place, he took a start of six hours and reached Ekaterinburg in time to play his part in the weaving of the complicated net of death.

The travelers began their journey on April 26. It was a horror. No conveyances were available except the peasant tarantass, consisting of a large wicker basket resting on poles in place of springs. Passengers lie or sit on the straw-covered floor, at the mercy of every jolt. The roads were what all country roads in Russia are in early spring — quagmires of clinging mud. The horses floundered about, up to their knees in ooze and to their chests in water when crossing rivers. Wheels were broken, horses exhausted, and passengers bruised and sore. But at last the two hundred and eighty versts to Tiumen, the nearest railroad station, were covered in safety, and an assuring message came back to Tobolsk on April 28: "Traveling in comfort. How is the Boy? God be with you."

But dead silence thereafter until May 7. Then a letter, from Ekaterinburg, with the laconic announcement that they were well. Nothing more. Why Ekaterinburg? An agony of fear descended on the children at Tobolsk. Ekaterinburg was the headquarters of the Ural Soviets. What and who had diverted their parents to the stronghold of the Reds? The mystery remained unsolved, — as, in fact, it remains to this day, — until, on May 8, the officers and men of the guard who started out with Jakolev returned to Tobolsk and told a story which, while it does not explain, at least describes the occurrence.

Once on the open road, Jakolev manifested a feverish desire to hasten forward without losing an instant. He seemed possessed by some secret, driving fear. Despite the appalling condition of the roads, he would permit neither halts nor relaxation of speed. En route, the cavalcade passed the house of Rasputin in Pokrovskoie; the wife and children of the murdered *staretz* were standing in the doorway and made the sign of the cross over the royal couple as they swept by. Arriving at Tiumen on the evening of the twenty-seventh, Jakolev conducted his prisoners to a waiting train and started westward toward European Russia by the line passing through Ekaterinburg. But on approaching that city, with no intention of stopping, he learned, no one knows how, that the local authorities would not permit him to pass, but intended to arrest him. He doubled on his tracks and sped at full steam back to Tiumen and took the alternative, but longer, Cheliabinsk-Ufa route to Moscow. At the station of Koulomzino, the last stop before Omsk, his train was again halted, this time by a massed contingent of Red Guards who declared that the Soviet of Ekaterinburg had pronounced him an outlaw for having attempted to rescue Nicholas Romanov and transport him to a foreign land.

The spy, Zaslavsky, had arrived in time! And even had he failed, Boris Nicolaievich Soloviev was still on the lookout. This man, a revolutionary — and, like his father-in-law, a hypnotist — had married Rasputin's daughter, Matrona, not from any love he bore her, but to exploit her position as daughter of the former court favorite. Incidentally, he was aware that the murdered " prophet " had left his daughter a considerable sum of money. Trading on his wife's influence with the Tzarina, Soloviev stationed himself at Tioumen and pretended to act as confidential agent for the loyal monarchists who sought to establish contact with the prisoners in the hope of effecting a rescue. It was later ascertained that Soloviev had betrayed every attempt to the Bolshevist authorities.

Jakolev then uncoupled his engine and rode into Omsk, where he spoke by direct wire with someone in Moscow. He was ordered to proceed via Ekaterinburg. This he did, with train and passengers. The convoy had barely steamed into the station of that city when this amazing game of hare and hounds came to an abrupt end. Jakolev was surrounded by Red soldiers, his own guard disarmed and thrown into a cellar. Jakolev himself went to the office of the local Soviet for a conference; he soon came out, crestfallen, his authority gone. The three royal prisoners were conducted to a house that had been hurriedly requisitioned from a wealthy Siberian merchant named Ipatiev and there imprisoned. It was to be their death chamber. After a few days the soldiers imprisoned in the cellar, Jakolev's Tobolsk detachment, were released; Jakolev himself left for Moscow and from there sent a message to his private telegraph operator at Tobolsk : —

Gather together the company and come back. I have resigned. I take no responsibility for the consequences.

With the exit and disappearance of the mysterious Commissar charged with his mission of "particular importance" vanished the key of that bewildering performance. He is never to be heard from again; report had it later that he had been killed in battle, fighting on the side of the Whites. At the end of this narrative I shall hazard a guess as to who Comrade Jakolev really was.

CHAPTER X

THE HOUSE OF SPECIAL DESIGNATION

On May 23 the Tzarevitch Alexis and his three sisters arrived at Ekaterinburg from Tobolsk; the entire family was thus reunited, never again to be separated. But the two foreign tutors, Gilliard and Gibbs, were not permitted to continue in attendance on their pupils. They remained in Ekaterinburg, however, until the arrival of the White troops.

The imprisonment which now began was far different in character and severity from the preceding periods. Brutality replaced respect, and the thirst for vengeance became increasingly apparent in the attitude of the jailers. Two hoardings of rough logs and planks were erected around the Ipatiev house, the outer one a short distance from the first stockade, leaving a walking space between. These barricades reached to the level of the second-story window-tops, thus completely isolating the prisoners from sight and the outside world from them. To ensure a complete screen, the windows themselves were painted. The Grand Duchess Anastasia, driven desperate by the isolation, once opened her window and looked out. She was driven back by a shot from a sentry, the bullet lodging in the woodwork of the window frame. A machine gun was mounted on the roof of the house directly opposite and trained on the Ipatiev house; guards were posted at every corner of the stockade as well as at the doors of the rooms where the prisoners ate, slept, and congregated. The first floor was occupied by the Bolshevist guards; the royal family was quartered on the second.

For the first time the prisoners were subjected to personal search. Avdeiev, the Commandant of the "House of Special Designation," rudely snatched a reticule from the hands of the Empress. Nicholas protested: "Until now I have had honest and respectful men around me."

Didkovsky, one of the searchers, retorted: "Please remember that you are under arrest and in the hands of justice."

Tchemodourov, the Tzar's faithful valet who accompanied the family throughout their imprisonment, has left, under oath, a deposition the bare recital of which makes comment superfluous: —

Night and day three Red guards were posted on the first floor, one at the door, one in the vestibule, and one at the door of the [only] toilet. The conduct of these men was gross; cigarettes hanging on their lips, vulgar and half-clothed, their looks, actions, and habitual manners inspired fear and disgust. . . . When the young Grand Duchesses passed on their way to the toilet room the guards followed, under pretense of watching them; they addressed indecent remarks to the girls, asking them whither they were going and for what purpose. While the girls were inside the guards lounged against the door. . . . The food was bad, coming all prepared from a Soviet dining room. [Later they were allowed to have their own cook.] Their Majesties always ate in company with the domestics . . . They would put a soup tureen on the table, but there would not be enough spoons or knives or forks. The Red guards sat by our side and ate from the same dishes. One day a soldier plunged his spoon into the soup tureen, saying, "Enough for you — I will be served." Another day Avdeiev [the Commandant] kept his hat on and smoked a cigarette. As we ate our cutlets, he took his plate and, interposing his arms between the Emperor and the Empress, helped himself. As he took the meat, he managed to bend his elbow and strike the Emperor on the chin.

The very walls of the Ipatiev house, particularly in the lavatory, were made to contribute something to the mental suffering of the helpless victims. The guards, under the tutelage of a certain Bielomoine, covered them with ribald verses and gross sketches caricaturing the Empress and Rasputin. On another occasion Faya Safonov, one of the most offensive of the guard, climbed a fence to the level of the Tzarina's window and sang filthy songs at her.

The girls had a swing in the garden; the soldiers carved indecent words on the seat. Under the moral torture and physical confinement, — toward the end the prisoners were allowed but five minutes in the garden each day, — the ex-Tzar maintained that astonishing external calm and passivity which characterized his whole life. His health did not seem to weaken, nor did his hair whiten. During the few minutes allowed for exercise in the open air, he carried the Tzarevitch in his arms, as the boy was unable to walk, and marched stolidly up and down until his precious five minutes were over. But the Empress never left the porch; she aged visibly, her health failed, and gray hairs appeared.

The first days of July brought important and ominous changes in the personnel guarding the prisoners. Avdeiev, together with his colleagues, Moshkin and all the peasant-soldiers who had been recruited locally from the Zlokazov and Sissert factories, were dismissed or removed to a position outside the house. All "key" stations were taken by "reliable" guards, a sure indication that murder was contemplated. Three entirely new figures glide into the picture — Jankel Mikhailovich Jurovsky, who assumed the duties of Commandant vacated by Avdeiev, Chaia Isaacovich Golostchekin, an active and influential member of the Bolshevist Party, and Alexander Georgevich Bieloborodov, the twenty-five-year-old peasant who served as President of the Soviet of the Ural region. Jurovsky and Golostchekin were of Jewish birth, while Bieloborodov was of purely Slavic origin. All three were leading spirits in the local organ of

EXTERIOR BEFORE THE OUTER PALING WAS ERECTED

THE CELLAR (x) WHERE THE MURDER TOOK PLACE
THE IPATIEV HOUSE, EKATERINBURG

terrorism, the *Chrezvychaika*, commonly called the "Cheka" or secret police, and had contributed their share to its final roll call of 1,800,000 victims. All, particularly Golostchekin, were in close relation with another Jewish Commissar, Jankel Sverdlov, who was, at that time, undisputed master of Moscow as Chairman of the Central Executive Committee of the All-Russian Congress. It was to Sverdlov that reports would be directed from Ekaterinburg.

The new arrivals were accompanied by ten Lettish soldiers — that is, by a detachment of those hardened shock troops whose ruthless brutality won for them the reputation of being the bashibazouks of the Russian Revolution. In the present case certain circumstances would indicate that this group were really Magyars. In any case, the Cheka simply followed its common practice in thus removing all strictly Russian guards from immediate participation in the most comprehensive act of regicide in the history of a people whose annals reek with deeds of violence and bloodshed.

Golostchekin had been in Moscow for the two weeks preceding the night of the murder, remaining absent until the fourteenth of July. During that time he was closeted in frequent conference with Sverdlov, with whom he lodged. Bieloborodov kept him informed by wire of events at the Ipatiev house. Thus in early July, the following telegram was dispatched : —

Moscow. Sverdlov for Golostchekin. . . . Jurovsky replaces Avdeiev. The indoor guard has been entirely changed.

BIELOBORODOV

In the meantime, Jurovsky had been seen by townsfolk on several occasions surveying the woods in the suburbs of Ekaterinburg; a week before the murder he was discovered in the same occupation near the locality which subsequent investigation determined as the spot where the funeral pyre had been erected.

On July 14, the day of Golostchekin's return from Moscow, an Orthodox priest of Ekaterinburg, Storojev by name, was permitted to celebrate Mass for the prisoners. He testified later that Jurovsky had remarked : —
"You have said Mass here before?"
"Yes."
"Well and good. You will do it once again."
Storojev further deposed : —

According to the liturgy governing a low Mass, at a determined moment the following prayer must be read : "May the souls of the departed rest in peace with Thy saints." I do not know why he did it, but my deacon, instead of merely reading the prayer, began to chant it. [This prayer is never *sung* except at funerals.] I followed suit, though somewhat irritated at his violation of the canons. We had barely begun when we heard, behind us, the noise of the whole imperial family throwing themselves on their knees. . . . At the end of the service they all approached to kiss the Cross and the deacon gave the Blessed Bread to both Emperor and Empress. . . . The deacon and I left in silence. . . . Suddenly, in front of the School of Fine Arts, the deacon said to me, "Do you know, something has happened to them." As his words corresponded exactly to what I was thinking, I stopped and asked him why he thought so. "I am sure," he said ; "they seem so changed, and not one of them sang to-day." He was right, because for the first time, on July 14, not one of the Romanovs accompanied us by singing.

On Monday, the fifteenth, four women were admitted into the death house and ordered to scrub the parquet floors. Their testimony, taken before the Commission of Inquiry, establishes the fact that the entire imperial family was alive on that day and in good health. On the same day, two lay sisters from a local institution, Antonina Trinkina and Maria Krokhaleva, presented themselves as usual with milk for the prisoners. Jurovsky himself received the charitable offering and informed them that on the morrow, July 16, they should bring not only milk but fifty eggs, carefully packed in a basket. This the good Samaritans gladly did on the sixteenth, all unconscious of the cynical preparation Jurovsky was making to ensure a luncheon for his executioners in the woods after the deed of blood was done and the traces removed. During the minute examination of the ground in the forest at the spot where the bodies were cremated, the indefatigable Nicholas Sokolov discovered a mass of broken eggshells.

Final preparations seem to have been completed by Tuesday, July 16. On that day the boy Leonid Sednev, a playmate of the Tzarevitch, was removed from the house and transferred to an adjoining building. He was never seen again, except for a brief moment next day as he sat in tears at an open window. Five motor lorries were requisitioned from the official Bolshevist garage and the chauffeurs were instructed to have them in readiness outside the Ipatiev house at midnight. On one of these trucks were placed two barrels of benzine and a few smaller jugs containing a supply of sulphuric acid. The Commission of Inquiry which gathered and laboriously analyzed every scrap of evidence bearing on the gruesome happenings of those twenty-four hours was able to establish, from the confiscated receipts delivered by Jurovsky for these supplies, that the barrels held more than three hundred litres of benzine and the jugs one hundred and ninety kilogrammes of the deadly acid. These destructive precautions had been obtained on mandates signed by Voikov, who paid for his zeal with his life; he was assassinated by a Russian exile at Warsaw, in June 1927.

The instruments of death were provided; the grave was ready; the executioners were resolved, and the victims were asleep in their beds. It was Tuesday night, July 16, 1918.

CHAPTER XI

THE TRAGEDY ENDS

THE knell sounded shortly after midnight, when Jurovsky knocked at the door of the ex-Emperor and bade Nicholas arise and dress. The same summons was delivered to the Tzarina, the children, and their suite. Jurovsky explained to Nicholas that the Siberian army, under Admiral Kolchak, and the Czechoslovak troops, those former prisoners of war who had succeeded in arming themselves and were now a serious menace to the Soviet régime in Siberia, were approaching Ekaterinburg; an engagement was imminent, and bullets would be flying in the streets. In his solicitude for the safety of the royal family he must insist that they come below stairs, where they would be secure from accident or injury.

The ex-Tzar, seemingly, was satisfied, credulous as always, and did not appear to suspect a trap. The women dressed and washed, not omitting, however, to put on the specially prepared clothes into the lining and hems of which they had previously sewn jewels and bank notes against the hoped-for day of escape. Several cushions had likewise been filled with precious stones and money; in all, one million rubles, something over $500,000, had been secreted in this manner.

To reach the safe place designated by Jurovsky, they descended a flight of steps, passed into the open courtyard, and thence approached a semibasement, eighteen by sixteen feet in dimensions. The single door was open, awaiting their coming; there was no other exit, as the inside door entering into a second room was barred and obstructed on the far side. The only window, opening on to the Vosnesensky Lane that skirted the side of the house, was protected by a heavy iron grille. Outside this window stood sentries, their faces pressed against the grimy glass, able to see all that passed within, especially as the room had been lighted for the better aim of the executioners. The testimony of these onlookers forms one of the strongest elements in the convincing depositions gathered during the inquiry.

There was, moreover, another window, opening not directly into the room, but into a lobby before it; this window commanded a view of the interior, and here too stood a sentry who witnessed the butchery. The deposition of Medvedev, one of the actual participants in the murder, later captured by the Whites; the description given to Yakimov by Klescheev and Deriabin, the sentries who gazed spellbound through these windows; and the account of Proskouriakov, the Red Guard who removed the blood-stains from the floor with water, mop, and sawdust, make it possible to reconstruct the tragedy in all its hideous detail.

The midnight procession, in passing through the dim courtyard, must have seen the motor trucks silhouetted against the summer sky. In that northern latitude it is light until after 10 P.M.; it is never wholly dark, especially on clear nights, and dawn appears as early as two in the morning. They doubtless imagined the vehicles were for their escape in case of danger, or possibly for the baggage. Not one of the victims seems to have suspected what lay beyond that open door through which light was streaming into the courtyard. Above, nothing to be seen but sharp points of light, like a myriad watching eyes in a clear blue sky; below, shadowy figures lurking at corners and along the inner stockade; no sound, except the shuffling of many feet on the dirt walk. Jurovsky marshaled them, leading the way and beckoning toward the open door; behind followed Medvedev and the scowling Letts, eleven men, fingering their pistols as they closed in on their unsuspecting victims.

As it is the last time we shall look upon their faces before the fiery acid burns away all traces of a human countenance, let us note them carefully as they pass into the shambles : —

1. *Nicholas Romanov*, fifty years of age, late Tzar of All the Russias, carrying in his arms,

2. *The Tzarevitch, Alexis*, a boy of fourteen years, heir to the throne ;

3. *Alexandra Feodorovna*, forty-six years old, late Empress, born Princess Alice of Hesse, favorite granddaughter of Queen Victoria of England ;

4. *The Grand Duchess Olga*, eldest daughter, twenty-three years of age ;

5. *The Grand Duchess Tatiana*, daughter, twenty-one years of age ;

6. *The Grand Duchess Maria*, daughter, nineteen years of age ;

7. *The Grand Duchess Anastasia*, youngest daughter, seventeen years old ;

8. *Dr. Eugene Sergeievich Botkin*, physician to the royal family, a stout, gray-haired man, between fifty-five and sixty years of age ;

9. *Anna Demidova*, a chambermaid, tall, thin, dark, about forty years of age ;

10. *Ivan Haritonov*, cook to the imperial family, a short man, slightly bald, with black hair and moustache, aged forty years ;

11. *Alexis Troupp*, a footman, tall, thin, dark, thirty-five years of age.

Once having entered, exit for them is barred by the executioners, who mass themselves before the door, awaiting the prearranged signal. Nicholas, still believing that the family is about to be conveyed to a place of safety, requests

OLGA   TATIANA

ANASTASIA   ALEXIS   MARIA

THE CHILDREN OF THE IMPERIAL FAMILY

that chairs be brought for the Empress and the children. It is done. They rest, waiting in simple expectation, hats on and clad in traveling clothes.

At this point the available testimony, which covers volumes, diverges slightly, but only in unimportant chronological details. According to some witnesses, Jurovsky, standing at the head of his file, suddenly produced a paper and read what purported to be a death warrant which authorized him to execute "Nicholas the Bloody and all his family"; others, not mentioning the death warrant, depose that Jurovsky suddenly addressed Nicholas and said: —

"Your relatives have sought to rescue you, but it could not be managed by them and so we ourselves are obliged to kill you."

The ex-Tzar did not seem to understand and asked: "What do you mean?"

"This is what I mean!" cried Jurovsky, firing point-blank at the Emperor with his automatic revolver, killing him instantly.

The scene that followed must await its own proper Dante. Twelve revolvers bellowed thunder and spat tongues of fire; the hollow chamber, reverberating with the explosions, filled up with smoke and acrid fumes; not once nor twice, but again and again each Lett, frenzied with primeval blood-lust, fired, choosing his own particular victim. With twelve men letting loose the pent-up hatreds of three hundred years, it is not unreasonable to expect that each emptied the clip of his automatic, which would make nearly a hundred shots. Medvedev, a participant, confessed that the sight, with the blended smell of blood and powder fumes, nauseated him. The petrified onlookers at the windows were harrowed by the shrieks of women and the groans of men; Alexis, the Tzarevitch, was not killed outright, but moaned and writhed over the bodies of his dead parents. It was Jurovsky who finally dispatched him with his revolver.

Those who still breathed were bayoneted to death. The floor was chipped and torn with bayonet thrusts driven through the soft bodies. A little dog, a King Charles spaniel, pet of the Grand Duchess Anastasia and brought down by her in her arms, ran hysterically about, darting between the legs of friend and foe, barking furiously. Floor and walls were spattered with blood and bits of clinging flesh.

Twenty-three living persons had entered that narrow cellar — eleven prisoners and the twelve guards conducting them to a place of greater safety. As dawn began to streak the sky, twelve persons came out, leaving eleven corpses safely within, lying in pools of blood that trickled in widening circles out into the corridor. Such evidence must be removed; Jurovsky called for Proskouriakov to mop up the floor, scatter sawdust about, and cleanse the walls. Sheets were then brought from upstairs; into them the bleeding bodies were rolled and then piled pell-mell into the waiting motor truck, precedence no longer observed.

Twelve miles northwest of Ekaterinburg, on the shores of Lake Isset, stands the secluded little village of Koptiaki in the centre of a heavily wooded forest. Once the site of extensive mining operations, it was now deserted, save for the scattered peasant families who remained unaffected by the coming and going of miners and engineers. Off the beaten track, forgotten and insignificant, the Siberian hamlet slumbered in obscurity — until July 17, 1918.

Early that morning, Anastasia Zykova, a peasant, accompanied by her son Nicholas and her daughter-in-law Maria, started before sunup for Ekaterinburg, with horse and cart, to sell their catch of fish. They had barely passed one of the abandoned mines, — the one known as "Four Brothers" because of the four pine trees that once stood there, — when they perceived a procession of some sort approaching them. It took the form of several vehicles guarded by Red horsemen. Barely recovered from their surprise at the early morning apparition, they were further dismayed when two of the horsemen galloped swiftly forward to intercept them. The soldiers reined up before the Zykovi, ordered them curtly and with menace in their voices to turn back to their village, and, above all, not to dare to look behind. The simple peasants obeyed, turned their horse's head toward home, and retreated. But one of the women looked back, whereupon the two Red Guards galloped in pursuit and with drawn revolvers accompanied the party nearly a mile, threatening them with instant death if they attempted to see what was going on behind them.

In a short time the village of Koptiaki was buzzing with excitement. Men crept out on all fours across the fields in the direction taken by the motor truck and carts of the cortège; the tracks led across open ground toward one of the shafts of the old Isetsky mine. But the village scouts found that sentries had been stationed in a wide circle, completely isolating the locality; frightened and wondering, they crawled back and awaited developments. Toward evening they saw in the heavens glowing reflections from a great bonfire kindled on the spot where the Bolsheviki had finally halted. The hidden rite, whatever it was, continued throughout the next day; only on Thursday, July 19, were the woods deserted and silent.

Then, and only then, did a group of peasants venture to approach the scene. They found the space around the shaft littered with débris of various kinds — disturbed foliage, remnants of a fire, charred wood, and piles of ashes. But on poking under the ashes with sticks they encountered a collection of burnt objects that gave rise to horrible suspicions: first, a Maltese cross set with emeralds, six corset steels from women's corsets, a miscellaneous collection of charred buttons, buckles, parts of slippers, hooks and eyes, beads, parts of women's clothing, and a number of small, dirty pebbles which, on being cleaned and treated chemically, turned out to be pure diamonds. Francis McCullagh, that brilliant and supremely daring journalist who visited these scenes a few weeks after the murder and interrogated the peasants and even Jurovsky himself, spent many weeks — trying weeks — with the present writer in Moscow. He recounted his findings at Ekaterinburg in considerable detail. It was the discovery of that Maltese cross that led to the ghastly truth. Such a decoration was worn only by personages high in the Imperial Service. Pometkovsky, one of the searchers, who was in reality an escaped royalist officer in hiding, knew that there was but one such person in Ekaterinburg. As other metallic and stone objects that had resisted the fire but plainly revealed their late owners were placed before him, he cried aloud: "God Almighty! Can they have burned the whole family alive?"

He was right, but not entirely so; they had burned them, but not while alive.

The spot for the cremation of the bodies had been chosen in advance by Jurovsky and extraordinary precautions taken to destroy the *corpus delicti*. Subsequent events, however, have proved that, though the bodies of the victims can never be produced as primary evidence of the crime, the boast of Voikov, "The world will never know what we have done with them," has not been justified. The elaborate technique of concealment overshot its mark and ignored a number of obvious possibilities. Jurovsky had added to his staff two new assistants whose particular function seems to have been to dismember the bodies. Arrived at the pit, which was thirty feet deep, the regicides set to work to finish their gruesome task. The corpses were drenched with benzine, the countenances having probably first been destroyed by the sulphuric acid, and the human bonfire was then ignited. Acid was likewise used to dissolve the larger and tougher bones which were likely to resist the flames. When fire had consumed all the flesh and reduced skulls and skeletons to ashes, the débris was swept up and cast into the yawning mouth of the iron pit. An attempt was made to rearrange the scarred face of nature by scattering the embers and foliage carelessly about, so as to simulate the appearance of an ordinary camping ground or picnic place. But the wound was too deep; the executioners were tired and probably hurried. They sat down at last beneath the pine trees to eat their lunch, letting fall the telltale eggshells.

The Commission of Inquiry found hundreds of clues and articles definitely identified as belonging to the imperial family: the six sets of corset steels, exactly the number for six women; precious stones in great numbers; the belt buckles of both Tzar and Tzarevitch; the buckles of the women's shoes; hooks and eyes and other metallic parts of feminine wear; the broken lense of the Empress's eyeglasses; a set of artificial teeth identified as those of Dr. Botkin; fragments of chopped and sawed human bones; and one human finger, long, slender, well-shaped, probably cut from the Empress's hand to get at a ring. This pathetic collection of relics, the meagre débris of a fallen dynasty, this admixture of human bones and ashes, corset steels and diamond dust, was transported in a single trunk to Harbin and from thence to "a sure place." That is all the record shows; where or how far they wandered after crossing into Mongolia I know not.[1]

So passed Nicholas II and the Romanovs, to be followed by a third Nicholas, called Lenin, and the House of the Soviets.

Eight days after these events, on July 25, 1918, Ekaterinburg was evacuated by the Bolsheviki, and the combined Kolchak and Czechoslovak troops entered the city. Five days later, on July 30, an orderly investigation, conducted in a scientific and judicial spirit, was instituted, first under

[1] See Appendix XI.

the direction of Judge Nametkin, of that territorial jurisdiction, but later — and fortunately — committed to the very capable hands of Judge Nicholas Sokolov of the Omsk Tribunal. On the evacuation of the town by the Bolsheviki, someone had the presence of mind to rush to the telegraph office and secure possession of the official telegrams that passed between Moscow and the Ural capital during those eventful days; from these records, fortified by the sworn statements of the scores of witnesses and the mute testimony of the hundreds of recognizable clues that had been trampled into the clay in the forest or found at the bottom of the shaft, Sokolov was enabled to publish to an expectant world in 1925 his precious report of 295 pages, totaling 120,000 words. With infinite difficulty, patience, and hazard, he managed to smuggle his material out of Russia to Western Europe, where in peace and safety he edited and published his findings. His work done, he died of hardship and exhaustion.

These documents, of inestimable importance for students of the Russian Revolution, are a monument to the painstaking judicial mind of their author. They set at rest, definitely, all doubt as to the fate of the Romanovs,[1] not only with respect to the immediate family of the Tzar, but also of his near relatives, the grand dukes and princes who were murdered about the same time, either at Petrograd or in the environs of Perm. The murders at Alapaevsk, near Perm, bear a striking resemblance to the Ekaterinburg tragedy.

[1] Following historical precedent, claims are now being made in monarchist circles that not all the family perished. At Castle Seeon, in Bavaria, a certain young woman called Frau Von Tchaikovsky has been proclaimed as the Grand Duchess Anastasia, who, it is pretended, managed to escape from Ekaterinburg to find refuge, eventually, in Germany. Similarly, a young man calling himself Eugene Michaielevich Ivanov, resembling Alexis, — he is even afflicted with hæmophilia, — has been discovered in Bydgosz, Pomerania, Poland, and hailed as the true Tzarevitch. According to the legend, he too escaped the slaughter, his place having been taken by the son of a cook. This is not the place to subject these claims to minute investigation. Royalist circles are divided. The evidence is far from being convincing and shows glaring inconsistencies.

THE DEATH CHAMBER

SVERDLOV

JUROVSKY

Twenty-four hours after the death of Nicholas, six other Romanovs were officially murdered in that city by the Bolsheviki, their bodies thrown down the shaft of an unused mine, and hand grenades dropped down to ensure complete destruction of life. But the bodies of the Perm victims were eventually recovered and identified.

The moral responsibility for the wholesale butchery of the imperial family would now seem to rest fairly and squarely on the shoulders of the Soviet Government, and can no longer be charged off to an alleged uncontrollable fanaticism on the part of local Ekaterinburg authorities. It was decided upon, approved, and arranged by Jankel Sverdlov at Moscow; Bieloborodov, Golostchekin, and Jurovsky were merely the executors — most willing executors — of a matured governmental policy. To be sure, contrary protestations have been made and pretexts advanced as fictitious as the inhuman charge of incest brought against Marie Antoinette by Hébert during her trial. But, in the copious light shed upon events by the official telegrams confiscated at Ekaterinburg, such evasion is no longer tenable.

There was but one telegram sent by the Ekaterinburg "Cheka" to Moscow on July 17, the day following the murder; it was signed by Bieloborodov, President of the Ural Soviet. Written in code, the combinations of numbers defied the best cypher experts of Europe for two years. But when human ingenuity had unraveled what other human ingenuity had contrived, the cryptic groupings of numbers fell into the following indictment of Moscow as having had a clear understanding with Ekaterinburg before the murder :—

To Moscow, KREMLIN, for GORBOUNOV, Secretary of Council of People's Commissars
Please confirm receipt

Tell Sverdlov that the entire family has met the same fate as its head. Officially, they will perish during the evacuation.

BIELOBORODOV

On the following day, July 18, Sverdlov announced to the Central Executive Committee at Moscow that the Tzar had been killed, adding — falsely — that the remaining members of his family had been moved to a safe place. He knew, by prearranged convention, the exact meaning of the sentence " the whole family has met the same fate as its head." Two days later he gives Golotschekin assurance by telegraph that the Central Government approves the execution and authorizes his friend to publish these facts in Ekaterinburg. On the evening of the twentieth, in a meeting of the regional Soviet of the Urals, public announcement was made of the execution to its members — who were supposed to have ordered the deed on their own initiative. On the following day placards were posted throughout the town informing the inhabitants of the Tzar's death and repeating the falsehood concerning the rest of the family. Every single step was ordered, controlled, and approved from Moscow, by Jankel Sverdlov and his colleagues of the Central Executive Committee.

CHAPTER XII

WHO WAS COMRADE JAKOLEV?

In an earlier chapter I promised to hazard a guess as to the identity of Commissar Jakolev and the nature of his mission of "particular importance." It will be only a deduced conclusion, in the realm of conjecture, quite distinct from the facts before narrated, which have been juridically established and historically authenticated. The only persons capable of fully substantiating my thesis are dead; the remaining principal actors in that unsuccessful episode are still dumb, though they have contributed valuable hints.

It will be necessary to recall the military history of the Great War and to visualize the situation on the Western Front at that time. Germany had suffered a fatal check by the entrance of the United States into the arena on the side of her adversaries. With fresh and seemingly unending American forces pouring into the trenches and massing before Saint-Mihiel, the German High Staff prepared for that supreme drive on Paris that caused the world to hold its breath in agonized expectation. The scales of war hung even.

The disappearance of Russia from the Allied line was followed by the Treaty of Brest-Litovsk, which reduced Bolshevist Russia to the status of a sullen vassal of the Teutonic Powers. The interpreter of Germany's will and the virtual dictator of Russia's foreign policy was Count Mirbach, the German ambassador in Moscow. Fully aware of the fundamentally revolutionary character of Bolshevism, with its threat to German monarchism as well as to Russian autocracy, and perfectly willing to repudiate the dubious alliance which military necessity had obliged her to contract with Communist Russia, Germany decided on a bold move. She would restore monarchy in Russia and place Alexis on the throne — provided the Tzar would consent to sign the treaty of Brest-Litovsk and align Russia with the Teutonic Powers!

The Tzar's spontaneous and indignant reaction to Jakolev's very first proposals and his outspoken resentment against Germany support this view: "I will let them cut off my hand before I do it." The coachman who drove the team to Tiumen reported that Jakolev had sought in vain to win the Tzar over to some weighty project. Although unable to hear the exact words, the driver made out that Nicholas always refused; he did not "scold the Bolsheviki, but somebody else."

General Ludendorff, in his *Memoirs*, gives solid ground for a similar surmise. Guardedly, vaguely, as if unwilling yet to admit the full truth, he says: —

We could have deposed the Soviet Government, which was thoroughly hostile to us, and given help to other authorities in Russia, which were not working against us, but indeed anxious to coöperate with us. This would have been a success of great importance to the general conduct of the war. If some other government were established in Russia, it would almost certainly have been possible to come to some compromise with it over the Peace of Brest.

These are significant words. If Mirbach was authorized to sound out Nicholas on this important possibility, he must get the Tzar back to Moscow, or, better still, out of Russia. Sverdlov, already under the domination of Mirbach, may have been obliged to acquiesce — or feign acquiescence — in the plan to move the Tzar. It was noted at Tobolsk that Jakolev was not the usual type of Bolshevist Commissar; he was suave, well spoken, versed in foreign languages, showed breeding, "had clean hands and thin fingers," in the words of Khobylinsky, and treated the former monarch with courtesy and deference. He did not omit to salute Nicholas as the Emperor entered the cart for the trip to Tiumen. His nervous haste and ill-concealed anxiety to get his prisoner out of the danger zone indicates knowledge of some *coup d'état* ahead.

But something went wrong. Either the Tzar refused point-blank to accede to the Teutonic advances, as we may reasonably assume from his own condemnatory utterances, and was flung back into the hands of the Soviets by the infuriated Mirbach, or Mirbach himself was double-crossed by Sverdlov, who permitted the escape as far as Omsk and then ordered the farce to be ended at Ekaterinburg. In any case, the final decision was abrupt and unexpected; no preparation had been made for the imprisonment at Ekaterinburg and Ipatiev's house was requisitioned at a moment's notice; no properly constituted guard was on hand, but had to be recruited from a local factory; the encircling stockade was hurriedly erected after the arrival of the prisoners. Neither Sverdlov nor Mirbach is available to affirm or deny; they were assassinated too soon.

If my main hypothesis be true, which only time and the opening up of more European archives can determine, then Comrade Jakolev was an agent of the German High Staff; and Nicholas II, redeeming an inglorious past by one heroic choice, was murdered because of his unshakable loyalty to the cause of the Allies.

III

FLOOD TIDE

" Ce qu'il nous faut faire pour vaincre, c'est l'audace, encore de l'audace, toujours de l'audace."

DANTON, September 1792

CHAPTER XIII

THE PROVISIONAL GOVERNMENT

It is time to retrace our steps, return to Petrograd, and resume the strictly historical sequence of events which we have interrupted, advisedly, in order to follow the imperial family, step by step, to its pitiable end. Both narratives might have been continued, as it were, in parallel columns, as they run concurrently; but it has been judged more satisfactory for the reader — if admittedly less chronological — to close the history of the Romanovs before depicting the complicated phases upon which the Revolution itself now enters. These two currents diverged almost immediately; the fortunes of the deposed monarch and the mass movements of the capital never crossed, but swept farther and farther apart. Both ended in catastrophe for the principal actors, though, in point of time, the monarch survived longer than the Constitutional Democracy which had unhorsed his autocracy.

Beginning on the tenth of March, fully five days before the formal abdication of the Tzar, a series of events occurred which were destined to exercise an important and permanent influence on the direction which the Revolution ultimately took. With the workmen of the Petrograd factories and shops on general strike, revolutionary meetings and street demonstrations increased in number and frequency; no one as yet seemed to have formulated a constructive political programme, intent as all were on destroying every hated vestige of the old régime. Loosed from the traditional restraint of the Cossack, — who now joined the universal revolt, — Petrograd gave full vent to an ancient Russian characteristic and indulged an inhibited, centrifugal passion which craved destruction and found satisfaction in mere negation.

"At last! At last!" shouted a demonstrator, pointing at a red glow in the direction of the Nicolaevsky station.

"What is burning?"

"The police station."

"But there is a fire station in the same building."

"That won't help. We are going to destroy all government offices, burn, smash, kill all police, all tyrants, all despots."

On the Liteiny a new blaze breaks out and is unchecked. It is the Okroujny Soud, the magnificent building of the High Court of Justice.

"Who started that fire?" someone asks. "Is it not necessary to have a court building for new Russia?"

As the frenzy spreads, rioters and looters fall on their natural enemies, the policemen. The Social Revolutionary, Pitirim Sorokin, tells us that he came on a group of men pitilessly beating a prostrate policeman with butts of revolvers and grinding their victim's body into the pavement with their boot heels. "Stop that, you brutes!" cried Sorokin's companion. "Arrest the man if you like, but don't kill him."

"Who are you to hinder us from killing a Pharaoh?" the mob yelled. "Are you also a counter-revolutionary?"

A few moments later, from a window on the fourth floor of a house where a Tzarist general lodged, a man was tossed to the pavement beneath by revolting soldiers. His piercing shriek of agony was drowned by shouts of exultation. "As the body crashed on the stones," Sorokin writes, "men rushed forward, stamping on it, lashing it with whatever they held in their hands. Deathly sick with the hideousness of the sight, I ran on, my companion following." . . . But someone plucked desperately at his sleeve: "Sorokin! I know you are generous. Save me! In the name of God, save me." In this trembling fugitive Sorokin recognized a spy of the Secret Service who, two years previously, had denounced and secured the arrest of the very man from whom he was now begging sanctuary. "Go home quickly," answered Sorokin. "Destroy your uniform and then, if you can, change your lodging. . . . If anything happens, let me know."

Kerensky passes at the head of a squad of soldiers leading one of the Ministers of the Tzar to prison. The mob yells imprecations and attempts to tear the victim limb from limb. "In the name of the Revolution," cries Kerensky, "I forbid you to touch this man. It is not for you to judge him. He and all the others will be tried, and I swear to you that they will receive justice."

Meanwhile, what of the Duma, the legally elected, representative assembly which alone could claim to voice the collective will of the Russian people? Much and heated controversy centres about that body, apologists of the monarchy assailing it bitterly as a hotbed of treasonable conspiracy, while neutral historians blame its members severely for the feebleness and indecision of its policy. Truth is, no one had a clear idea or a political programme, much less a determined will to assume leadership at a moment when the mounting passion of the populace created disorders which needed, above all else, cool heads, alert minds, and eyes that saw something more relevant to Russia's future than the welcome vision of a toppling throne, burning police stations, and jail deliveries. Everyone foresaw the Revolution, and no one prepared for it. Gutchkov's frank admission is the key to the kaleidoscopic variations that are to follow: ". . . The destruction of old forms of life was faster than the creation of new forms to replace them."

The Revolution was everyone's special business in Russia, and hence its excesses became no one's responsibility.

Ordered by the Emperor to dissolve and disperse on March 12, the Duma obeyed the letter of the ukase by transforming its sessions into "unofficial" sittings called by authority of a Temporary Executive Committee of Members acting on their individual liability. With the supreme authority of the monarch already repudiated in fact, though not announced in public until seventy-two hours later, this technical abdication by the Duma of its legal headship left the State virtually at the mercy of the highest and the most daredevil bidder. Although in the popular imagination the Duma remained the focal point of the Revolutionary movement, its halls and corridors inundated by surging masses who gravitated toward it in search of inspiration, advice, and active leadership, its overlegalistic hesitation on receipt of the Tzar's ukase furnished just the necessary interlude for a Jacobin *coup d'état*. To be sure, it boldly reassumed its authority at midnight, March 13, only to find that, Russian-like, it was again too late!

The interval brought forth a rival claimant. The Union of Coöperative Workers of Petrograd — the only legal labor union then in existence — had already, on March 10, summoned delegates from different quarters of the capital to a conference in their headquarters at 144 Nevsky Prospekt. About thirty-five workmen and a few Social Democrats responded. There for the first time was heard a demand for the formation of "Soviets" along the lines of the abortive Soviet of Khroustalev Nossar which made itself master of St. Petersburg for a brief space in 1905. Couriers were dispatched to every factory in the metropolitan area with instructions to organize elections of delegates according to trades and occupations, one representative to be chosen from each thousand workmen, while factories of less than a thousand hands were invited to send one spokesman. By

March 12 the Soviet was ready to bid for the control of Russia.

On that morning several revolting regiments, in conjunction with insurgent civilians, took possession of the Arsenal, the Central Artillery Bureau, and the prison called "The Crosses." From the latter the mob and the troops liberated, not only political prisoners, but all common-law criminals as well. They then rushed to the Tauride Palace, where the Duma sat; Tcheidze, Skobelev, and Kerensky, Socialist members of the Duma, welcomed them, Kerensky himself undertaking to find a room for the accommodation of this self-elected and heterogeneous parliament. He secured Room No. 12,[1] into which crowded a dozen labor leaders, including the Social Democrats from the Duma; a group of factory delegates; Bogdanov, and Gvozdev, just out of prison; Grinievitch, of the local Menshivist organization; Volkov, and Kamensky, delegates of the Union of Petrograd Labor Coöperatives; and N. D. Sokolov, who is described by an informed narrator of the events as "representing only himself." The inevitable proclamation to the people was the first business of the day : —

Citizens! The representatives of the workmen, the soldiers, and the population of Petrograd, sitting in the building of the State Duma, by the present give notice that their first session will take place this evening at seven o'clock. All troops that have gone over to the people must elect on the spot a representative for each company. Factories must elect one representative per thousand workmen. Those with less than a thousand workmen send one representative.

The appeal was signed by the temporary Executive Committee of the Soviet of Labor Deputies.

---

[1] Mr. Kerensky in his account mentions Room 13; other witnesses maintain that Room 12 was the first chosen. In point of fact, three rooms were eventually used — 11, 12, 13.

The second proclamation of the Soviet organizers — as yet no plenary session had been held — was a stroke of genius. The attitude of the army toward this new form of political control was uncertain and gave rise to anxiety in Room No. 12. There must, then, be a special gesture in the direction of the Petrograd Garrison, which, admittedly, held a Pretorian balance of power. It was forthcoming immediately : —

Citizens! The soldiers who have made themselves watchmen of the people's interests are, since this morning, in the streets, hungry. The Soviet of Workmen Deputies and Soldiers makes every effort to feed the soldiers, guardians of the people's interests, but the immediate organization of a commissariat for the troops is very difficult. The Soviet appeals to you, citizens, begging you to provide for the soldiers' nourishment, devoting to this purpose all provisions in your possession.

Toward evening, Room 12 began to fill up; the two adjoining rooms, 11 and 13, were requisitioned. Generals and military commanders began to drift in, tiring of the perfervid oratory in the Chamber of the Duma, where parliamentarians vied with sociologists in endless discussion of the psychology of the masses — and missed it. The realists in Room 12 appointed two of the first-comers to immediate command of the ultimate arguments of Revolution : the land forces were assigned to Colonel Maslovsky, the navy to Lieutenant Philippovsky. At 9 P.M., with the Duma still sitting, — and debating as usual, — Tcheidze rang a bell and declared the Soviet of Workmen convened in their first formal session. It now numbered one hundred and fifty persons. A Council was appointed, including the Duma Members, Tcheidze and Kerensky ; an Executive Committee was elected, and various commissions created. After an all-night session, this parent Soviet issued its first official pronouncement in the pages of a newspaper founded overnight, to be known thereafter as *Izvestia*.

News of the

PETROGRAD SOVIET OF WORKMEN DEPUTIES

No. 1 — March 13, 1917   No. 1

To the Population of Petrograd and Russia
From the Soviet of Workmen's Deputies

The old authorities brought the country to ruin and the people to starvation. It became impossible to endure it longer. The population of Petrograd came out in the streets to express its discontent. It was met with guns. Instead of bread, the government of the Tzar gave the people bullets.

But the soldiers have refused to go against the people and have revolted against the government. Together with the civilians, they have seized the armories, the military stores, and many impor_ tant government institutions.

The struggle is still going on; it must be brought to an end. The old power must be deposed and replaced by a people's government. This is the salvation of Russia.

To secure a victorious end of this struggle in the interests of democracy, the people must create an organization of its own power.

Yesterday, March 12, a Soviet of Workmen Deputies was formed in the Capital. It consists of representatives elected from the shops and factories, the revolting military detachments, and also from democratic and socialistic parties and groups.

The Soviet of Workmen Deputies now in session at the Imperial Duma faces, as its basic problem, the organization of the people's forces in the battle for permanent political freedom and self-government in Russia.

The Soviet has appointed district commissars to execute the people's authority in the districts of Petrograd.

We call upon the inhabitants of the capital to rally around the Soviet, to form district committees, and to take the administration of local affairs in their own hands.

All together, we unite our forces to fight for the complete destruction of the old government, and for the calling of a Constituent

Assembly, elected on the basis of a universal, equal, direct, and secret ballot.

THE SOVIET OF WORKERS' DEPUTIES

On the following day, March 14, representatives of the military units took their places in the Soviet, the title of which was straightway enlarged into "Soviet of Workmen and Soldiers' Deputies."

Outmanœuvred at the starting post, the Duma took alarm — and compromised. An "Executive Committee of the State Duma" was formed, consisting of Rodzianko, Kerensky, Tcheidze, Milyukov, Karaoulov, Konovalov, Nekrassov, Schidlovsky, Dimitrioukov, Rjevsky, Shulgin, and V. Lvov. These names were communicated to Room 12 with an invitation to consolidate and coöperate. The Soviet placidly ignored the message and continued to address the people over the head of the Duma, urging the formation of regional Soviets for the administration of local affairs. The only means of contact between the two competing bodies was the liaison effected by Kerensky and Tcheidze, who retained their membership in both. Learning that the military section of the Soviet was about to take measures that looked seditious, Rodzianko, at three o'clock in the morning, went in person to their session and proposed a fusion with the military commission of the Duma Committee. With no available funds of their own, the Soviet leaders judged it opportune to accede to this limited coalition and agreed to the nomination of Colonel Engelhardt, a Duma member, to the Presidency of the Joint Commission.

The following days were spent in endless and complicated negotiations between the legally elected Duma of the land and the illegal Soviet, representing a fraction of the inhabitants of Petrograd; the issue was the personnel of the forthcoming Ministry. For two days the bargaining continued. Finally, on the fifteenth, a compromise Cabinet was agreed upon and published as "The Provisional Government of Russia": Premier and Minister of the Interior, Prince G. E. Lvov, the venerable and veteran leader of the Zemstvo movement; Minister of Foreign Affairs, Paul L. Milyukov, leader of the Constitutional-Democratic Party (Cadets); Minister of War and Marine, A. I. Gutchkov, member of the Duma and a leader of the Oktobrist (Conservative) Party, and representative of the Moscow merchant class; Minister of Finance, N. B. Terestchenko, a free lance in politics, one of the wealthiest men in Russia and noted as a philanthropist; Minister of Agriculture, A. I. Shingariov, Constitutional-Democrat, member of the fourth Duma; Minister of Education, Professor A. I. Manuilov, Constitutional-Democrat, well-known University lecturer; Minister of Commerce and Industry, A. I. Konovalov, Progressive, publicist, member of the Duma, one of the foremost industrialists and commercial leaders of Moscow; Minister of Railways, N. Nekrassov, member of the Duma, leader of the left wing of the Constitutional-Democratic Party; Procurator of the Holy Synod, V. Lvov, Moderate Conservative, landed proprietor, and member of the Duma; State Controller, Godnev, Oktobrist, veteran publicist from the Volga districts; Vice Premier and Minister of Justice, A. F. Kerensky, Social Democrat, an active participant in anti-Tzaristic propaganda among the working and peasant classes.

The first official act of the new Provisional Government was the issuance of its declaration: —

1. Full and immediate amnesty for all political, religious, and terroristic crimes, military mutinies, and agrarian offenses, et cetera. (Followed by abolition of capital punishment on March 25.)

2. Freedom of speech, the press, meetings, unions, and strikes. Political liberties to be granted to all men serving in the army within the limits of military requirements.

3. Cancellation of all restrictions of class, religion, and nationality.

4. Immediate preparation for the convocation of a Constituent Assembly elected by universal, equal, direct, and secret suffrage for the establishment of a formal government and of the Constitution of the country.

5. The police to be replaced by a people's militia, with elective chiefs subordinate to the organizations of local self-government.

6. Members of local self-governing institutions to be elected by universal, equal, direct, and secret suffrage.

7. The units of the army that have taken part in the Revolutionary movement not to be disarmed or removed from Petrograd.

8. Military discipline to be preserved on parade and on duty. Soldiers, however, to be free to enjoy all social rights enjoyed by other citizens.

The Provisional Government deems it its duty to add that it has no intention of taking advantage of war time to delay carrying out the aforesaid reforms and measures.[1]

Thus, on the arrival of Gutchkov and Shulgin from Pskov bearing the text of the Tzar's abdication, the ancient régime had completely disappeared; its ministers had either been placed under arrest or were in hiding, and a new, *de facto*,

---

[1] No mention is found of two basic problems: land and the Church. On April 2, however, the Provisional Government promulgated its "Agrarian Reform," designed to hand over the land to those who worked it. In numerous cases they had already taken it. Simultaneously, a Central Land Committee began work on a basic "Land Law" for submission to the Constituent Assembly; but the peasants regarded the Cadet programme as a half-measure, in no way meeting the land hunger of the moujik. With the accession of Kerensky to the Premiership, more radical expropriation was contemplated and the decrees prepared. It remained, however, for the new Bolshevist Government to enact finally the long-awaited confiscatory legislation.

In the sphere of Church administration, the Provisional Government moved with greater dispatch. The ecclesiastical authorities were encouraged to convoke a National Sobor (Council) with a view to reëstablishing the independent functioning of the Church destroyed by Peter the Great through the abolition of the office of Patriarch. The Council met in the autumn; in the early days of November, while firing in the streets announced the downfall of the Provisional Government, the Sobor elected Archbishop Tikhon, Metropolitan of Moscow, to the office of Patriarch of the Orthodox Russian Church, and thus revived an office that had been defunct for two hundred years.

government existed.   But it was a dual government composed of two irreconcilable elements, one bourgeois and democratic, the second proletarian and socialistic, both contending for mastery, neither in complete control of the Revolution.

This duality of control, never fully abolished until November 7, gave time for one deadly stroke that completed the demoralization of the army and unloosed the anarchy that had been seething in its ranks for a year.   I mean the notorious and much discussed "Order Number One."

On March 14 there was promulgated to the troops of the Petrograd Garrison and wirelessed to the front the following extraordinary command : —

ORDER NUMBER ONE.   MARCH 14, 1917

To the garrison of the Petrograd District, to all guardsmen, soldiers of the line, of the artillery, and of the fleet, for immediate and strict observance, and to the workmen of Petrograd for information.

The Soviet of Workmen and Soldiers' Deputies has decreed : —

1. That committees be elected of representatives of the men in all companies, battalions, regiments, artillery parks, batteries, squadrons, and separate services of various military institutions and on the ships of the fleet.

2. All military units not yet represented on the Soviet of Workmen's Deputies to elect one representative from each company. These representatives to provide themselves with written certificates and to report to the Duma at 10 A.M. on March 17.

3. In all its political activities the military unit is subordinate to the Soviet and to its respective committees.

4. The orders of the Military Commission of the Duma are to be obeyed only when they are not in contradiction with the orders and decrees of the Soviet.

5. All arms — rifles, machine guns, armored cars, etc. — are to be at the disposal and under the control of company and battalion committees and should never be handed over to the officers even should they claim them.

6. On parade and on duty the soldiers must comply with strict military discipline; but off parade and off duty, in their political, social, and private life, soldiers must suffer no restriction of the rights common to all citizens. In particular, saluting when off duty is abolished.

7. Officers are no longer to be addressed as "Your Excellency," "Your Honor," etc. Instead, they should be addressed as "Mr. General," "Mr. Colonel," etc.

8. Rudeness to soldiers on the part of all ranks and, in particular, addressing them in the second person singular is prohibited, and any infringement of this regulation and misunderstandings between officers and men are to be reported by the latter to the company commanders.

This order is to be read in all companies, battalions, regiments, batteries, and other combatant and noncombatant formations.

(*Signed*)
THE PETROGRAD SOVIET OF WORKMEN
AND SOLDIERS' DEPUTIES

From the military point of view, this "printed charter of license" meant practically the transfer of the actual command of operations to committees of soldiers and opened the way for the dismissal of officers by their men. Who were the authors of this final folly which destroyed discipline and initiated that "melting away" process which was to ensue? Interrogated by the present writer, Mr. Kerensky put the entire blame on the Soviet and pointed out that, as the Provisional Government did not come into existence until the night of March 15, no responsibility can be laid on its shoulders.

He insists, moreover, that Colonel Engelhardt, the Temporary Chairman of the Joint Military Commission, had refused categorically to sanction its promulgation.

"Very well," answered the Delegates to the Soviet, "if you refuse, we will draft it ourselves."

Intended, moreover, primarily for the soldiers of the

Petrograd Garrison, it was radioed to the front by persons whose identity has never been discovered.

Influential members of the Soviet likewise disclaim responsibility for the fatal effects which followed.

"Pilates," retorts General Denikin, "they washed their hands of the writing of their own credo. For their words are placed on record, in the report of the secret sitting of the Government, the Commanders-in-Chief, and the Executive Committee of the Workmen and Soldiers' Deputies, of May 4 (17), 1917: —

TZERETELLI: You might, perhaps, understand Order Number One if you knew the circumstances in which it was issued. We were confronted with an unorganized mob, and we had to organize.

SKOBELEV: I consider it necessary to explain the circumstances in which Order Number One was issued. Among the troops that overthrew the old régime, the commanding officers did not join the rebels. In order to deprive the former of their importance, we were forced to issue Order Number One. We had inward apprehensions as to the attitude of the front toward the Revolution. Certain instructions were given, which provoked our distrust. To-day we have ascertained that this distrust was well-founded.

A member of the Soviet, Joseph Goldenberg, editor of *New Life*, was still more outspoken. He said to the French journalist, Claude Anet, "Order Number One was not an error, but a necessity. It was not drafted by Sokolov. It is the expression of the unanimous will of the Soviet. On the day 'we made the Revolution,' we understood that if we did not dismember the old army it would crush the Revolution. We had to choose between the army and the Revolution. We did not hesitate — we chose the latter, and I dare say that we were right."

Alarmed by the flood of protesting telegrams from the front recounting the disastrous effects of the Prikaz, the Provisional Government, on March 19, attempted to undo the harm by a proclamation to the army which declared that the Order was not universal and that troops should obey only commanders acting under authority from the Provisional Government.

"The Russian is clever, but always too late."

The mischief was done and was never undone; both Russia and the Allies were soon to feel the results. Again — as in every conflict with Room No. 12 — the Provisional Government found itself on the losing side.

Was it a bloodless transformation? If compared with its historic prototype, the French Revolution, the answer must be a half affirmative. There was no storming of a Bastille, no taking of a Tuileries, no Vendée. The nearest approach to a pitched battle was the last stand made by four companies of infantry one company of Cossacks, two batteries, and a single platoon of machine gunners who took up a position at the Admiralty under the joint command of General Havalov, Commander of the Petrograd Garrison, Beliaev, Minister of War, and the Tzar's own brother, the Grand Duke Michael. Their position, though strategically a commanding one for even a thousand men, became untenable because of lack of food and ammunition, but mainly because of the overwhelming artillery power of the revolted garrison, which numbered nearly one hundred and fifty thousand men. The Royalists retired without battle, leaving the Capital in undisputed possession of the revolutionaries.

But there were frightful acts of vengeance, cowardly slaughter of officers at Kronstadt and in Petrograd, coupled with mob violence of bestial brutality directed against police, public officials, and alleged counter-revolutionaries in the Capital and elsewhere. The lives lost may have reached a total of five thousand.

Russia now enters upon its first summer as a free nation. From the Allied Powers came congratulations and expressions of confidence. On March 22, one week after the abdication of Nicholas II, Mr. David Francis, American ambassador in Petrograd, acting under instructions from Secretary of State Lansing, waited on Milyukov and announced America's recognition of the Provisional Government as the *de jure* Government of Russia. The same afternoon, to lend solemnity and formality to that historic event, Mr. Francis, accompanied by the entire personnel of the Embassy, returned to the Marensky Palace to meet the assembled Council of Ministers and convey the recognition in official form : —

Mr. President of the Council of Ministers, I have the honor as American ambassador, and as representative of the Government of the United States accredited to Russia, to hereby make formal recognition of the Provisional Government of All the Russias and to state that it gives me pleasure officially and personally to continue intercourse with Russia through the medium of the new government.

May the cordial relations existing between the two countries continue to obtain and may they prove mutually satisfactory and beneficial.

Mr. Francis felt a just pride in being the spokesman of the first people to welcome Russia into the family of free, sovereign, and independent nations. England, France, and Italy followed suit, within forty-eight hours. On the second of April, President Wilson, in his memorable speech to the Congress of the United States, confirmed America's friendship for the Russian people, in words that electrified his hearers : —

Does not every American feel that assurance has been added to our hope for the future peace of the world by the wonderful and heartening things that have been happening within the last few weeks in Russia ? Russia was known by those who knew her best to have been always in fact democratic at heart, in all the vital habits of her thought, in all the intimate relationships of her people that spoke their natural instincts, their habitual attitude toward life. . . . Here is a fit partner for a league of honor.

On the second of April, the veteran labor leader, Samuel Gompers, cabled the greetings of the American Federation of Labor : —

WASHINGTON, *April* 2, 1917

. . . We send greetings. The establishment of the liberty of Russia finds a warm spot in the hearts of America's workers. . . . In the name of America's workers, whose watchwords are "Justice, Freedom, and Humanity," we plead that Russia's workers and masses shall maintain what you have already achieved and practically and rationally solve the problem of to-day and safeguard the future from the reactionary forces who would gladly take advantage of your lack of unity to reëstablish the old régime of royalty, reaction, tyranny, and injustice. Our best wishes are with Russia in her new opportunity.

SAMUEL GOMPERS

President, American Federation of Labor

The effect of the Revolution within Russia was comparable only to the joy created by the emancipation of the serfs in 1861. "Life is flowing in a heaving, purifying torrent," wrote an English correspondent from Petrograd. "Never was any country in the world as interesting as Russia now is. Old men are saying, 'Nunc dimittis'; young men are singing in the dawn; and I have met many men and women who seem walking in a hushed sense of benediction." The sunshine of freedom flooded men's souls and exalted their spirits. It was the romantic moment of the Revolution. Mr. Kerensky, Minister of Justice and Vice Premier of the Soviet, believed the hour had come for a generous act of universal clemency. "Send a telegram," he said to Sorokin, "to the governors of prisons throughout Russia to liberate all political prisoners." When written, he signed it: "Citizen Kerensky." The politicals come trooping into Petrograd, followed, alas! by criminals, hooligans, and international adventurers.

Professor Ross, of the University of Wisconsin, found himself in Siberia during these times. He reports that something like twenty thousand sledges were needed to transport the exiles out of Northern Siberia. "It is certain," he writes, "that up to June 23, 1917, more than a thousand refugees had passed in through Yokohama alone. I had an opportunity to observe many of these, and their appearance boded ill for their native land. For the most part, they were of the lowest class of Russian Jews, dirty, sordid, repulsive, not genuine revolutionists at all, but ignorant, self-seeking proletarians. One of them on our boat tried to smuggle into the country twenty-three pairs of shoes and fifteen pairs of gloves, and made great outcry when he was required to pay duty on these goods. It was his sort which, on leaving the quarters which had been provided for them at Vladivostok, stole the silver from the table and the blankets and pillows from the beds. The real revolutionists in New York, Pittsburgh, and elsewhere had protested against the repatriation of these impostors at Russia's expense, but their protests went unheeded. It seemed as if the Russian consuls — appointees of the old régime, be it noted — took a malicious pleasure in sending back persons certain to make trouble."

The news of amnesty, spreading beyond the western frontiers of Russia, penetrates to America, France, England, Germany, and Switzerland. The tidings reach an undersized, bald-headed Russian exile, of a semi-Mongolian cast of countenance, living at the moment in a second-story room over Herr Kammerer's cobbler shop, at No. 14 Spiegelgasse, Zurich. His left eye narrows and a half smile parts his lips as he reaches for a battered valise kept ready for many years against the arrival of just such a summons. His true name is Vladimir Ilyich Ulianov; but he is known in the Revolutionary circles of Europe — and will go down in history — as Nicholas Lenin.

CHAPTER XIV

LENIN AND A SEALED CAR FROM GERMANY

ASTRAKHAN, on the northwestern shore of the Caspian, was the birthplace of Lenin's father, Ilia Ulianov, who came from a respectable middle-class stock which had somehow been crossed with Mongolian blood; miscegenation was clearly visible in the future dictator's countenance. But it was at Simbirsk on the Volga that Vladimir was born, April 10, 1870, while his father was acting as Inspector of Rural Schools, a position which entitled him to be addressed as "Your Excellency." In the same city lived the family of Alexander Kerensky, whose father was principal of the local high school and hence exercised supervision over the Ulianov boys — including Vladimir — during the period of their secondary education. The friendship between the two families which gave Russia its rival claimants for supreme power in 1917 must have been intimate, for when old Ulianov died it was Kerensky's father who became guardian of the children and completed their schooling. Kerensky records the coincidence in his writings and recalls an accidental meeting with Ulianov's sister in 1914. The conversation naturally centred upon her brother, then living as a political exile in Western Europe. "But don't worry," Kerensky assured her, "you will soon see him again. There will be a war and it will open to him the road to Russia." "My prophecy," he adds, "half serious and half in jest, was realized. Alas! to Russia's sorrow."

The school reports of the district of Simbirsk contained flattering comments on young Ulianov's scholarship and conduct : "Excellent," "assiduous," "perfect," are frequent notations. Lenin's biographer, Isaac Don Levine, finds the following estimate from the headmaster of the Classical High School from which Lenin was graduated : —

Very gifted, always punctual and diligent, Ulianov was first in all the classes and received a gold medal upon the conclusion of his studies as the most deserving of all the students, in progress, development, and conduct. Neither in school nor outside of it has there ever been registered a case in which the school authorities had occasion to censure him. His parents always followed carefully his studies and moral development, and from 1886, after his father's death, his mother all alone concentrated her efforts on the education of her children. Religion and prudent discipline were the basis of this education. The good fruits of it were evident in Ulianov's perfect behavior. Examining more closely the life which he led at home, and his character, I could not fail to notice an excessive reserve and gruffness, even with acquaintances, and also with his comrades at school.

But the classical philosophers of Greece and Rome were not to retain their fascination for the honor student of Simbirsk. Though always retaining a fondness for the terse forcefulness of Latin proverbs, Lenin discarded the idealism of the Greeks. Plato, in particular, he repudiated because of his teleology; hence the works of that master were included in the index of one hundred and thirty-four prohibited works drawn up for Soviet Russia by the Main Committee for National Education presided over by Krupskaia, Lenin's widow. Democritus, materialist *par excellence*, was permitted to survive, however, as the only safe philosopher of antiquity. One can understand how the atomic theory of the Grecian Iconoclast, which pictures the cosmos as a whirlwind of bellicose particles in perpetual flux, would be particularly welcome in Bolshevist circles as a satisfactory description of the universe.

The turning point in Ulianov's character development seems to have come just after he passed his seventeenth year. Who was it that said, "At eighteen a man will join any party that attacks?" In 1887 his elder brother, Alexander Ulianov, a shy, reserved university student, became ringleader in an attempt to assassinate Alexander III; the attempt was frustrated and Ulianov was executed. From that day Vladimir was an implacable rebel and never relented until his agent, Jurovsky, first slew and then dismembered the body of Nicholas II, the executioner's son.

Expelled from the University of Kazan for radicalism, forbidden to reside in Moscow, forbidden to leave the country to reside abroad, Vladimir Ulianov finally succeeded in passing the examinations of the Law School of the University of St. Petersburg, in 1891, and was admitted to the bar in Samara in 1892. Returning to St. Petersburg, he there embarked on his life work of indoctrinating workmen with the theories of Karl Marx, meeting with such success that in 1896 he was condemned to exile in Eastern Siberia. On the banks of the Lena — from which he took his pseudonym of Lenin — he toiled unremittingly for three years on his most pretentious work, *The Development of Capitalism in Russia*, and returned to clandestine social warfare on the expiration of his three-year sentence.

The ensuing years, until 1905, were passed in an extraordinary manifestation of dogged, persevering, and calculating propaganda. Pamphlets, tracts, theses, lectures, dialectics, drafts of revolutionary warfare, and philippics marked by biting sarcasm, poured from his fertile pen. From Munich he edited *Iskra* ("The Spark"); in Paris he lectured before the Institute for Social Sciences; in London, at the 1903 convention, he split the Social Democrats by converting the majority to his programme of direct action and advocated immediate uprising of the proletariat in armed revolt. Here the name "Bolshevik" first appeared; the word merely designates the purely historical fact that the left and more radical wing of the Social Democratic Party succeeded in obtaining a majority vote. (*Bolshoi* in Russian means "great," "large," and is, in itself, an innocuous term.) The more conservative right wing was henceforth to be known as "Mensheviki," the defeated or minority group. The accidental fact that the Bolsheviki also advocate a maximum of radicalism is a secondary connotation.

Back in Petrograd, under an assumed name, Lenin fanned the fires of the abortive Revolution of 1905, and on its failure continued unabated his undermining of the established order of things from Finland, Germany, Galicia, France, and, finally, Switzerland. Temporary setbacks but served to harden his heart, sharpen his tongue, whet his purpose, and dehumanize his soul. Advancing years, far from mellowing his character, rather limited his capacity to think or breathe except in terms of class consciousness. His whole being was seared and grooved by a network of scars, the result of his unending mental conflict with God and His creation. Every new thought or impression, every emotion, every reaction from the physical world, even in the domain of art and beauty, was diverted, as it were, into some one or other of these runnels and emptied into a central reservoir of hate. He had a genius for unifying unrelated phenomena and discovering underlying social significances in the most disparate and indifferent acts.

Trotsky, just escaped from Siberia, takes a walk with his chief one day through the streets of London. "He showed me Westminster Abbey (from outside) and some other famous buildings. I no longer know how he expressed himself, but the meaning was: 'That is *their* famous Westminster.' The 'their' meant, naturally, not the English, but the enemy. Not emphatic at all, rather deeply organic and revealed by the pitch of his voice, this meaning was always obvious when he spoke of any kind of cultural values or new conquests, whether it was about the edification of the British Museum or the richness of information of the *Times,* or, many years later, German artillery or French aviation. '*They* understand' or '*They* have,' '*They* have accomplished or succeeded,' but always as enemies! The invisible shadow of the shareholders of society lay, as it were, in his eyes, on all human culture, and this shadow he felt as incontestably as the daylight."

Lenin became a personification of will power devoid of the control of conscience and consecrated to world revolution. His mind became a sealed book, except for three thoughts : Russia, Revolution, the World on Fire. In *What Is To Be Done?* he states his platform baldly : —

Workingmen are not and cannot be conscious of the antagonism of their interests to those of the existing order. Only the educated representatives of the possessing classes are conscious of it. The history of all countries shows that the working classes alone can create but trade-unionism. The workingmen can be saved only by an organization of revolutionaries which, unlike the labor unions, must consist exclusively of people whose profession is revolutionary activity. Such an organization must not be too wide and must be as secret as possible.

"Unmoral" best describes his ethics, as human acts to him were only good or bad in the relation they bore to the inevitable class struggle, not to any objective norm of morality, which he despised. "For Lenin," writes one who knew him, "moral principles do not exist, just as there is no music for a deaf person. . . . Morality or humanity do not exist in Lenin's vocabulary except in such phrases as 'capitalist morality,' or 'slobbering humanity.'"

In the words of another of his colleagues, Minsky : "One might say Lenin lived outside of his own personality, and this is why he had no intimates. He was a devotee of his cult, a hermit of his vow. He met and parted with people only on party grounds.

NICHOLAS LENIN (Vladimir Ulianov)
Sketched from life by a Bolshevist artist

"Men and conditions meant nothing to Lenin but means to accomplish his aims. This is why some of his former associates now call him a 'hangman.' But he is really a monomaniac — a man with a fixed idea.

"Whoever met for the first time this ungainly, poorly dressed, somewhat round-shouldered, bald-headed man with his impenetrable Mongol face and slow movements, would take him for a small bureaucrat, and would never believe that he was face to face with one of the most fearless, crafty, and willful maniacs of our time. Only after recognizing his narrow, sharp eye and unforgettable smile might one guess the extraordinary will-power concealed behind the ordinary mask of his face."

Posterity will never understand the phenomenal influence which this man was destined to wield in his own day and generation, unless men explore the sources of his power. His aims and principles — for he did have a very definite group of guiding motives — must be examined from his point of view, or else the ensuing conflict reveals only the dust and fury of a dog fight. Precisely because his theory seemed eminently reasonable, coherent, and justified, he was enabled to endow it with vitality and persuasive appeal. First and foremost must it be remembered that Lenin made Communism a religion. Karl Marx was its divinity; *Das Kapital* and *The Communist Manifesto* its inspired writings — its Bible; and he, Nicholas Lenin, was its master missionary. "We are rock-ribbed Marxists" was his unvarying credo. On this human trilogy a faith was founded and propagated which, in its psychological reactions, supplied an earth-born substitute for that natural instinct and need which humanity feels for a divine revelation. Beginning with one pivotal dogma, — false, as most men believe, — the apostles of Communism have elaborated a set of doctrines, conclusions, and rules of conduct which furnish them with weapons of daily propaganda. Of these its

adherents are intimately, and often sincerely, persuaded —
at least, your true Communist is, that one sincere believer
of whom Lenin spoke in the First Moscow Congress, when
he said: "Among one hundred so-called Bolsheviki there is
one real Bolshevik, with thirty-nine criminals and sixty fools."

Now, the basic doctrine upon which the whole structure
rests, and upon whose validity Communism stands or falls,
is the assertion that the purely economic motive has been
the determining element in all human activity and that
the development of humanity has been determined and
limited by the production, consumption, distribution, and
exchange of material goods. The Marxian Socialist is an
economic monist. For him the wisdom of Plato and Aristotle and Aquinas is economic waste; the genius of a Phidias,
the sublime poetic raptures of a Homer, a Dante, and a
Shakespeare, are universally immortal only if interpreted in
a proletarian sense; the laws of a Solon, the juridical monu-
ments bequeathed by Justinian and Blackstone and Kent,
the principles of human freedom established by Magna
Charta and the Declaration of Independence, have contributed nothing to purer government; the exquisite charity of
a Damien, — that whitened saint among the leprous shadows
of Molokai, — the blood of Christianity's first social revolutionaries shed in the Coliseum, the writings of Paul and
Matthew and Mark and Luke and John, the life and sacri-
ficial death of the Word made Flesh, the subsequent miracu-
lous progress of Christianity — all these and similar manifestations of mind and Spirit are ineffectual gestures, wasted
energies, which left no serious impression on the heart of
man nor influenced the course of human affairs! Or, if they
did, the mainspring of their motivation was purely economic!

Underlying this economic determinism we find, however,
still another postulate, equally famous and equally at vari-
ance with human experience. It is the Marxian notion of
value. According to Marxian reckoning, the value of a

given object, the quality in the article which makes it capable of being exchanged for another object, or for money, is solely the amount of human labor that has been expended in producing it or modifying the raw material into a marketable form. And by labor Marx means, of course, the purely manual labor of the workman who produces the ultimate form. "The quantity of labor," he says, "is measured by its duration . . . but labor which constitutes the substance of value is equal, uniform human labor, the expenditure of the same intensity of labor power." Hence, three hundred working hours spent by two workmen in producing two objects should determine an identical value for those products; both should bring the same price because of the amount of physical labor, measured in terms of time, that has been consumed in producing them. By such reckoning it would seem to matter very little what was produced. One of the workers, a skilled laborer, may have contrived an excellent gold watch, whereas the other produces a fully dressed, bizarre rag doll with a painted face, crinkly hair, and shoe buttons for eyes, but which has taken the same time and labor to complete as did the gold watch. These efforts, according to the Marxian postulate, have the right to equal compensation. The conclusion is manifestly untenable. No reputable economist now holds it.[1]

Then, too, under this hypothesis the intellectual worker, the author, the research professor, the mathematician, obliged to work from twelve to fourteen hours a day, after

[1] The author is familiar with the explanations advanced at this point by Communist writers who seek to rescue Marx from the consequences of his theory by insisting that he does not mean the individual, quantitative labor of a particular workman, but the average period usually necessary, under given social conditions, to produce the commodity in question: "socially necessary hours of labor." But the distinction proves too much; it introduces an element of quality and of utility, both of which are extraneous to Marx's original intention. A "socially necessary labor hour," to mean anything, would have to be accepted by all men and nations concerned in the complex processes of modern industrial life; it is an ideal entity, corresponding to nothing objective and tangible. There is no other self-operating criterion conceivable beyond the law of supply and demand.

spending all their youth and most of their manhood in the acquisition of the necessary qualifications, become worthy only of the consideration accorded to the linotypist who puts their thoughts and findings into print for eight hours a day — with time and a half for overtime.

The theory ignores the numerous other elements entering into the production of exchangeable articles, such as the furnishing of raw material, of tools, machinery, and work-shops, the payment of taxes and overhead, the technical administration and direction of the labor — in a word, all those factors entering into the involved process of produc-tion which are furnished at the risk and expense, not of the laborer, but of the so-called capitalist. Both capital and labor, employer and employee, brain worker and manual worker, have a definite and legitimate function to perform, and one without the other is powerless.

But with dogged, undaunted persistence the Communist repeats that it is only the actual physical labor that creates value, refusing again to face the cold, inescapable fact that if there is no one who wants the object it has no value what-soever in exchange. The psychological state of the buyer is as important as the labor expended. A marooned sailor on a desert island sees a ship looming over the horizon. He has at hand a crude rowboat hollowed out of the trunk of a tree, made in a couple of days. But he also has on hand, as salvage from the wreck, several Rolls-Royce automobiles that probably took many months to fabricate and may be worth eight to ten thousand dollars apiece — elsewhere. The boat has acquired a superior "place value," independ-ently of human labor. As the celebrated economist, Gide, expresses it, "The value of things grows by scarcity and diminishes by abundance. Abundance may decrease it to zero. A superabundance of goods is always valueless when we cannot make use of the surplus, for then it is entirely useless." Benjamin Franklin reveals the same common sense in the terse and homely philosophizings of Poor Richard: "When the well is dry, we know the value of water." Robinson Crusoe accumulated an important collection of intrinsically valuable commodities on his desert island as proof of his labor. But they had no value, did not become economic wealth, until somebody *wanted* them to supply a definite personal need.

Then, too, value frequently exists where labor is entirely absent. Many objects have a value of their own without the slightest intervention of human labor, such as springs of mineral water, a sperm whale cast up on the seashore, and guano deposits. And there are objects which undergo extraordinary increase in value without the slightest touch of manual labor. For example, a wine cellar, assembled before the Federal Prohibition Act.

But with a display of dialectics and an array of industrial statistics, by frequent appeals to the emotions, your orthodox Communist continues to assert that the capitalist system, like a vampire, appropriates what justly belongs to the laborer and pays him only a miserable, minimum salary, whereas the entire exchange value should accrue to the manual producer. All financial gains over and above that of the labor value imbedded, as it were, within the commodity, Marx calls "surplus value," and it is the unwarranted accumulation of surplus values that creates the *bête noire* of Communism, which is capital. Playing cleverly and bitterly on the injustices that have undoubtedly arisen from the indefensible greed of individual capitalists since the world began, Marx next deduces as a permanent working principle his so-called "class warfare."

Assuming that his premises are sound, he recognizes only two entities in the human race — the employing and the employed classes — and from the "inevitable" conflict arising between these eternal antagonists he derives every social, economic, religious, political, and industrial evil that history has recorded. These classes he calls the "bourgeoisie" (employing class) and the "proletariat" (employed or wage-earning class). This conception of industrial life as a daily class struggle is then enlarged and transferred until it embraces every form of human activity. Everything centres about that stormy petrel. It is the only explanation of history and alone can interpret historical variations, account for the rise and fall of empires, explain the domination of given races, and is the ultimate principle of wars, plagues, and famines. It penetrates the realms of philosophy, metaphysics, economics, and the political sciences. It has not as yet fully embraced the natural sciences and pure mathematics, but, as one commentator truly points out, there is hardly another known field of human knowledge from Totemism to the origin of Greek tragedy which your orthodox Marxist will not undertake to explain on the basis of the class struggle between the bourgeoisie and the proletariat. The panacea of mundane ills is therefore to be sought in an application of Marx's principles to the root of human diseases. And as, for the Marxist, the root of all evil is private property, so the first tremendous blow must be struck at that institution. Then industry must be nationalized and expropriated in favor of the operatives; the bourgeoisie must be disarmed, then disenfranchised and destroyed, as you would exterminate parasitic insects.

Education, art, literature, music, and similar manifestations of human genius must be cultivated only in so far as they serve to increase the class consciousness of the proletariat and ensure the dictatorship of that class. Religion, in the Marxist scheme of life, is an opiate only, invented to drug the proletariat into unthinking submission to their capitalistic overlords; hence it should be deliberately identified in the minds of the masses with the patent and more repulsive abuses of capitalism in order that it may then be destroyed with impunity.

So far Karl Marx and Engels and Bebel, the doctrinaires. Now enters on the scene Nicholas Lenin, the doer of deeds, the Mohammed of Marxism, who applies the doctrine with fire and sword, first to Russia, then *in spe* to the entire world. As one of Lenin's admirers, Losovsky, points out, "Marx directed against capitalism the weapon of criticism. Lenin employed the criticism of weapons. . . . Lenin had the same genius for making history as Marx had for explaining it."

In one important respect did Lenin surpass his master. It would appear that Marx admitted, as a natural transition, that the proletariat would pass through democracy to supreme victory, gaining political ascendancy by the legal path of the ballot. He does not seem to make particular mention in any place of that immediate dictatorship of the proletariat which became the battle cry of the left wing of the Social Democrats and is still the avowed goal of the Third International.

The exiled Lenin, realistic opportunist that he was, and alert strategist, recognized in the World War and its attendant confusion an opportunity, as unparalleled as it was unexpected, to launch at once the World Revolution. He became feverishly active. At the Zimmerwald and Kienthal conferences, convoked by anti-war Socialists in 1915 and 1916, he preached local defeatism, sabotage, general strikes, and domestic revolt, as sure means of transforming the "imperialist war into a civil war." But internationalism capitulated to nationalism, and his last hope, the Socialist Party of Germany, supported the Reichstag by voting war credits. Bullets, not ballots, for the bourgeoisie, had been Lenin's hope; with bitter scorn and sarcasm he now turns on his former colleagues, such as Kautsky, Leo Deutsch, Plekhanov, and all Mensheviki, — who relied on pacific evolution rather than bloody revolution, — and poured savage ridicule on their Fabianism. "Boot-lickers of the capitalists," "Cowards," "Lily-livered milksops," and such descriptive epithets fill the pages of Lenin's philippics against the Mensheviki, as they do Stalin's later work on Leninism. War, implacable war, with no mercy shown, organized terrorism, complete physical annihilation of the bourgeois opponent — such was the all-inclusive strategy of this impatient Hotspur.[1]

His opportunity was not long in coming and from an unexpected quarter.

The political attitude of Germany toward Russia, naturally enough, had undergone a complete transformation in August 1914. Previously German foreign policy included, as one of its major objectives, the gradual enticement of Russia into the Teutonic alignment by weaning the Tzar away from his English and French alliances. Then, too, the preservation of the monarchical principle, as vital to the Hohenzollerns as to the Romanovs, was a serious deterrent to the natural hostility felt by the Kaiser at the growing Pan-Slavic aspirations of his Eastern neighbor. He limited his eager diplomats, therefore, to two Machiavellian courses: they urged Russia toward her disastrous adventures in the East, counting on Japan to keep the Russian Bear occupied on his Eastern frontier, and, as a collateral precaution, they poured an occasional supply of oil on the nationalistic fires forever smouldering among the non-Slavic elements of the Tzar's empire. But with open warfare declared, neither the family ties between the reigning houses nor the inviolability of the monarchical principle could stand in the way of Russia's downfall. The stubborn resistance of the Russian armies seriously upset the war lord's strategy, divided his forces, and in the long run undoubtedly saved the Allies in the West. Hence copious recourse was had to the arts of

[1] Lenin is said to have often repeated that, in the event of his being forced to go, he would rather surrender to restored autocracy than to a bourgeois republic — *i.e.*, to stabilized democracy. — Milyukov, Lowell Lectures, Boston, 1921

propaganda, both within Russia and among revolutionaries living abroad. The disaffection of Finland offered a convenient "back-door" entrance into Russia for German spies, and the suspicions of Sweden were cultivated by whispering in her ears the rumor that Russia planned to seize a strip of Scandinavian territory. The elaborate Intelligence Service tolerated in Sweden was the result. Similar propaganda centres had already been established by Austria at Cracow and among the Ukrainophiles in Vienna.

The abdication of the Tzar and the subsequent uncertainty of command at Petrograd presented a superb opportunity to the German High Staff for progressive demoralization of the enemy's rear guard. Orders went out from Headquarters that Russian exiles, particularly revolutionaries, should be urged to return to their homeland, bringing their defeatism and socialism with them. Funds and transportation were provided from the War Chest and presumably charged off as legitimate expenditures for poison gas. The Secretary of the Swiss Socialist Party, Fritz Platten, acted as party whip and rounded up thirty or more Russian radicals, including Lenin, Zinoviev, Kamenev, Lunacharsky, Radek, Krylenko, and Voikov. German agents handed over a generous supply of gold to Lenin, who received it as readily from German hands for the destruction of Russia as he would have taken it from English or French sources for the destruction of Germany. "Of course," writes Radek, one of the returning exiles, "we knew perfectly well that the German authorities had their own designs in granting us the permission to travel across Germany. . . . We did not pay much attention to this, for we knew that if a true revolution developed in Russia its influence would spread far beyond our borders."

The German High Command felt the same. They had no delusions as to the seriousness of the step they were taking. Hence, the car bearing the Bolshevist "bacillus" was guarded by detectives and a strong military contingent, and no communications permitted with outsiders as the train passed through German territory en route to Finland.

The "Sealed Car" takes its place in history beside the Wooden Horse of Troy.

"By sending Lenin to Russia," writes General Ludendorff in *My War Memories*, "our Government had moreover assumed a great responsibility. From a military point of view his journey was justified, for Russia had to be laid low. But our Government should have seen to it that we also were not involved in her fall."

General von Hoffmann, Chief of the German General Staff on the Eastern Front, in his memoirs, *The War of Lost Opportunities*, defends the action of the German Government in these words: —

We naturally tried, by means of propaganda, to increase the disintegration that the Russian Revolution had introduced into the army. Some man at home who had connections with the Russian revolutionaries exiled in Switzerland came upon the idea of employing some of them in order to hasten the undermining and poisoning of the morale of the Russian army. He applied to Deputy Erzberger and the Deputy of the German Foreign Office. And thus it came about that Lenin was conveyed through Germany to Petersburg in the manner that afterward transpired.

In the same way as I send shells into the enemy trenches, as I discharge poison gas at him, I, as an enemy, have the right to employ the expedient of propaganda against his garrisons.

As for Lenin, this kindly act of the German High Staff was a veritable *deus ex machina;* it was the fruition of thirty years of waiting and dreaming and planning. Controlled, obsessed, transformed, by his single idea of world revolution, he had driven straight for his goal with unshakable pertinacity; and here he was rolling swiftly toward Russia under military escort! The vision of this hour had been the cloud by day and the pillar of fire by night that led him through the

Leon Trotsky (Bronstein)

darkness and drab monotony of prison days in that house of the dead, Siberia. It sustained him during his exile in Switzerland, where he ate with it, slept with it, walked with it, and talked with it, until, like the magnetic North, it was now drawing him back to Petrograd, at precisely the opportune moment. No Roman conqueror leading captives at his chariot wheels ever made a more triumphant entry than did this Third Nicholas into the demoralized Muscovite capital on April 16, 1917. He was the Russian Marius, and the whole world should be his Jugurtha.

Leon Trotsky was also on his way across the ocean from New York. British authorities detained him at Halifax; but the Provisional Government of Russia protested to its ally, and Mr. Trotsky was allowed to proceed.

CHAPTER XV

PISTOLS FOR TWO, COFFEE FOR ONE

I⊤ would be a superficial understanding of the facts in the case, and a futile explanation of the Second Russian Revolution, to picture the next scene in the Finland Station as the triumph of a Jewish conspiracy or as the entry of a mere unprincipled adventurer in the pay of German military opportunists. The garlands, the streamers, and the pennants that gave to the platform a holiday color were not all symbols of Israel — though Jewry was as much in evidence at Lenin's arrival as it would be, under similar conditions, at Paddington, St. Lazare, or at Forty-Second Street, New York. The military and naval detachments that stood stiffly at salute in the square before the station had not been drafted from Potsdam; nor can the tens of thousands of enthusiastic citizens who rushed the incoming train be described as German sympathizers. The shabbily dressed exile who stepped blinking into the glare of the searchlights and fumbled awkwardly with a bouquet thrust into his hands owed allegiance neither to Germany nor to a Hidden Council of Elders of Sion. Exponent of a denationalized idea and prophet of a rationalistic religion, he would have alighted at Friedrichstrasse in Berlin or at the Ostbahnhof of Vienna as confidently as now he entered upon the conquest of Russia's soul. It was a fortune of war and an accident — a very welcome accident to be sure — that made Russia the first laboratory for his social experimentation. Certain difficulties of approach might have had to be overcome elsewhere, language problems might have been more annoying, and psychological barriers based on racial prejudices might have been harder to overcome, but the essential procedure in all cases was identical and the objective clearly laid down, irrespective of the territory in which it was to be achieved.

Participants in that extraordinary greeting, which assumed the proportions of a triumphant procession as it flowed through the streets, noted that Lenin seemed surprised at the sea of faces before him.   But during Tcheidze's address of welcome he had time to decide upon his next and characteristically daring move.

"Comrade Lenin," said the Representative of the Soviet, "we welcome you to Russia in the name of the Soviet of Workmen and Soldiers' Deputies and of the whole Revolution. . . .   But we think that the main task of the Revolutionary Democracy is the defense of the Revolution against external and internal dangers. . . .   We hope you will pursue, together with us, the same aims."

With his eyes fixed, not on the spokesman of the official delegation, but wandering from the insignia of the Tzar, which decorated the waiting room, to the throng outside, Lenin's active mind leaped over the heads of the decorous group before him and fixed itself upon the massed workers. He was never to let go. . . .   He knew his Russia.

"The piratical, imperialistic war is the beginning of civil war in all Europe," he replied, and turned his back on Tcheidze.   "The dawn of the World Socialist Revolution is breaking. . . .   All Germany is boiling. . . .   Any day the collapse of the entire European Imperialism may come."

The same speech was repeated at a dozen street corners on the way to the Soviet headquarters, in the sumptuous palace of Kshesinskaia, the ballet dancer and former favorite of the Tzar.

L'audace, encore de l'audace, toujours de l'audace.

That evening two hundred representative members of the Bolshevist Party sat down in the hall of the palace to hear the first pronouncement of their returned leader. "I will never forget," writes Sukhanov, the only outsider present, "that thunderlike speech which shook and amazed not only me, an accidental heretic, but all the orthodox Bolsheviki. I assert that no one expected anything like it. It seemed as if the elements had been let loose from their depths and a spirit of all-destruction, knowing no obstacles, doubts, human difficulties, and calculations, was sweeping through the hall of Kshesinskaia's house over the heads of the spell-bound disciples.

"Lenin is generally a very good speaker, not an orator of the finished, round phrase, or the striking figure, or gripping pathos, or clever pun, but an orator of tremendous driving force, dissolving complicated problems into their most simple elements.

"A year and a half afterward, changed from a demagogue and a rebel into a statesman, a defender of statutes, a guardian of his governmental property, Lenin lost his force and individuality as an orator. His speeches were all alike, all harping on the same subject, with trivial variations. But all happened as a result of being in power. In the early days Lenin could shake one thoroughly. But he moved the entire Bolshevist audience then. Not only with his eloquence, but with the unheard-of contents of his speech. Lenin spoke for about two hours. He sharply attacked the Soviet as belonging to the enemy's camp. This alone was enough to make the most radical hearers dizzy."

If a direct challenge to the Provisional Government, this opening manifesto was no less astounding to the conservative members of his own party. The eight months which followed witnessed fluctuations, complications, defeats, and victories that would merit a series of separate volumes for adequate historical treatment and stand an enduring monument to the crystal clearness of programme, the inflexible will, and the superhuman driving power of one man. For a solid month Lenin stood alone in his demands for the immediate assumption of political power by the Soviet, meaning always the controlling wing of the Soviet, the Bolshevist Party. Opposed on prudential grounds by Kamenev, Rykov, Nogin, Zinoviev, and Trotsky, — who had arrived after his brush with the British authorities at Halifax, — he beat against the opposition with telling argument, scorn, personal ridicule, and flaming appeals to the revolutionary instincts of the mob. In May was held the First National Conference of the Bolshevist Party, attended by one hundred and forty delegates. The test came — and Lenin won. His theses were adopted. It was to be Socialism, not by evolution, but by revolution. It was not to be Fabianism, but Socialism *hic et nunc*. From the balcony of Kshesinskaia's palace he proclaims his panacea in four simple, understandable, and wonderfully hypnotic phrases: *immediate peace, the land to the peasant, the factories to the workers, all power to the Soviets.*

Already, on March 27, the Petrograd Soviet had sent a wireless message to all the peoples of the world appealing for an immediate peace, instructing the populations of belligerent countries to act over the heads of their governments. Seizing time by the forelock, but giving Comrade Lenin a fair margin behind the lines, German propaganda planes began to shower down on the Russian trenches multitudinous offers of separate peace: "The Russian Revolution wants peace. Then why tarry?" The enemy promised, too, that not another shot would be fired by the Germans unless provoked by the Russians.

Harassed by the unending demands made upon their resources and ingenuity by the crushing burden of creating a new administrative machinery to replace the old governmental personnel that had simply vanished overnight throughout the empire, the Provisional Government was faced with a task which the sequel showed to be beyond their endurance and outside their foresight. From each province, city, and village, telegrams came pouring into Petrograd making frantic demands for competent officials to direct into orderly channels the tempest of irresponsibility whipped up by the intoxicating winds of the new-found freedom. Upward of one hundred and seventy million people, prone to spontaneous anarchy, left without a visible organized government! These telegrams, Mr. Kerensky reports, seemed written by the same hand. "They all told the same story: the old administration, from the governor to the last town policeman and village bailiff, had disappeared without trace, and everywhere were being formed, instead, all sorts of self-appointed organizations — Soviets, committees of public safety, conferences of public leaders, etc., etc."

In despair, Prince Lvov, the Premier, authorized the chairmen of the local zemstvo organizations to assume, temporarily, the functions of governors; it was a case of naming the first honest man who walked the road as executive and the first strong man or the village blacksmith as chief of police. The result was foreordained by the nature of things. Conservative men held office for a week and gave way to assertive and unscrupulous adventurers. Villages ruled themselves. The scum began to rise to the surface as the aroused peasantry made a mad rush for the land and the nearest manor.

From one village comes a telegram asking for a picture of the new sovereign, *Revolutzia*. They imagined him some new, benevolent Tzar.

Paralleling the domestic ferment ran the external menace. The war was not abandoned outright, but indecision and demoralization prevailed; drills and military operations were replaced by political meetings in the trenches as the centre of interest shifted.   The troops were no longer concerned with the common enemy, — who, on his part, sent over an occasional invitation to fraternize, — but with reports from home.

"What is happening in our village on the Volga?"

"Has the division of land begun while we remain rotting here in the swamps?"

A Russian soldier creeps out toward the German lines, unmolested by the watchful enemy.   He reaches a crude post-box, set up near the German position, and takes out the latest number of *The Russian Messenger* (printed in Berlin or Vilna, then in German hands), and plods sullenly back to the trenches.   He reads aloud from the "news" sheet: "The English want the Russians to shed the last drop of their blood for the greater glory of England, who seeks her profit in everything. . . .   Dear soldiers, you must know that Russia would have concluded peace long ago had not England prevented her. . . .   The Russian people demand it; such is their sacred will."

An oath is heard from the corner of a trench.

"Don't you wish for peace?   *They* make peace, the —— ; we shall die here, without getting our freedom."

From the trenches rises a solid roar : —

"To the devil with the war!   Let us go home."

Guns were thrown down, and the great *katabasis* began.   Deserters swarmed over every road leading to Petrograd and the provinces.   The Russian front grew stiller and stiller; the German High Staff applauded and began to transfer divisions to the Western Front.   The Allies cable to Washington, "Hurry, hurry."   And his foreign colleagues ask General Pershing, "When will you be ready to attack?"

The Allies grow anxious and ask Mr. Milyukov for a statement of Russia's intentions.   The Prime Minister replies with a pronouncement that advanced the Bolshevist cause enormously and paved the way for the first governmental crisis. After reiterating the Government's unshakable concurrence with the common cause, he continues : —

As it is known, President Wilson on the question of the Straits did not only take the position of their possible neutralization, but also their transfer to Russian control. In the establishment of Russian domination over the Straits there must be in no wise seen a manifestation of tendencies of conquest, but exclusively the existence of a national objective — the necessity of commanding the gate to Russia without which it is impossible to guarantee the safety of the Black Sea. When this gate shall have been firmly fortified, we shall not be obliged to increase the defenses of the shores of the Black Sea or to maintain a powerful battle fleet. As far as the neutralization of the Straits is concerned, this solution of the questions would give access to the Black Sea to foreign battleships, which is precisely the consideration impelling Russia to prefer to a neutralization the retention of the Straits in the hands of a weak Power. Occupying Constantinople as mere parasites and ruling by the sole force of conquest, the Turks cannot, in opposition to the Russian claims, allege their national rights.

This declaration of war aims proved to be a boomerang. It furnished Lenin with a new pretext for mounting the balcony of the Kshesinskaia palace and shouting, "Imperialism — capitalistic warfare! No annexations — no exploitation of the working classes!"

A storm of opposition broke out in the Soviet. Crowds demonstrated, and even loyal regiments paraded in the streets; cries of "Down with the Government!" "Down with Milyukov!" were heard on all sides.

Counter-demonstrations, organized by anti-Leninites, supported the Government, and on the Nevsky several people were killed. For the first time, blood was flowing within the Revolution.

Anxious times begin. The Soviet's claim to possess exclusive right to dispose of the government troops gives rise to Prince Lvov's epigrammatic description : —

The Government is an authority without power and the Workmen's Council a power without authority.

Unable to tolerate the dual control, Gutchkov, Minister of War, resigns, describing the Provisional Government as being "perpetually under domiciliary arrest"; General Kornilov, military commander of Petrograd, follows suit, declining to accept further responsibility for the maintenance of discipline. Kerensky assumes the portfolio of War; the leaders of the Provisional Government drop into their usual frame of mind, and a compromise is voted to be the order of the day : the Soviet is too powerful to be ignored and the Government is unwilling or unable to accept its challenge. A coalition Cabinet is suggested ; three Socialists, Tzeretelli, Chernov, and Skobelev, come over from the Soviet and take equal rank with the members of the Provisional Government. Milyukov refuses to be relegated to the post of Minister of Education and follows the example of Gutchkov and Kornilov. Tereschenko becomes Minister of Foreign Affairs, and the Allies grasp at the forlorn hope that harmony and confidence have been restored.

Lulled possibly by a sense of false security, and responding to the moral pressure of the Allies, Mr. Kerensky now begins preparations for a grandiose Russian offensive and starts in person for the front. He finds "neither the crack of machine guns nor the exchange of artillery fire." "The trenches," he writes, "were deserted. All preparatory work for offensive operations had been abandoned. With their uniforms in ludicrous order, thousands of troops were devoting their time to interminable meetings. Most of the officers seemed completely confused. The local Galician population was looking on in surprise and amusement."

With admirable energy the Minister of War flits from the

Galician front to Odessa and Sebastopol, thence to Kiev and Dvinsk and Moscow, patching up quarrels, restoring morale, and galvanizing, with his ringing oratory, the war-weary legions into willingness for one final heave of their bodies against the German gun. His tasks are varied : —

We entered a dugout, unobservable from the enemy's position, and called a number of troops from the trenches.

Weary, growling faces surrounded us in a ring. We began to converse. Standing aloof, the little soldier (agitator), who had won the ears of his regiment, made no effort to reply. His comrades thereupon pushed him forward. (Voices: "Well, what is the matter? Here's your chance to speak in the presence of the Minister himself.") Finally, the little soldier spoke up: "What I want to say is this : You say we must fight so that the peasants may have the land, but of what use is the land to me, for instance, if I am killed?"

I realized immediately that all discussion and logic were of no use in this case. What confronted me here was the dark inside of a human being. The case was one in which personal interest, in its most naked form, was being preferred to sacrifice for the common good. The desirability and wisdom of such sacrifice does not lend itself to proof by word or reason. It can only be felt. The situation was rather difficult. To leave the little soldier without a reply was unthinkable. Where the logic of reason seems powerless it was necessary to resort to the logic of emotion.

Silently I took a few steps forward in the direction of the little soldier.

Turning to Radko-Dmitriev, I said : —

"General, I order you to remove this soldier immediately; pack him off at once to his village. Let his fellow villagers know that the Russian Revolution has no need of cowards."

My surprising reply created a moving impression on all those present. The little soldier himself stood trembling, dumb and pale. And then he fell in a deep faint. Soon after I received a request from his officer to countermand the order for his removal. A profound change had now come over him. He was now an example to others.

But Lenin is losing no time. He too is mobilizing his forces in step with the Minister of War at the front.

In June an All-Russian Congress of Delegates of Soviets was summoned; representatives from Workmen's Councils throughout Russia were invited to Petrograd for the purpose of transforming the local Petrograd Council into a national organization. Lenin, with all proletarian Russia as an auditor before him, delivered an impassioned attack upon the Provisional Government in phrases which subsequent comparison revealed as taken word for word from the latest German wireless propaganda.

On the second of July, the long-prepared offensive was launched on the Southwestern Front. On July 8, General Kornilov routed the Austrians at Halicz and Kalusz; optimism ran high, and the fortunes of the Provisional Government rose with the rise of the national pride.

This is not the place to enter upon a technical history of the ultimate failure of this last heroic effort of the Russian army; it must suffice for our present purpose to record the outstanding fact that optimism gave way to chronic pessimism when, on July 18, the enemy counter-attacked, broke the Russian front, and completed the disintegration already prepared by the clandestine activities of the Bolshevist emissaries in the ranks.

General Denikin again describes what he saw: —

Afterward?

Afterward, "the molten element" overflowed its banks completely. Officers were killed, burned, drowned, torn asunder, and had their heads broken through with hammers, slowly, with inexpressible cruelty.

Afterward — millions of deserters. Like an avalanche the soldiery moved along the railways, waterways, and country roads, trampling down, breaking, and destroying the last nerves of poor, roadless Russia.

Afterward — Tarnopol, Kalusz, Kazan. Like a whirlwind,

robbery, murder, violence, incendiarism, swept over Galicia, Volhynia, Podolsk, and other provinces, leaving behind them everywhere a trail of blood and arousing in the minds of the Russian people, crazed with grief and weak in spirit, the monstrous thought: "Oh, Lord! If only the Germans would come quickly."

Retreat became general rout, and the standards of the Leninites advanced one step nearer their domestic goal in Petrograd.

Was it the opportune moment for a decisive frontal attack on the Provisional Government? The very streets invited a Bolshevist *coup d'état*, filled, as they were, with masses of parading regiments on the verge of revolt and Red Guards (armed workmen mobilized by the Soviet) demanding the overthrow of the Government. Motor lorries packed with unidentified soldiers dashed in apparent confusion through the streets; a red banner appeared with the inscription, "The first bullet for Kerensky." Twenty thousand sailors are landed from Kronstadt and thirty thousand strikers arrive from the enormous Putilov works, converging upon the centre of the city and threatening the Tauride Palace, seat of the Duma.

The Ides of March have returned. Only now the Revolution has turned on its own creators and demands their heads.

An all-night parley is going on in the Soviet. Curious enough, it is Lenin himself who wavers, wondering if it be really his destined hour. He might indeed have taken the power, but could he hold it? Kerensky, absent at the front, was yet to be heard from, and might return with enough loyal troops to crush the insurrection. . . . Lenin's caution prevails, and a proclamation in the *Pravda* calling for an uprising on July 17 was deleted at the last moment — the matrix was cut out — and the Bolshevist organ carried a gaping blank space on the first page of its morning edition.

Zɪɴᴏᴠɪᴇᴠ (Apfelbaum)   Kᴀᴍᴇɴᴇᴠ (Rosenberg)

Lᴜɴᴀᴄʜᴀʀsᴋʏ   Bᴜᴋʜᴀʀɪɴ

Lᴇɴɪɴ's Lɪᴇᴜᴛᴇɴᴀɴᴛs

Sketched from life by a Bolshevist artist

Kerensky, advised by telegrams of the mutiny, returns on July 19 and orders the arrest of all the Bolshevist leaders, beginning with Lenin, Trotsky, Zinoviev (who escaped), Kamenev and Madame Kollontai. But when the arresting party arrives at Lenin's lodgings they find that he too has forestalled them and is on his way across the Finnish border. He will not appear publicly again until he enters the Smolny Institute as undisputed master of Petrograd, on November 7.

On July 20 the gentle Prince Lvov resigns in despair from the Cabinet, and Kerensky becomes Premier, still retaining, however, his post of Minister of War and Marine. The new Government sets about to emancipate itself from control of party factions, whether Soviet or bourgeois, and declares itself a coalition, pledged to represent all creative forces in the country, irrespective of party affiliations. The Soviet admits tactical defeat in the frank statement of Tzeretelli, in the next meeting of the All-Russian Executive Committee of the Congress of the Soviets : —

We have just experienced not only a Cabinet crisis, but a crisis of the Revolution. A new era in the history of the Revolution has begun. Two months ago the Soviets were stronger. Now we have become weaker, for the correlation of forces has changed to our disadvantage.

The State had triumphed and could afford now to be magnanimous. Premier Kerensky ordered the release of Mr. Trotsky and all the Bolshevist prisoners. They promptly resume their attack, but in the old, underground fashion. Contact is established with their absent leader in Finland, and the agents sent from Petrograd find Lenin on a farm pitching hay by daylight and drawing up plans for a new campaign by night.

The phase upon which the Revolution now enters is comparable only to the buoyant period that followed the abdica- tion of the Tzar. It was the second honeymoon of the Revolution. To meet the popular impatience for a Constituent Assembly, the convocation of which had been postponed until December 16, a National Conference is called for August 26, to be held in ancient Moscow, better suited to recall Muscovite traditions than the surcharged political atmosphere of Petrograd. "Held in the Bolshoi Theatre, it presented," writes Mr. Kerensky, "a most pleasing picture. Running from the stage to the main entrance was the middle aisle, dividing the conference into two equal sides: on the left was Democratic, peasant, Soviet, socialist Russia, and on the right was Liberal, bourgeois, capitalist Russia. The army was represented on the left by army committees and on the right by members of the Commanding Corps. Exactly opposite the main entrance on the stage sat the Provisional Government. My seat was precisely in the middle. On my left were the Democratic-Socialist Ministers. On my right were the Ministers from the bourgeoisie. The Provisional Government was the only centre uniting both Russias into one. In this centre I was the mathematical point of unity."

It was precisely that straight line of demarcation running down the main aisle that drove a wedge into these foundations of unity, split the state organization into a right and left faction, and nullified the effects of that mid-July victory by transforming the final struggle into a three-cornered contest.

Adroitly, persistently, and with all the art of seasoned fishers in troubled waters, the underground Bolshevist emissaries undermined confidence in the coalition government and played on the quick suspicions and volatile emotions that flare into hot passion when nerves are frayed and quivering. They found an excellent target in that "mathematical centre of unity" provided by Kerensky, between the two opposing wings.

From his Finnish G. H. Q. in the hidden hut at Razliv,

ONE OF LENIN'S PROPAGANDISTS DISTRIBUTING LITERA-
TURE TO KERENSKY'S SOLDIERS, NOVEMBER 1917

Lenin poured revolutionary tracts into Petrograd; armed with his torrents of words, indefatigable lieutenants penetrated factories, workshops, and barracks, disseminating dissatisfaction and whispering seductive reasons for revolt against "the dictator, Kerensky" — "the servant of the bourgeoisie" — "the traitor to the working classes."

Winter was approaching with all its old hardships — and the enemy, too. On the first of September the Germans broke the Russian lines on the Dvina and threatened Petrograd. Mr. Kerensky decided to transfer the seat of government to Moscow and issued a proclamation to that effect. A storm of protest resulted and tension was increased. Then came the final blow, from within, from the Right, in the shape of the Kornilov uprising.

The inner history of this *cause célèbre* still remains obscure, although copious explanations are available, ranging from unqualified defense of the attempt by monarchist and bourgeois apologists to bitter denunciations of its folly by Kerensky. To the former, Kornilov is the incarnation of Russian patriotism, stabbed in the back by Mr. Kerensky, as he rose in one final, desperate effort to save the country from anarchy; to Mr. Kerensky, on the contrary, Kornilov is the villain in the piece, the last guard of reactionary monarchism whose treasonable thrust at Petrograd threatened the very life of the revolution and foreshadowed a restoration of the Tzarist régime. But to the Bolsheviki Kornilov was an open blessing, and his name should be a benediction; he engaged their chief adversary in civil war and raised a new, distracting issue while they stood, *tertium gaudens*, on the side lines sharpening their swords to slit the throat of the exhausted victor, whichever it might be.

It appertains to the historian of Russian military operations to unfold the complete record of that revolution within a revolution. In our account of the fall of the Provisional Government it is but an episode, though the last and most characteristic one, as it concentrates within itself all known elements of misunderstanding, distrust, indecision, compromise, and tactical blundering.

General Lavre Kornilov, a brave and popular Cossack officer, fifty years of age, had long been a heroic figure in public life, his popularity dating from the days of his captaincy, when, alone and in the disguise of a traveling merchant, he penetrated the contiguous buffer State of Afghanistan — forbidden then to foreigners — in quest of military information. It was said at Petrograd that he could speak eighteen of the languages that made Russia a polyglot empire. Appointed by Kerensky Commander in Chief of the Russian Armies, on August 1, 1917, the General rapidly became a symbol of nationalism and was presumably the one dominating personality capable of commanding the personal loyalty of the army at the front. His direct, soldierlike speech at the Moscow Conference still remains its outstanding feature and increased his prestige enormously, much to the annoyance of Mr. Kerensky. Around him from that day centred the conservative elements, army leaders, Constitutional Democrats, financiers, and the industrialists, all of whom sensed in Kerensky that perpetual conflict of will between his duties as head of the anti-Bolshevist movement and his known instincts as a Socialistic idealist.

At a Cabinet meeting held in Petrograd on August 16, the bluff and forthright General laid before the Ministers his views on the military situation, which was then none too hopeful. But he was prepared to attack along certain designated sectors where he believed his troops were sufficient and willing. It is related by E. H. Wilcox, a war-time correspondent in Petrograd, that when Kornilov reached the point of naming the specific sectors where he intended to launch his attack Kerensky leaned over to him and in a whisper advised that that question should be treated with caution. "Simultaneously," writes Wilcox, "Savinkov [Deputy Minister of

War] passed across to Kerensky a slip of paper on which was written, 'Is the President sure that our state secrets and those of the Allies communicated by Kornilov will not become known to the enemy by way of comradeship?'

"The effect which this incident had on Kornilov may be given in his own words : 'I was astounded and horrified that, at a sitting of the Council of Ministers of Russia, the Commander in Chief could not without danger touch on questions of which, in the interest of national defense, he thought it necessary to place the Government in cognizance.'"

The mutual distrust between the Premier and the Commander in Chief rapidly hardened into ill-concealed and reciprocated enmity. Kerensky, conceding the soldierly qualities of his own appointee, suspected him of ambitioning the Napoleonic rôle of dictator; Kornilov, schooled to direct action in camps and on firing lines, chafed at the dilatory tactics of the Premier and, spurred on by the Right, was all for crossing swords with the Bolsheviki and forcing a decision once for all. Two Russias were thus in the field, drawn up against each other at a moment when two equally determined foes were closing in on the Fatherland. Riga was taken by the Germans, and Lenin was soon to slip back to the scene of action, losing himself in the Viborg Quarter, Petrograd's *St. Antoine.*

The final rupture was hastened by the misunderstanding caused, deliberately or unintentionally, by Vladimir Lvov, who acted as Kerensky's delegate in the negotiations with the recalcitrant Commander in Chief. Sent by the Premier to Kornilov with an invitation to discuss various possibilities for ensuring order in the Capital, Lvov, according to the account published by Savinkov, laid three courses before Kornilov. The bluff General received the proposals in good faith as coming from Kerensky : —

1. Kornilov to form a Government, with Kerensky and Savinkov respectively Ministers of Justice and War.

2. A triumvirate, with dictatorial powers, composed of Kerensky, Kornilov, and Savinkov.

3. Kornilov to declare himself dictator.

Lvov, on returning to Petrograd on Saturday, September 8, reported to Kerensky *that Kornilov had decided on the third course and would declare himself dictator;* he furthermore informed Kerensky that Kornilov desired the Premier to come to Mohilev, the General Headquarters, as he wished Kerensky to serve as Minister of Justice under his Dictatorship, and Savinkov should accompany him, as it was desirable that he should serve as Minister of War. Kerensky interpreted this message as an ultimatum; Kornilov probably intended it merely as a proposal.

To assure himself of the authenticity of Lvov's report, Kerensky established telegraphic connections with Kornilov at the front. The record of this conversation, preserved on the ribbon of a Hughes recording instrument, is a valuable document revealing the curious formalism that had replaced frank confidence : —

KERENSKY: Here is the Minister-President Kerensky. He awaits General Kornilov.

KORNILOV: General Kornilov is at the apparatus.

KERENSKY: Greetings, General! At the telephone are Vladimir Nicolaievich Lvov and Kerensky. We beg you to confirm that Kerensky may act in conformity with the communication transmitted by Vladimir Nicolaievich.

KORNILOV: Greeting, Alexander Feodorovich! Greeting, Vladimir Nicolaievich! Once more confirming my sketch of the position of the country and the army as it appears to me, — a sketch made by me to Vladimir Nicolaievich, with the request that he would report it to you, — I again declare that the events of the past few days, and those which are becoming apparent, imperatively demand an absolutely definite decision within the shortest possible term.

KERENSKY: I, Vladimir Nicolaievich [Kerensky pretends Lvov

is now speaking], ask you: Is it necessary to carry out that definite decision as to which you requested me to inform Alexander Feodorovich only quite privately? Without this confirmation personally from you, Alexander Feodorovich hesitates to trust me fully.

KORNILOV: I confirm that I begged you to transmit to Alexander Feodorovich my urgent request to come to Mohilev.

KERENSKY: I, Alexander Feodorovich, understand your answer as a confirmation of the words communicated to me by Vladimir Nicolaievich. To-day it is impossible to do that and leave. I hope to leave to-morrow. Is Savinkov needed?

KORNILOV: I urgently beg that Boris Victorovich [Savinkov] should come with you. What I say to Vladimir Nicolaievich applies in like measure to Boris Victorovich. I fervently beg you not to postpone your departure beyond to-morrow. I beg you to believe that only my sense of the responsibility of the moment compels me to importune you.

KERENSKY: Should we come only in the event of the rising, of which rumors are in circulation, or in any case?

KORNILOV: In any case.

KERENSKY: Au revoir! We shall soon see one another.

KORNILOV: Au revoir!

It will be recalled that the Tzar, — also speaking from Mohilev, — once held an important conversation by telephone with the Tzarina, on the eve of his abdication. The decisions he took as a result of that *pourparler* made the Russian Revolution inevitable. So this parley between Kerensky and Kornilov was the prelude to Bolshevism. For, convinced that his own Commander in Chief intended to proclaim himself dictator, Kerensky, on September 9, sought and obtained authority from the Government to deprive Kornilov of his command and order him back to the Capital. On September 10 the morning papers of Petrograd published a proclamation from the Central Executive Committee of the All-Russian Soviet, declaring Kornilov a traitor to his country and the Revolution and calling on the army to resist his orders. The fat was in the fire, and the Provisional

Government added fuel to the flame; next day their official proclamation denounced Kornilov and, for the first time, used officially the word "treason."

Kornilov replied with his Orders of the Day, which he posted at Mohilev on September 10 and 11, in which he disclaimed all personal ambition, or intentions of a one-man dictatorship, or a projected restoration of the monarchy; but he refused to surrender to the Government, which had, he maintained, requested him, through Savinkov, to concentrate the Third Cavalry Corps in the environs of Petrograd. Furthermore, he recounted his belief that treasonable agencies in Petrograd "working for German money and exercising influence on the actions of the Government . . . intended to seize power, if only for a few days, and declare an armistice . . . take the decisive and irretrievable step toward the conclusion of a shameful peace, and consequently destroy Russia."

He ended by refusing to surrender his position and ordered General Krimov to advance with his "wild division" of Cossacks on Petrograd. Kerensky declared the Capital in danger of a counter-revolutionary attack, proclaimed a state of siege, brought in reënforcements of sailors from Kronstadt, and distributed arms to additional workmen's units, thereby increasing the power of the Red Guards. He was to hear the ironic barking of those rifles later — pointed in his own direction.

The advance of Krimov's Cossacks was a fiasco; hesitating between two masters, confused and perplexed by subtle agitators in their ranks, and finally convinced that they were but pawns in an unpopular game, they were turned back without a shot being fired. Krimov committed suicide; Kornilov was arrested and court-martialed.

But it was a barren victory for the Kerensky Government. New enemies were created and old foes strengthened. "General Kornilov," announced Lenin, "has opened for us

THE VICTOR IN THE KERENSKY-KORNILOV AFFAIR

quite unexpected perspectives. We must act at once."
The first action came on September 18, six days after Kornilov's failure, when the Petrograd Soviet swept out its Moderate and Menshevist members and put the Bolshevist faction
in supreme control. Trotsky was instructed to redouble his
efforts to win over the garrison troops. Hopeless chaos resulted within the Government as disorders, strikes, lockouts,
massacres of landowners, seizure of estates, breakdown of
transportation, and rumors of a bread famine developed in
waves throughout the country. Left alone by the increasing
resignation of his colleagues, Premier Kerensky resorted to
a Directorate in which he and the Minister of War, Verkhov-
sky, were the principal members, its mandate consisting in a
charge to conduct negotiations with all parties with a view to
a new coalition. The Soviet declined to recognize its authority and drove straight for its own unchanging goal — "all
power to the Soviet."

In the middle of September occurred that last futile
gesture by the Provisional Government, ordinarily lost sight
of in this confused and anarchic period of disintegration:
a Republic was declared on September 15 in order to assure
Russia that the Revolution had come to stay. This explains
the references to a subsequent "Council of the Republic"
which now begin to appear.

A General Congress of Soviets had been convoked by the
Bolsheviki for the month of November, and elections for the
Constituent Assembly had been announced by the Provisional Government for November 25; the first session was
scheduled for December 13. Lenin's strategy, however,
required him to anticipate both.

"It is necessary to seize power as soon as possible," he
wrote, "otherwise it will be too late. . . . History will
never forgive us if we do not take power now. . . . To wait
for a formal majority is naïve; no Revolution ever waits

for this. . . . We shall come out victorious without a doubt."

With his finger on the feverish pulse of the nation, he knew how much more persuasive it would be to confront both Congress of Soviets and Constituent Assembly with a *fait accompli* than with a petition for authority to execute a *coup d'état*. The date for the uprising was set for October 28, though technical difficulties caused a postponement. But not for long. On October 23 a German squadron penetrated the Gulf of Riga and engaged the remnants of the Baltic Fleet. The Provisional Government prepared to evacuate Petrograd; the Soviet press seized on the opportunity to shout "Treason!"

The Government is abandoning the Red Capital in order to weaken the Revolution. Riga has been sold to the Germans; now Petrograd is being betrayed.

Rodzianko, leader of the Right Wing of the Constitutional Democratic Party contributed to the irritation.

"Petrograd is in danger," he wrote. "I say to myself, 'Let God take care of Petrograd.' They fear that if Petrograd is lost the Central Revolutionary organization will be destroyed. To that I answer that I rejoice if all these organizations are destroyed; for they will bring nothing but disaster upon Russia. . . . With the taking of Petrograd the Baltic Fleet will also be destroyed. . . . But there will be nothing to regret; most of the battleships are completely demoralized."

The same night, the Bolshevist General Staff held a most important council of war. Present: Lenin, Trotsky, Zinoviev, Kamenev, Stalin, Sverdlov, Dzherzhinsky, Uritzky, Buvnov, Sokolnikov, Lamov, and two women, Kollontai and Yakovleva, the latter of whom acted as secretary: "Lenin arrived when all were present, and was beyond recognition [he still wore his Finland disguise]. Smoothly

shaved, in a wig, he resembled a Lutheran Minister. . . . I
was entrusted with keeping the secretarial minutes, but on
account of the conspiratory nature of the meeting they were
very brief."

The session lasted all night. The final resolution was
written in pencil by Lenin himself and reads as follows : —

The Central Committee recognizes that the international situation of the Russian Revolution (the mutiny in the German navy
and the extreme signs of growth throughout Europe of the universal
socialist revolution, finally the threat of peace among the imperial-
ists for the purpose of strangling the Russian Revolution) and the
military situation (the unquestionable decision of the Russian bourgeoisie and of Kerensky and Co. to surrender Petrograd to the
Germans), as well as the majority gained in the Soviets by the party
of the Proletariat, all this in connection with the peasant risings and
the turn of popular confidence toward our party (the elections in
Moscow) ; finally, the obvious preparation of a second Kornilov
stroke (the removal of the Petrograd Garrison, the dispatch of
Cossacks to Petrograd, the encircling of Minsk by Cossacks, and
so forth) — all this makes an armed revolt the question of the day.

Having recognized thus that an armed revolt is inevitable and
the time fully matured for it, the Central Committee proposes to
all the party organizations to be guided by this fact and to consider
and decide all questions (the conventions of the Northern Soviets,
the removal of the Petrograd Garrison, and the demonstration of
Moscow and Minsk Workers) from this viewpoint.

The execution of the revolt was committed to Trotsky,
and Lenin returned to his hiding place to continue work on
his pamphlet, *Will the Bolsheviki Retain Power?*

Mr. Kerensky, realizing that the fate of the Provisional
Government was sealed, counted his forces — and made a
serious miscalculation. He relied on the Cossack troops,
whose loyalty was traditional, but was deceived. They had
already declared their neutrality — they had not forgotten
that Kornilov was a Cossack — and the last pin was knocked

from under the already tottering régime. But one hope remained — the army in the field. The sequel proved that on this count Kerensky was equally deceived.

His decision to leave Petrograd in a last effort to mobilize sufficient troops outside the city to justify battle with the Bolsheviki has exposed his next move to the scorn of his adversaries. They describe it as "flight," and his "temporary absence" as "abandonment of his post." The accounts of his exit from the city on November 7 are obscure. His own version follows : —

I do not know how it happened, but the news of my proposed departure reached the Allied Embassies. Just as we were about to leave, representatives of the British and, as far as I can remember, of the American Embassy arrived saying that the Allied envoys desired that I be accompanied by an automobile flying the American flag. Although it was more than evident that the American flag could not save me and my companions in the event of our failure, and that, on the contrary, it would only attract unnecessary attention to our passing through the city, I accepted the suggestion as evidence of the interest of the Allies in the Russian Provisional Government and their solidarity with it.

Shaking hands for the last time with Kishkin, who took upon himself the direction of the defense of the Capital in my absence, I went out into the yard of the Staff Building, together with my companions. We entered my car. Close at hand was the American machine. One of my officers, unable to find room in my car, decided to travel alone, but on the condition that in passing through the city he was to keep his machine, flying the American flag, at a respectful distance from ours. Finally we moved. We followed closely all the details of my daily travel through the city. I occupied my usual seat — on the right. I wore my customary semimilitary uniform, which had become so familiar to the population and to the troops. The automobile moved at the usual city speed.

A somewhat different version is given by Mr. Francis, the American ambassador : —

Photo by Arnold Genthe, N. Y.

ALEXANDER KERENSKY

Shortly after receipt of this message [a routine communication from the Foreign Office], Secretary Whitehouse rushed in in great excitement and told me that his automobile, on which he carried an American flag, had been followed to his residence by a Russian officer, who said that Kerensky wanted it to go to the front. Whitehouse and his brother-in-law, Baron Ramsai, who was with him, accompanied the officer to General Headquarters in order to confirm his authority for making this amazing request. There they found Kerensky — the Headquarters are across the square from the Winter Palace, where he lived, surrounded by his staff. Everyone seemed to be in a high tension of excitement and all was confusion. Kerensky confirmed the officer's statement that he wanted Whitehouse's car to go to the front. Whitehouse asserted: "This car is my personal property and you have (pointing across the square to the Winter Palace) thirty or more automobiles waiting in front of the Palace." Kerensky replied: "Those were put out of commission during the night and the Bolsheviki now command all the troops in Petrograd except some who claim to be neutral and refuse to obey my orders."

Whitehouse and Ramsai, after a hurried conference, came to the proper conclusion that, as the car had virtually been commandeered, they could offer no further objection. After they had left the Headquarters, Whitehouse remembered the American flag, and, returning, told the officer who had originally asked for the car that he must remove the American flag before using the car. He objected to doing this, and after some argument Whitehouse had to be content with registering a protest against Kerensky's use of the flag, and left to report the affair to me.

In the face of this perplexity the present writer can do no more than fall back upon the phrase of a certain commentator on the French Revolution: "Il n'est rien de plus honorable pour un historien que de dire, ' Je ne sais pas.' "

Through the Moscow toll gate at breakneck speed Mr. Kerensky flies, headed for Gatchina, twenty-nine miles from Petrograd, leaving the firing and manœuvring Bolshevist troops behind. Then follows a mad hunt for loyal troops, supposedly en route from Mohilev to Gatchina, in answer

to the Premier's appeals for help. But the local commandant of the town knows nothing of their arrival. . . . Thence
to Pskov, — some hundred miles and more away, — under a
shower of bullets from an automobile flying a Red flag; a
tire is pierced and the chauffeur wounded. At Pskov, the
general in command replies coldly that he is not inclined to
associate his fate with a "doomed Government." He adds
incisively that he cannot be responsible for Mr. Kerensky's
life if he remains longer in the vicinity. . . . At last General Krassnov reluctantly supplies a paltry force of six
hundred Cossacks and a few cannon. . . . It was the
handwriting on the wall.

Returning to Gatchina with his corporal's guard of the
Imperial Russian Army, Kerensky finds himself faced by a
new and ominous condition. General Krassnov's attitude
changes and his replies become evasive. The reënforcements
from the front? They were either on the way or about to
leave. And would Mr. Kerensky please not remain on the
battlefield. . . . His presence was interfering with the military operations . . . and disturbing the officers. . . . Mr.
Kerensky, looking about, notices that the Cossacks are
forever "saddling their horses," but never advancing.

After thirty-six hours of agony, during which some slight
reënforcements dribble through from the front, light dawns
on Mr. Kerensky. He has been trapped! Gatchina had
become his Philippi where the memory of Kornilov hung
over the Cossack tents. He writes a farewell letter to M. D.
Avksentiev, President of the Council of the Republic, transferring to him the rights and duties of Premier of the Provisional Government; then in company with one loyal aide,
Lieutenant Vinner, he shuts himself in one of the upper
chambers, — there were six hundred rooms in the Palace, —
prepared to "settle accounts with life by means of our revolvers. At that time, on the morning of November 14, 1917,
this resolve seemed quite simple, logical, and inevitable."

Below stairs the Cossacks are bargaining with the Bolsheviki as to the terms on which they will turn over their prisoner. While the conditions are being arranged, two unknown and unidentified figures, a soldier and a sailor, slip into the room where Kerensky and Lieutenant Vinner are waiting for the end; they hand Mr. Kerensky a sailor's coat, a sailor's hat, and a pair of automobile goggles. This "masquerade attire" strikes Mr. Kerensky as supremely ridiculous; when clothed in it he remarks, "I certainly do look ludicrous." But it serves; one of the unknown rescuers whispers that an automobile is waiting at the Egyptian Gates. After a passage of breathless suspense across an open space, — where another unknown friend faints and falls to the ground in order to distract the attention of a suspicious guardsman, — the automobile is located. A moment later, as a delegation of Cossacks mounts the stairs to deliver to the victors the price of their amnesty, Mr. Kerensky is safely on his way to Paris, London, and New York.

On November 7, Lenin, still disguised, — his face bandaged with a large handkerchief as if suffering from a toothache, — enters the Bolshevist Headquarters in the Smolny Institute, leaving the street fighting to his Field Marshal, Trotsky. The members of the Provisional Government are bombarded out of the Winter Palace and imprisoned, one after another, in the Fortress of St. Peter and St. Paul; the Women's Battalion has made its last, ineffectual stand, and the students of the Military Academy, refusing to surrender, are overwhelmed and hundreds of them massacred by the Red Guards.

CHAPTER XVI

A REVERY ON THE ROAD FROM GATCHINA

THE central character in the story now finished—the advent
of the Bolshevist régime marks the opening of a new tragedy
—has every right to sympathetic and understanding consideration by the critics as he makes his hurried and unheroic exit.
There will be little applause and much execration, even from
his colleagues in the losing struggle with the Soviet, who may
complain that he should have remained at his post until the
end and not escaped through a side entrance. That particular insinuation would, I am convinced, be unjust, as there
is no evidence thus far available to convict Mr. Kerensky
either of cowardice or of duplicity. He was the victim of a
conjunction of superior forces that rose like a tidal wave and
tossed him and his government into the discard. But there
is considerable ground for laying many fundamental and
far-reaching blunders to his charge, some of which were the
results of his own impetuous choice, others imposed upon him
by circumstances which he could neither control nor dominate. The pity is that so much depended on one man's
judgment in a crisis when so many Russians — the Bolsheviki alone excepted — suffered from a paralysis of the
intuitive faculties. Mr. Kerensky had no lieutenants or
counselors capable of matching wits with the Machiavellian Cabinet that surrounded Lenin. Mussolini doubtless
learned much wisdom from observation of the Russian Revolution and dared mightily. Had he flinched, there might
have been a second Russia in Italy to-day.

In the first place, I believe Kerensky was miscast for a rôle which was, however, practically of his own choosing. His antecedents as a professed revolutionary of socialistic tendencies naturally drew him into the first Soviet, if not by political choice, at least by instinctive sympathy. As a consequence, during the period of uncertainty which followed the disappearance of the Tzar's government, his personal allegiance was cast as much with the self-appointed Soviet as with the Provisional Government. It was pure rhetoric for any single party to assume to speak in the name of the Russian people; the nation, politically dumb for centuries, had not yet spoken — except in one thundering shriek of exultation at finding itself free. Least of all did it give a mandate to the 45,585 members who composed the Bolshevist Party in early 1917.

That Kerensky's stand would have great weight with public opinion is attested by the fact that it was largely his influence that caused the Grand Duke Michael to refuse the throne after the abdication of his brother, and issue his own renunciation.

The appearance, then, at such a critical moment, of an alternative government claiming equal jurisdiction with the Duma was the first deadly blow at national unity, so essential under the circumstance. If Mr. Kerensky had fathomed the psychology and the predominantly anarchic tendencies of his own people, he would have hesitated long before lending his person to a policy of challenge that eventually divided the country hopelessly. Freed from the age-old control of the *tchinovniki*, the broad masses of the people found themselves in a mood to experiment with their new and unaccustomed liberty. With no political training, without competent federal or municipal administrators, at the mercy of every silver-tongued orator, however radical or destructive, they fell an easy prey to demagogy. It seems to me, therefore, that it was an initial blunder on Mr. Kerensky's part to have remained a member of the competing Soviet, much less to have sponsored its creation, particularly as he held a seat in the Duma as the elected representative of a constituency in Saratov.

The five days from March 10 to March 15 were the most critical period in the history of modern Russia, and the direction which the state organization took during those days was to determine in a large measure the ultimate destiny of its people. The only legal depository of power and the sole executive entrusted with a popular mandate was the Duma, and it would seem that all farsighted men should have strengthened in every possible way the principle of legitimate authority as concentrated in that Assembly. The local Soviets could claim no more legal competency than might the Club of the Nobles or any similar private organization. Their claim to represent the working masses of Russia was seriously challenged by other revolutionary parties; but their voice prevailed, simply and solely because their leaders had the shrewdness and will-power to impose their programme on less organized though equally representative groups of citizens. They dared to be strong before the nation could make up its mind who was right.

Mr. Kerensky defends his adhesion to the Soviet and his participation in its activities on the ground that the Duma had virtually ceased to function and had practically abdicated its leadership by dissolving at the command of the Tzar. Although, technically, the Duma may be said to have dissolved, in reality it never accepted the ukase of the Tzar and never actually dispersed. In point of fact, the authority of the Tzar had actually vanished, and his ukase was, to my way of thinking, absolutely void and harmless. The Duma, therefore, furnished the only basis of organized control then visible in Russia. In fostering the Soviet, in actually providing a room in which its members might meet, and by retaining his membership in both parliaments, Mr.

Kerensky attempted to ride two horses, neither of which was trained or inclined to run with the other. The catastrophe which followed was inevitable.

The second fatal mistake — not so much Mr. Kerensky's as that of the Provisional Government as a whole — was the ill-advised speech of Milyukov, with its claims for territorial annexations and its demand for the ultimate restoration of Constantinople to Russia. It was a mistake in psychology, as it missed entirely the state of mind prevailing among the people, war-worn and fatigued as they were, and unwilling to listen to any further imperialistic programmes. Better psychologists and more in touch with the realities, the Bolsheviki turned this pronouncement of the Foreign Minister into a strong argument for the overthrow of the Government. It must, however, in justice be said that Mr. Kerensky opposed this pronouncement, and his opposition led to the first crisis in the new Government.

The blame for Prikaz Number One, the order which destroyed discipline at the front and paved the way for the progressive demoralization of the army, was undoubtedly a prime cause leading to disunion and disaffection among the troops. Here again Mr. Kerensky disavows both responsibility and participation. The blame, according to his explanation, is to be placed exclusively at the door of the Soviet. However, reverting to my first contention, Mr. Kerensky as a leading member of the Soviet when this order was issued cannot be absolved from at least a proportionate blame for the disastrous effects which followed.

But whether or not the presence of Mr. Kerensky in the councils of the Soviet can fairly be interpreted as coöperation and condonation, he did at least have an unparalleled opportunity to suppress the menace entirely after the July uprising. He was never stronger and the Bolsheviki were never in greater discredit. Fully conscious, as he must then have been, of the ultimate goal and destructive programme of the Soviets, he yet found it possible to release all his Bolshevist prisoners in a moment of exuberance and permit them to return to their underground activities. Questioned by the present writer as to his reasons for not taking drastic action at that time, the ex-Premier insisted that the emotional and nervous state of the population cannot be left out of consideration. One of the first acts of the triumphant Revolution was to abolish the death penalty so often applied by the previous Government. How would it have been possible, he argued, to impose the ultimate punishment during those first months of freedom when men were ready to die to show their abhorrence of Tzaristic practices? Such an act would have shocked and probably alienated the masses from the new Government!

The explanation is an interesting example of an ingrained Russian characteristic which is prone to fasten on the opposite extremes of conduct. There is a wide range of colors lying between the red at the end of a rainbow and the modest violet with which the spectrum begins. Mr. Chesterton, in mild satire, puts his finger on the same fact when he introduces into one of his essays a Russian who explains quite simply that he was obliged to kill his sister because her boots squeaked. The golden middle was never a favorite ground for Russian philosophy or Russian politics. Believing it inadvisable to apply the death sentence to the mutineers, — though in time of war they had struck at the very heart of the existing Government, — Mr. Kerensky proceeds to the opposite end of the possibilities and lets them all go scot-free. He must have known that they would have been the first to apply drastic measures to himself and to the whole Government, if the fortunes of war had placed them in the saddle. More than one student of Russian affairs regards this act of exaggerated clemency as a fatal error on the part of the

Provisional Government, which should have taken protective measures to prevent the further activities of these avowed counter-revolutionaries. This does not mean that execution was inevitable, but that imprisonment and safekeeping were advisable.

Was it not another error to have postponed so long the convocation of the Constituent Assembly? Against that free expression of the popular will not even Lenin's magic could have prevailed. That master of divination knew as much; he anticipated the date of the elections and launched his *coup de surprise* before the Assembly came into existence. When it did convene, he quietly sent the delegates back home — at the point of a bayonet.

The July offensive must also be enumerated among the contributory causes leading to the final disaster. To be sure, extraordinary pressure was brought to bear on Mr. Kerensky by the Allies, who urged him to give a practical proof of Russia's solidarity with the war aims of the Entente. That solidarity and loyalty could, they argued, be best demonstrated by an offensive along the whole Russian front. We know that Mr. Kerensky responded to this idea with his usual ardor and inexhaustible energy. It is an open question, however, if he could not have served Russia better by plain talk to Sir George Buchanan and the other Allied ambassadors, who demanded the offensive. Here was a country which had suffered more than any other combatant through war casualties, moral bankruptcy, and domestic revolt. Not only the army, but the rear guard of every army, the civil population, was sick unto death and weary of suffering. To this must be added the administrative chaos that reigned within the country, where the collapse of the old régime had progressed so fast and so completely that no new machinery of government had as yet been substituted. For the nation to live, it was imperative that its vital organs should first be strengthened. Instead, tremendous losses were inflicted, discontent revived, and additional reasons provided for the Bolsheviki to demand a change of government. All that Mr. Kerensky could offer the troops was a renewal of warfare and a very shadowy hope of victory. But in case of defeat the most elemental political foresight might have prophesied exactly the revulsion which followed.

Then came the Kornilov affair; the scales sank — on the left side, as confidence in Mr. Kerensky's leadership evaporated on the right. He missed entirely the *status quæstionis*. He imagined the issue to lie between himself and Kornilov. He was wrong; the people chose neither the one nor the other, but voted, constructively, for Lenin. The merits of the defense set forth by the parties to that historic dispute must await the decision of impartial Time; but it would appear, even in the limited perspective of ten years, that Mr. Kerensky's divided allegiance — one half to Socialism and one half to a strong national government — weakened his powers of judgment. In any case, the results of that unfortunate misunderstanding destroyed his already tenuous hold on the popular imagination, and opened the way for the flight from Gatchina.

The pursuit continues; but the fugitive automobile draws farther and farther away, as the "friendly" chauffeur of the pursuing car suddenly discovers that his engine has "broken down."

As the tumult and the shouting dies, it becomes possible — at least for a nonpartisan observer — to disentangle the confused and intertwined causes of success and failure, in an endeavor to strike a balance between wisdom and folly.

Our conclusions are no reflection on Mr. Kerensky's valor, but on his statesmanship. And even in that capacity he

can fairly offer, as he disappears from the scene, Macbeth's
defense : —

> Who can be wise, amazed, temperate and furious,
> Loyal and neutral, in a moment? No man.

For eight weary months Russia had been on the auction
block. Lenin, nearer to the soil from which armies and electors are recruited, offered an alluring programme of peace,
land, bread, ownership of factories, and supreme political
power for the proletariat. Kerensky's appeal for popular
support was more nebulous, because less daring. His government, in the eyes of the impatient masses, stood for none
of these fundamental necessities, despite the fact that a cred-
itable array of basic reforms, civic, industrial, and agrarian,
had been sponsored and many of them actually introduced by
the Provisional Government. But his intent could not be
clothed in the colorful language of his opponent. His rule
suffered from the inevitable limitation which conscience and
a sense of responsibility impose on dominant parties, but
which a desperate minority ignores when unrestrained by
moral or legal scruples. As morality and legality are of
" bourgeois origin," the pragmatic Bolshevik, rejecting both,
enters every contest with an immense advantage over all
comers.

The experience of the Provisional Government was a confirmation of certain historical analogies. How often has it
happened in the past — it will probably happen again —
that a small and relatively insignificant proportion of a population has swept out an honest but irresolute majority by
appealing nakedly to primitive instincts and elemental
passions? Did not the power once before descend from a
Mirabeau to Danton, to Carrier, to Marat, and finally to
Robespierre and Fouquier-Tinville, each of them of a deeper
red than his predecessor? So in Russia the control passed
from Lvov and Milyukov to Kerensky, and then was

wrested from his hand by Lenin and Trotsky and Felix Dzherzhinsky.

In 1789, as Paul Bourget reminds us, the Parliamentary theorists and Rules-of-Order experts spent the month of November wrangling endlessly over the most perfect type of Constitution. Should there be one chamber or two? Should the King have the right to a veto? And, if he had, should it be absolute or merely suspensory? They deliberated and voted and deliberated on the vote. In the meantime, Paris starved; the red days of October dawned, and the merciless logic of Madame Guillotine put a sharp end to the debates and the debaters.

The harangues of the Duma spellbinders were protracted without end in 1917, until, as Sorokin assures us, the orators dropped in their places, asleep. Kerensky himself was no exception. Indeed, as one foreign diplomat, then resident in Petrograd, puts it, "The only real Kerensky was the orator. Only when speaking did he exist — then he was Cæsar to himself and the throng . . . he spoke more and more, until at last he spoke all the time: from windows, from balconies and church doors, from automobiles and at theatres, for ministers, diplomats, delegations, soldiers, man and beast."

While the Duma orators slept and Mr. Kerensky perorated, Lenin mounted Kshesinskaia's balcony and repeated his five stereotyped words: "Bread, land, peace, factories, power." It was meaty diet for stomachs that had been starved politically for three centuries, and terminated in delirious outbursts of collective psychosis.

And as for the Kornilov affair, did not that ill-starred adventure have historical precedents in the attempts of Lafayette and Dumouriez?

Mr. Kerensky's car slows down and stops. . . . Cautiously he explores the surrounding country with that penetrating look which, even to-day, arrests every eye that encounters it. . . . No one in sight. . . . He alights and disappears into the woods.

It is all over now — and astonishingly clear how and why it happened.

Lenin had simply outbid him, and Russia had dropped into his adversary's lap like an overripe apple. That plot of land by the Volga was immeasurably more enticing to the Russian moujik than six feet of earth under alien skies in a graveyard on the slopes of the Carpathian Mountains. Those factories in Petrograd promised better life by far to the workmen than the finest prison camp in Germany. And the shirt of the Russian soldier, patched and verminous though it might be, lay closer to its owner's heart than any hypothetical mantle of glory promised in the name of the Allies.

APPENDICES

APPENDIX I

LETTER OF THE EXECUTIVE COMMITTEE OF THE RUSSIAN REVO-
LUTIONARY PARTY TO THE PEOPLE OF THE UNITED STATES

EXPRESSING its profound sympathy for the American people, on the
occasion of the death of President James Abram Garfield, the
Executive Committee regards it as its duty to declare in the name
of the Russian Revolutionists its protest against such acts of
violence as that of Guiteau. In a land where personal freedom
gives an opportunity for an honest conflict of ideas, where the
free will of the people determines not only the law but also the
personality of the ruler, in such a land political murder as a means
of struggle presents a manifestation of that despotic spirit which
we aim to destroy in Russia. Personal despotism is as condem-
nable as group despotism and violence may be justified only when
it is directed against violence.

(*Signed*) THE EXECUTIVE COMMITTEE

September 10 (23), 1881

APPENDIX II

The following are a few sections from the "Rules Relating to the Measures for the Preservation of National Order and Public Tranquillity," approved by Alexander III on the 14th of August, 1881, and promulgated in an Imperial Command on the 4th of September of the same year.

Section 5. (*a*) When public tranquillity in any locality shall be disturbed by criminal attempts against the existing imperial form of government, or against the security of private persons and their property, or by preparations for such attempts, so that, for the preservation of order, a resort to the existing permanent laws seems to be insufficient, then that locality may be declared in a state of reinforced safeguard.

(*b*) When by reason of such attempts the population of a certain place shall be thrown into a state of alarm which creates a necessity for the adoption of exceptional measures to immediately reëstablish order, then the said place may be declared in a state of extraordinary safeguard.

Section 15. Within the limits of such places (places declared to be in a state of reinforced safeguard) governors-general, governors, and municipal chiefs of police may (*a*) issue obligatory ordinances relating to matters connected with the preservation of public tranquillity and the security of the Empire, and (*b*) punish by fine and imprisonment violations of such ordinances.

Section 16. Governors-general, governors, and municipal chiefs of police are authorized also (*a*) to settle by administrative process cases involving violation of the obligatory ordinances issued by them; (*b*) to prohibit all popular, social, and even private meetings; (*c*) to close temporarily, or for the whole term of reinforced safeguard, all commercial and industrial establishments; and (*d*) to prohibit particular persons from residing in places declared to be in a state of reinforced safeguard. (Remark. — Banishment to a specified place, even to one's native place, with obligatory residence there, will be allowed only after communication with the Minister of the Interior. Rules for such banishment are set forth in Sections 32–36.)

SECTION 32. The banishment of a private person by administrative process to any particular locality in European or Asiatic Russia, with obligatory residence there for a specified time, may not take place otherwise than with an observance of the following rules:

SECTION 33. The proper authority, upon becoming convinced of the necessity for the banishment of a private person, shall make a statement to that effect to the Minister of the Interior, with a detailed explanation of the reasons for the adoption of this measure, and also a proposition with regard to the period of banishment. (Remark. — The preliminary imprisonment of a person thus presented for exile to a specified place may be extended, by authority of the Minister of the Interior, until such time as a decision shall be reached in his case.)

SECTION 34. Presentations of this kind will be considered by a special council in the Ministry of the Interior, under the presidency of one of the Minister's associates, such council to consist of two members from the Ministry of the Interior and two members from the Ministry of Justice. The decisions of this council shall be submitted to the Minister of the Interior for confirmation.

SECTION 35. While considering presentations for exile the above-mentioned council may call for supplemental information or explanations, and in case of necessity, may summon for personal examination the individual nominated for banishment.

SECTION 36. A period of from one to five years shall be designated as the term for continuous residence in the assigned place of exile. (Remark. — The term of banishment may be shortened or lengthened, in the manner prescribed in Section 34, within the limits set by section 36.)

The following are the sections of the Russian penal code under which political offenders are prosecuted when brought before the courts: —

SECTION 245. All persons found guilty of composing and circulating written or printed documents, books, or representations calculated to create disrespect for the Supreme Authority, or for the personal character of the Gossudar (the Tzar), or for the Government of his Empire, shall be condemned, as insulters of Majesty, to deprivation of all civil rights, and to from ten to twelve years of penal servitude. (This punishment carries with it exile in Siberia for what remains of life after the expiration of the hard-labor sentence.)

SECTION 249. All persons who shall engage in rebellion against the Supreme Authority — that is, who shall take part in a collective and conspirative insurrection against the Gossudar and the Empire ; and also all persons who shall plan the overthrow of the Government in the Empire as a whole, or in any part thereof; or who shall intend to change the existing form of government, or the order of succession to the throne established by law ; all persons who, for the attainment of these ends, shall organize or take part in a conspiracy, either actively and with knowledge of its object, or by participation in a conspirative meeting, or by storing or distributing weapons, or by other preparations for insurrection — all such persons, including not only those most guilty, but their associates, instigators, prompters, helpers, and concealers, shall be deprived of all civil rights and be put to death. Those who have knowledge of such evil intentions, and of preparations to carry them into execution, and who, having power to inform the Government thereof, do not fulfil that duty, shall be subjected to the same punishment.

SECTION 250. If the guilty persons have not manifested an intention to resort to violence but have organized a society or association intended to attain, at a more or less remote time in the future, the objects set forth in Section 249, or have joined such an association, they shall be sentenced, according to the degree of their criminality, either to from four to six years of penal servitude, with deprivation of all civil rights (including exile in Siberia for life) . . . or to colonization in Siberia (without penal servitude), or to imprisonment in a fortress from one year and four months to four years.

These sections, it will be observed, are tolerably comprehensive. They not only include all attempts to overthrow the Government *vi et armis;* they not only cover all action "calculated to create disrespect for Majesty"; but they provide for the punishment of the mere intention to bring about a change of administration, at a remote time in the future, by means of peaceable discussion and the education of the people. Even this is not all. A man may be perfectly loyal; he may never have given expression to a single thought calculated to create disrespect for the Gossudar, or the Gossudar's Government; and yet, if he comes accidentally to know that his sister, or his brother, or his friend belongs to a society which contemplates a "change in the existing form of government," and if he does not go voluntarily to the chief of gendarmes and betray that brother, sister, or friend, the law is adequate to send him to Siberia for life.

From George Kennan's *Siberia and the Exile System*

APPENDIX III

BY fundamental conviction we are socialists and democrats. We are satisfied that only through socialistic principles can the human race acquire liberty, equality, and fraternity; secure the full and harmonious development of the individual as well as the material prosperity of all; and thus make progress. We are convinced that all social forms must rest upon the sanction of the people themselves, and that popular development is permanent only when it proceeds freely and independently, and when every idea that is to be embodied in the people's life has first passed through the people's consciousness and has been acted upon by the people's will. The welfare of the people and the will of the people are our two most sacred and most inseparable principles.

A

1. If we look at the environment in which the Russian people are forced to live and act, we see that they are, economically and politically, in a state of absolute slavery. As laborers they work only to feed and support the parasitic classes; and as citizens they are deprived of all rights. Not only does the actual state of things fail to answer to their will, but they dare not even express and formulate their will; they cannot even think what is good and what is bad for them; the very thought that they can have a will is regarded as a crime against the state. Enmeshed on all sides, they are being reduced to a state of physical degeneration, intellectual stolidity, and general inferiority.

2. Around the enchained people we see a class of exploiters whom the state creates and protects. The state itself is the greatest capitalistic power in the land, it constitutes the sole political

oppressor of the people, and only through its aid and support can the lesser robbers exist. This bourgeois excrescence in the form of a government sustains itself by mere brute force — by means of its military, police, and bureaucratic organizations — in precisely the same way that the Mongols of Genghis Khan sustained themselves in Russia. It is not sanctioned by the people, it rules by arbitrary violence, and it adopts and enforces governmental and economical forms and principles that have nothing whatever in common with the people's wishes and ideals.

3. In the nation we can see, crushed but still living, its old traditional principles, such as the right of the people to the land, communal and local self-government, freedom of speech and of conscience, and the rudiments of federal organisation. These principles would develop broadly, and would give an entirely different and a more popular direction to our whole history, if the nation could live and organize itself in accordance with its own wishes and its own tendencies.

B

1. We are of opinion, therefore, that it is our first duty, as socialists and democrats, to free the people from the oppression of the present Government, and bring about a political revolution, in order to transfer the supreme power to the nation. By means of this revolution we shall afford the people an opportunity to develop, henceforth, independently, and shall cause to be recognized and supported, in Russian life, many purely socialistic principles that are common to us and to the Russian people.

2. We think that the will of the people would be sufficiently well expressed and executed by a national Organizing Assembly, elected freely by a general vote, and acting under the instructions of the voters. This, of course, would fall far short of an ideal manifestation of the people's will; but it is the only one that is practicable at present, and we therefore think best to adopt it. Our plan is to take away the power from the existing Government, and give it to an Organizing Assembly, elected in the manner above described, whose duty it will be to make an examination of all our social and governmental institutions, and remodel them in accordance with instructions from the electors.

C

Although we are ready to submit wholly to the popular will, we regard it as none the less our duty, as a party, to appear before the people with our programme. This programme we shall use as a means of propaganda until the revolution comes, we shall advocate it during the election campaign, and we shall support it before the Organizing Assembly. It is as follows:

1. Perpetual popular representation, constituted as above described and having full power to act in all national questions.

2. General local self-government, secured by the election of all officers, and the economic independence of the people.

3. The self-controlled village commune as the economic and administrative unit.

4. Ownership of the land by the people.

5. A system of measures having for their object the turning over to the laborers of all mining works and factories.

6. Complete freedom of conscience, speech, association, public meeting, and electioneering activity.

7. Universal right of franchise, without any class or property limitation.

8. The substitution of a territorial militia for the army.

We shall follow this programme, and we believe that all of its parts are so interdependent as to be impracticable one without the other, and that only as a whole will the programme ensure political and economic freedom and the harmonious development of the people.

D

In view of the stated aim of the party its operations may be classified as follows:

1. *Propaganda and agitation.* Our propaganda has for its object the popularization, in all social classes, of the idea of a political and democratic revolution as a means of social reform, as well as popularization of the party's own programme. Its essential features are criticism of the existing order of things, and a statement and explanation of revolutionary methods. The aim of agitation should be to incite the people to protest, as generally as possible,

against the present state of affairs, to demand such reforms as are
in harmony with the party's purposes, and, especially, to demand
the summoning of an Organizing Assembly. The popular protest
may take the form of meetings, demonstrations, petitions, leading
addresses, refusals to pay taxes, etc.

2. *Destructive and terroristic activity.* Terroristic activity consists in the destruction of the most harmful persons in the Government, the protection of the party from spies, and the punishment
of official lawlessness and violence in all the more prominent and
important cases in which such lawlessness and violence are manifested. The aim of such activity is to break down the prestige of
governmental power, to furnish continuous proof of the possibility
of carrying on a contest with the Government, to raise in that way
the revolutionary spirit of the people and inspire belief in the
practicability of revolution, and finally, to form a body suited and
accustomed to warfare.

3. *The organization of secret societies and the arrangement of
them in connected groups around a single centre.* The organization
of small secret societies with all sorts of revolutionary aims is
indispensable, both as a means of executing the numerous functions
of the party and of finishing the political training of its members.
In order, however, that the work may be carried on harmoniously,
it is necessary that these small bodies should be grouped about one
common centre, upon the principle either of complete identification
or of federal union.

4. *The acquirement of ties, and an influential position in the
administration, in the army, in society, and among the people.* The
administration and the army are particularly important in connection with a revolution, and serious attention should also be
devoted to the people. The principal object of the party, so far
as the people are concerned, is to prepare them to coöperate with
the revolution, and to carry on a successful electioneering contest
after the revolution — a contest that shall have for its object the
election of purely democratic delegates to the Organizing Assembly.
The party should enlist acknowledged partisans among the more
prominent classes of the peasantry, and should prearrange for the
active coöperation of the masses at the more important points and
among the more sympathetic portions of the population. In view

of this, every member of the party who is in contact with the people must strive to take a position that will enable him to defend the interests of the peasants, give them aid when they need it, and acquire celebrity among them as an honest man and a man who wishes them well. In this way he must keep up the reputation of the party and support its ideas and aims.

5. *The organization and consummation of the revolution.* In view of the oppressed and cowed condition of the people, and of the fact that the Government, by means of partial concessions and pacifications, may retard for a long time a general revolutionary movement, the party should take the initiative, and not wait until the people are able to do the work without its aid.

6. *The electioneering canvass before the summoning of the Organizing Assembly.* However the revolution may be brought about — as the result of an open revolution, or with the aid of a conspiracy — the duty of the party will be to aid in the immediate summoning of an Organizing Assembly, to which shall be transferred the powers of the Provisional Government created by the revolution or the conspiracy. During the election canvass the party should oppose, in every way, the candidacy of *kulaks* of all sorts, and strive to promote the candidacy of purely communal people.

APPENDIX IV

"You have spoken, and your words are at present known everywhere in Russia; aye, in the whole of the civilised world. Until now you were unknown, but since yesterday you have become a definite factor in the situation of your country, about whom there is no room left for senseless dreams. We do not know whether you understand or realise the position which you have yourself created with your 'firm words,' but we believe that people whose position is not so high as yours, or so remote from the realities of life, and on that account are able to see what is going on in Russia just now, will easily understand what is your position and what is theirs.

"First of all, you are badly informed about these tendencies against which you decided to raise your voice in your speech. There has not been heard in one single assembly of any zemstvo one single word against that autocracy which is so dear to your heart; nor has one member of a zemstvo ever put the question on the basis upon which you have placed it. The most advanced thinkers among them have only insisted upon — or, rather, humbly begged — that a closer union might be inaugurated between the Monarch and his people; for the permission for the zemstvos to have free access to the Throne without anyone standing between it and them; for the right of public debate, and for the assurance that the law should always be observed and stand above the caprices of the Administration.

"In one word, the only thing that was in question was the desire to see fall and crumble to the ground that wall of bureaucracy and courtierdom that has always parted the Sovereign from the Russian nation.

"This was the desire of these people whom you, who have only just stepped upon the Throne, inexperienced and ignorant of the national needs, have seen fit to call 'senseless dreams.'

"It is clear to all the intelligent elements of the Russian people who has advised you to take this imprudent step. You are being deceived; you are being frightened by this very gang of bureaucrats and courtiers to whose actual autocracy not one single Russian man or woman has ever been reconciled. You, too, have reproached the zemstvos for the feeble cry that has escaped their lips against the tyranny of the bureaucracy and of the police.

"You have allowed yourself to be carried so far in your ideas of protecting that autocracy — your own — against which no one thought of rising, that you have considered as a danger thereto the participation of the zemstvos in the government of the country as well as of local needs.

"Such a point of view does not correspond even to that position in which the zemstvos have found themselves confirmed by your father's wishes; a position in which they appear as an indispensable organ, and participate in the internal government of the country.

"But your unfortunate expressions are not only a mistake in the way in which you have worded them, but appear as the definition of a whole system of government; and Russian society will understand quite well that on the 17/30th January it was not at all that ideal autocracy of which you believe yourself to be the representative that spoke through your mouth, but that omnipotent and jealous guardian of its privileges, *bureaucracy*.

"This bureaucracy, which begins with the committee of Ministers and ends with the meanest policeman, is odious to all those who desire the extension of real autocracy, even the one that is maintained by the present order of things. This it is that keeps the Monarch removed from free communion with the representatives of the nation. And your speech has proved once more that every desire on the part of the nation to be other than slaves kissing the ground before the Throne and bring to its notice the needs of the country — the most urgent needs — in a submissive form, is only met with a brutal rebuff.

"Many fundamental questions concerning the welfare of the nation have yet to be placed upon a satisfactory basis. Questions of moment have arisen since the great epoch of reforms initiated by your grandfather, and these lately have come to the front more acutely owing to the great famine which has weakened the country.

"Russian public opinion has been, and is, working hard, and with painstaking efforts, towards the solution of these; and it is just at such a time that, instead of words of comfort promising a real and beneficial union between the Tzar and his people, and of an acknowledgment from the heights of the Throne that for the future public discussion and a strong upholding of the law will mark the beginning of a new era in the public life of the country — the representatives of the different classes of society, gathered before you from all the corners of Russia, and expecting from you help and consolation, only heard from you a new expression of your attachment to the old system of a worn-out autocracy, and carried away the impression of the total separation of the Tzar from his people.

"Do believe, that even for the mildest of men, such a declaration, ill-timed as it was, could only produce a crushing feeling of betrayal. The 17th January has done away with that halo with which so many Russians had crowned your young inexperienced head. You have laid your own hand on your popularity, and have destroyed it.

"Unfortunately, the question does not touch your popularity alone. If in words and with deeds autocracy identifies itself with the all-powerful bureaucracy; if its existence is only possible when every expression of the public need is crushed, and it can live only when surrounded by an extra guard of police, then indeed it has outlived its time and lost the game. It has dug its own grave with its own hands, and sooner or later, but at all events at a none too distant period, it will fall under the weight of the real and vital forces of the nation. You have yourself by your own words and conduct put before society one clear question, which in itself alone is a terrible threat to the system of autocracy. You challenged not only the zemstvos but also the whole of Russian society to a mortal duel, and they have now nothing left them except to choose deliberately between a forward movement in the cause of civilisation or a blind obedience to autocracy. Truly, you have strengthened by your speech the detective-like proclivities of those who see the only possibility of serving their Sovereign in the crushing of every expression of public feeling and in disregard of the law. You have appealed to the enthusiasm of those who are ready to give their services to every kind of master, and who do not give one single thought to the public welfare, finding that tyranny serves their own narrow-minded views.   But you have turned against you all those who want to lead the country forward in the road of progress and civilisation.

"And what will become of all those who are unable to reconcile themselves with the concessions required from them, and with a long and mostly hopeless struggle with the present order of things ? After your sharp reply to the most humble and lawful demands that have been addressed to you, by what and through what means will Russian society be able to keep in quiet submission to your will those of its members who wish to proceed, further and further, on that road which leads to the amelioration of the nation's fate ? Yet this is the impression created for Russian public opinion and the Russian people by your first words to it, and your first reply as a Sovereign to the humble demands of its representatives.

"Without mentioning the feelings of discouragement and help-lessness of which you will very soon be convinced, your speech offended and revolted some who, however, will soon recover from their present depression and will begin a peaceful, quiet, but none the less determined struggle to obtain the liberties which they require.

"Likewise it has strengthened in others the determination to fight to the bitter end against a hateful order of things, and to fight it with all means they may have at their disposal and in their power.   You have been the first to begin the struggle, and it will not be long before you find yourself entangled by it.

"St. Petersburg, *January* 19th, 1895"

APPENDIX V

His friend Isvolsky recounts the various attempts made on his life

THE dissolution of the Duma gave the signal for a return to terrorism, and it was decided that it should be inaugurated by a most conspicuous deed of violence. On Saturday, the twenty-fifth of August, about three o'clock in the afternoon, a formidable explosion destroyed a part of the villa occupied by M. Stolypin on the islands. The Prime Minister was not injured, but some thirty people were killed and as many more wounded, several of them seriously, among these, two of M. Stolypin's children.

I was in town at the time, receiving at the Ministry of Foreign Affairs a visit from M. Nitroff, Master of the Court of the Grand Duke Wladimir, who had requested him to consult me on some matter of the protocol. This business being finished, I detained my visitor, whose artistic taste I knew and appreciated, about a half hour longer, in order to show him certain interior decorations that were in progress in the palace of the Ministry. After leaving me, M. Nitroff was to go to the residence of the Prime Minister on some other commission entrusted to him by the Grand Duke, and so it happened that this accidental delay saved him from the explosion at M. Stolypin's villa, where he would otherwise have arrived a few minutes before the catastrophe.

Informed by telephone of what had happened, I jumped into my carriage at the door of the Ministry, and in twenty minutes reached the scene of the disaster, the horror of which passed all description. About a third of the villa was blown to pieces, and if the destruction was not more complete it was only because the house had been built of wood; a stone or brick structure would have been entirely demolished and the number of victims would have been that much more numerous. Partly buried under piles of beams and wreckage one could see human bodies, some inanimate, while others still gave signs of life. Here and there were shreds of clothing and torn and bleeding limbs; cries of anguish and calls for help wrung the heart; before the entrance a shapeless mass of wood and twisted iron and the carcasses of two horses were all that was left of the equipage which had brought there the perpetrators of the horrible deed. Literally nothing remained of the vestibule and the three rooms on the ground floor leading to that occupied at the time by M. Stolypin; as if by a miracle the effect of the explosion terminated at the threshold of the Prime Minister's workroom. I found him in a little pavilion in the garden, pale, but quite calm and self-controlled, giving orders in a quiet voice for the succor of the wounded, among whom one of his daughters, a girl of fifteen years, had just been discovered. He himself had rescued his only son, four years of age, from a pile of débris with his own hands. He told me how he had been about to put his foot on the heap of plaster and splinters when he caught sight of a child half buried under it and recognized his son. The little boy was not seriously hurt, but his daughter's condition was very grave; she had been given such first aid as was possible, and the arrival of the distinguished surgeon Pavloff, who had been summoned by telephone, was anxiously awaited.

Among those killed were a former provincial governor, a marshal of the nobility, Colonel Schults, chief of police of the Tauride Palace, and a few others of high rank, but the majority of the victims were either police agents or humble petitioners, among whom was a poor woman in an advanced state of pregnancy, horribly *éventrée*. The force of the explosion was such that the trees along the banks of the Neva were uprooted and all the windowpanes in the houses on the opposite bank were shattered. For hundreds of meters round about were scattered the mangled remains of human limbs and bits of clothing, torn and stained with blood.

. . . On Sunday I arrived at Peterhof, where I was to breakfast with the Emperor; on leaving the train I perceived a great stir on the station platform, and found that the body of General Minn, who, as commanding officer of the Semenovsky regiment, had played a principal rôle in the repression of the Moscow revolt, had just been brought to the station. The General was killed by a woman, who fired repeated shots with a revolver and, when arrested upon the spot, warned the police not to jostle her because she was carrying a bomb, to have been used in case General Minn had escaped the revolver. The bomb, which was of the size and shape of a sardine box, was taken from her, placed carefully on a bench, and guarded by two policemen. A subsequent examination proved that it contained a very powerful explosive, the discharge of which would have produced terrible havoc.

. . . A group of terrorists were arrested by the police at the very moment that they were to carry it out, their plan being to launch a superb red automobile of German make, loaded with deadly explosives, at full speed against a door of the Winter Palace leading to the apartments of the Prime Minister. If this plot had not been discovered in time the destruction would have been formidable.

In order to give some idea of the excessive nerve of M. Stolypin I will mention here an episode which did not take place until three years later, but which is very characteristic of the entire period. He was present, together with several members of the Cabinet, at one of the first aviation trials in Russia, made by a group of pilots just returned from France, where they had learned to fly. One of the aviators begged M. Stolypin to go up with him, and his comrades joined enthusiastically in the request, declaring that they would all feel greatly encouraged by such proof of confidence in their skill. M. Stolypin, without a moment's hesitation, accepted the invitation of the pilot, an officer by the name of Matzievski, and accompanied him in a flight which lasted for about half an hour. When he landed he found all the police in a state of tremendous excitement, and with good reason, for information had been received a few days before to the effect that Lieutenant Matzievski belonged to one of the most dangerous terrorist organizations. M. Stolypin had cognizance of that information before going to the aerodrome, and when he consented to ascend with Matzievski he knew perfectly well to what a strange companion he was entrusting his life. On leaving the field he congratulated his pilot warmly and expressed himself as delighted with the experience. Shortly after, this incident had an unexpected epilogue. In the course of a flight Lieutenant Matzievski fell from a great height and was instantly killed. The cause of the accident was inexplicable, for the pilot had been seen to fall separately from the machine, which showed no trace of having sustained any damage before crashing to the ground.   This led to the firm conviction on the part of the police that Matzievski had committed suicide, and that this fate had been imposed by the terrorist committee as a punishment for having let the chance escape of doing away with M. Stolypin.

All these details, incredible as they may appear, were fully confirmed to me by M. Stolypin himself.   When I asked him why he had risked his life without necessity and with full knowledge of the danger incurred, he replied, after thinking a moment:

"I am inclined to believe that it was an instinctive act on my part but I recollect also having said to myself that they must on no account be allowed to think that I am afraid of them.   Besides," he added, "before I took my seat in the machine I looked squarely in the eyes of Lieutenant Matzievski, and saw plainly that he would not dare.   In fact, it is quite possible that it was the spirit of the sportsman, in love with his art, that prevailed over him at that moment, rather than that of the terrorist."

It was not until the 14th of September, 1911, after escaping a series of attempts upon his life, that M. Stolypin finally met his death at Kieff, having received several pistol shots during a theatrical representation at which the Emperor and all the Imperial Court were present. . . .

Nevertheless, as the assassinations became more and more frequent, and it was necessary to provide for the worst, I took pains to arrange so that the affairs of my Department need not suffer any interruption in case of my disappearance; a sealed envelope, lying upon my desk, contained all the necessary instructions to enable my eventual successor to enter upon his duties without delay. This precaution turned out to be quite superfluous; in spite of the sinister predictions of the secret police, I was never personally an object of terrorist attack.   I came very near, however, being the victim of a plot against the Grand Duke Nicholas, afterward commander-in-chief of the Russian armies in 1914.   It was on my return from Tzarskoei-Selo, the summer residence of the Court, where I had been to make my weekly report to the Emperor.   The Grand Duke Nicholas had also gone there that same day, and instead of returning to St. Petersburg in his special train he stayed to dinner with the Emperor. So it happened that I took his place in the empty train, and just before it arrived at St. Petersburg station the engine driver noticed a person putting something on the track and then running away. He brought the train to a sudden stop, only a few turns of the wheels from the infernal machine, the explosion of which would have destroyed not only the train, but a good portion of the railway station. This incident confirmed me in my fatalism, and I have never regretted refusing to be bothered with the protection of a police service which M. Stolypin never succeeded in completely reforming and whose agents, as was proved by M. Bourtzeff's revelations of the double rôle played by the notorious Azeff, were sometimes no less dangerous than the avowed terrorists. The murder of M. Stolypin appears to have been committed by one of those agents, who served and betrayed in turn, and even simultaneously, both the police and the revolutionaries.

The list of higher functionaries alone who met death at the hands of the terrorists during this period is too long to be related. The murder of General Minn was quickly followed by those of General Count Ignatieff, General Kozloff, General von der Launitz, Prefect of St. Petersburg, the Governors of Warsaw, Samara, Penza, the Commandant of the Black Sea Fleet, etc.

The terrorists carried out their plans with the utmost audacity, and contemplated willingly the sacrifice of their own lives when that was necessary to ensure success. For instance, a woman, who was arrested in the street where she was waiting to kill the Grand Duke Nicholas, wore a sort of jacket containing a considerable quantity of dynamite, which she intended, but lacked the time, to explode in case the Grand Duke escaped the shots of her revolver. I was a witness of two assassinations and was able to judge the *sang-froid* that characterized the terrorists' operations. General Kozloff was killed in the most frequented part of the Peterhof park, a few steps from the wing of the old Palace, where I had an apartment, and I saw the murder from my window. The poor General, who was a most retiring and harmless person, had the misfortune to resemble in appearance General Trépoff, whom the assassin really aimed to destroy. General von der Launitz, prefect of the capital, fell at my very side, after receiving a number of shots as we came away from the inaugural ceremony at the Pasteur Institute in St. Petersburg.

The Council of Ministers, held in the evening of August 25th, after the explosion at the town residence of the Prime Minister, was of great moment. M. Stolypin opened it with an address, in which he began by declaring in the most energetic manner that the attack upon him, which had barely missed depriving him of his children, could not influence in the slightest degree his political course; pitiless repression of all disorders and all revolutionary or terrorist acts; carrying into effect, with the help of the next Duma, a far-reaching plan of reforms in the direction of liberalism; immediate solution of the most urgent problems by executive decrees and, first of all, a settlement of the agrarian question. M. Stolypin added that we must expect the reactionary party to profit by the occasion and make it a pretext for inciting the Emperor to proclaim a military dictatorship, and even to annul the charter of 1905 and return to the old régime of absolute power. He announced that he would oppose with all his strength any such reaction and, rather than abandon his constitutional course, he would resign his office. He ended by expressing the hope that his colleagues would support him whole-heartedly in his effort to hold the Emperor to his word.

APPENDIX VI

The Empress and Rasputin

The exhaustive analysis made by Sir Bernard Pares for *Foreign Affairs* (October 1927) establishes beyond shadow of doubt the supremacy of Rasputin's influence over both Emperor and Empress. The following compilation from the pen of Sir Bernard appeared after the manuscript of the present work had been completed.

1915

Apr. 4. "Our Friend is shocked at the style of N.N." (the Grand Duke).

6. He though the Tsar should not have visited Galicia till after the War.

10. He is "rather disturbed about the meat stores."

May 11. He spends two hours with Bark (Minister of Finance).

Jun. 10. He says the second class of recruits should not be called in. The Empress adds, "Hearken unto Our Friend."

11. He is against the assembling of the Duma.

12. She objects to Polivanov, the new War Minister. "Is he not Our Friend's enemy? That brings bad luck." Rasputin likes Shakhovskoy (Minister of Trade). "Can influence him for good." He "begs most incessantly" for a one-day's prayer-giving to be ordered by the Tsar without the Synod. She adds "Be more autocratic, my very own sweetheart."

15. Message from Rasputin to the Tsar: "You are to pay less attention to what people say to you, not let yourself be influenced by them. They know much less than you . . . ." The Empress adds: "He regrets you did not speak to him more about all you think and were intending to do."

16. "Think more of Gr. (Gregory): ask Him to intervene before God to guide you right."

17. Rasputin begs to postpone the Duma.

18. Of Samarin, Procurator of the Holy Synod: "He is an enemy of Our Friend's and that is the worst thing there can be."

24. The Premier (Goremykin) is to tell Samarin and Shcherbatov (Minister of Interior) how they are to behave to Rasputin.

Aug. 22. Rasputin, after the replacement of the Grand Duke: "The worst is over."

28. He tells the Tsar to set free criminals and send them to the front.

29. He desires more munition factories. "Khvostov (candidate for Minister of Interior) spoke justly and well about Our Friend" (Khvostov told Rodzianko he intended to discredit Rasputin by making him drunk).

Sep. 7. She sends a list of possible successors to Samarin. Guriev (one of them) "likes Our Friend."

8. She asks to put Pitirim on the Synod. "He venerates Our Friend."

15. "Comb your hair with His comb" when about to receive the Ministers.

17. She recommends General Shvedov for Procurator, "He calls Our Friend Father Gregory."

Oct. 3. Rasputin begs the Tsar to telegraph to the King of Serbia. She adds "so I enclose a paper . . . put the sense in your words." Rasputin condemns the new stamp money. She will tell Bark.

8. Rasputin says the Grand Duke cannot be successful (in the Caucasus) "for going against Him." (On Sept. 19 Rasputin sent a message "There is little sunshine in the Caucasus.")

10. "He says you must give an order that waggons with flour, butter and sugar should be allowed to pass": no other trains for 3 days. He "saw the whole thing in the night in a vision." This is done.

Nov. 1. Rasputin is "very grieved at Trepov's nomination"

(as Minister of Commerce) "as He knows he is very against Him." "Our Friend was always against the war, saying the Balkans were not worth troubling to fight about."

8. "Our Friend is anxious to know . . . about your plans for Rumania." He dictates the course to be followed with Rumania and Greece, walking about and crossing himself. Gives his plans for the march into Constantinople.

10. Rasputin has recommended the dismissal of the Premier (Goremykin). Now he asks the Tsar to wait till He has seen the elder Khvostov "to form his impressions" of him as a possible successor.

12. He pushes Pitirim "as the only suitable man" for Metropolitan. He proposes Zhivakhov as Assistant Procurator of the Synod.

13. He spends 1½ hours with the Empress: tells the Tsar to wait as to the Premier "according to God." He suggests a surprise visit of the Tsar to the Duma to avert scandals (this is done later).

15. "Prompted by what He saw in the night," he bids an advance near Riga. He "says it is necessary: begs you seriously; says we can and we must."
He bids Tsar summon the Duma if there is no victory at the front. Tell the Premier to feign illness and let the Tsar make a surprise visit, though "He loathes their existence as I do for Russia." The Empress adds: "I feel sure you will agree to Gregory sooner than to the old man" (the Premier, who is her own choice).

Dec. 2. Among his instructions is one that "He cannot exactly remember, but He says that one must always do what He says."

16. "Always the first place for Gregory" (when entertained at Pitirim's).

19. She suggests Tatishchev as successor to Bark; he "knows and venerates Our Friend: hates Guchkov and those Moscow types."

22. Rasputin says "no more fogs would disturb."

31. He says, "always pay attention to the weather."

1916

Jan. 4. She recommends Stürmer for Premier (done).

6. Rasputin "regrets you began that movement (at the front) without asking Him." She sends "a petition from Our Friend, it is a military thing."

7. Rasputin says Stürmer (his protégé) is not to change his German name. She sends a budget of his requests.

30. Rasputin and the Empress urge Ivanov for Minister of War *vice* Polivanov.

Feb. 1. Rasputin objects to Obolensky (in charge of food supplies).

5. The Tsarevich ill. He says "it will pass in two days."

Mar. 4. "Remember about (dismissing) Polivanov."

6. Rasputin on a responsible Ministry: "It would be the ruin of everything."

12. She writes imploring the dismissal of Polivanov, "Lovey, don't dawdle." She receives the Tsar's consent and adds: "Oh, the relief." She objects to Ignatiev, Minister of Education.

13. She questions the Tsar's new choice for War Minister, Shuvaiev.

14. Rasputin is for Ivanov. She adds "In that He is certainly right."
The Synod has proposed to create 7 Metropolitan Sees. "Our Friend begs you not to agree."

15. "I wish you could shut up that rotten War Industries Committee."

Apr. 1. Ivanov appointed as military adviser at headquarters. Rasputin is pleased.

25. Rasputin on the trial of Sukhomlinov: "It is a bit not well."

May 23. He "begs very much not to name Makarov Minister of Interior."

Jun. 4. He "begs not yet strongly advance in the North."

5. "Our Friend says it is good for us that Kitchener died . . . as later he might have done Russia harm."

9. Rasputin wishes the Tsar to come for two days to Petrograd. She forwards 5 first-class requests transmitted to

her from him : prorogue the Duma ; dismiss Obolensky ; give the food supply to the Minister of Interior : don't thank the zemstvo Red Cross; the fifth request Mme. Vyrubov has forgotten. The Empress asks for a telegram, "Agree to your questions." She proposes a milder judge to try Sukhomlinov. Rasputin hopes "there will be a great victory, perhaps at Kovel," and wants Sukhomlinov then amnestied.

16. Rasputin is against the augmented tram prices. He wishes the Empress to take Mme. Vyrubov with her to headquarters (she does so).

17. He "predicts fatal results" if the 7 Metropolitan Sees are created.

18. He begs the Tsar to be "very firm with the Ministers."

25. The Empress wants Raiev as Procurator of the Synod.

Jul. 16. She protests at the nomination of Makarov (Minister of Justice : the Tsar's choice). "I must have Our Friend guaranteed against them."

24. Rasputin is against further advance.

Aug. 4. He objects to the liberation of the Slavonic prisoners of war (Poles, Czechs, Serbs, etc.). He "begs you to be very severe with the Generals," and to put off calling the recruits till September 1. He intervenes as to the supply of aeroplanes.

8. He warns against advance over the Carpathians.

9. He has a long talk with the Premier (Stürmer), and tells him to report to the Empress weekly.

13. The Empress recommends Raiev for Procurator and Beliayev for Minister of War (both done later).

18. Message from Rasputin : "A bad tree will fall whatever be the axe that cuts it."

Sep. 4. "Do not hurry with the Polish affair (the promised autonomy) . . . our full trust in Our Friend's wisdom endowed by God." (This advice is followed.)

6. "Our Friend would have liked to take the Rumanian troops in hand to be surer of them."

7. He says "all will be right." He "begs very earnestly to name Protopopov as Minister of Interior." She adds

"He likes Our Friend at least 4 years." He wishes an announcement of the promise of the Allies as to Constantinople: "then they must keep their word after." "About Poland he begs you to wait. Do listen to Him: He has more insight than all of them."

9. "Please take Protopopov."

14. "God bless your new choice of Protopopov."

15. He says, change Obolensky.

16. He tells the Tsar not to worry if he finds he has dismissed Generals wrongly.

17. He is given the military plans so as to pray over them. He sends a "paper."

18. The Empress asks the exact date of attack for the above reason.

19. She rejects all the Premier's (Stürmer's) candidates for Chief of Police; she tells him to "hurry up and think again."

21. "Since Catherine no Empress has received the Ministers . . . Gregory is delighted." "God inspires him and to-morrow I'll write what He said."

22. He says the food supply will go right. He advises to call up the Tatars to the army. Sukhomlinov "should not die in jail. . . . Otherwise things will not be smooth."

23. Rasputin is "very satisfied with Father's orders (*i.e.* from the Tsar to Brusilov)."

28. Obolensky abases himself to Rasputin and begs to be Governor-General of Finland.

29. "Did you remember about mobilising the Tatars?"

Oct. 14. "Tell him (Protopopov) to go on seeing Gregory."

16. Rasputin advises to call up young men, not old.

26. He says that when asked about Polish autonomy the Tsar is to answer, "I do all for my son, will be pure before my son."

30. She countermands, on her own authority, an order of Protopopov (on the food supply) because "Our Friend said it was absolutely necessary." Rasputin says: "Protopopov will finish off the Unions (zemstvo and town Red Cross) and by that save Russia." She describes

their wish for a responsible ministry as "colossal impudence."

31. He says the Sukhomlinov trial must be "absolutely stopped." "All my trust lies in Our Friend." The profiteer Rubinstein must be "at once" released.

Nov. 3. Message from Rasputin. "Calm papa. Write that everything will be right." She asks again for Rubinstein.

7. Rasputin and Protopopov want the Premier (Stürmer) to be "rested."

9. Rasputin says Stürmer can go on.

10. The Tsar, however, has dismissed Stürmer altogether. She is shocked. "Thanks for Sukhomlinov." Rasputin wants a new Minister of Communications (Trepov is now Premier).

11. Trepov has asked for the dismissal of Protopopov. The Empress writes to save Protopopov. "He venerates Our Friend and will be blessed."

12. "It is the question of the monarchy and your prestige . . . You were alone with us two" (herself and Rasputin).

Dec. 4. Rasputin has prophesied great times coming for the Tsar and Russia. "Our Friend's dreams mean so much."

5. "He has kept you where you are." "He entreats for Makarov (Minister of Justice) to be quicker changed." "The good is coming — the turn has begun."

8. She urges Shcheglovitov for President of the Council of State (done later). "Only have the Duma cleverly shut."

10. She begs to withdraw the case against the swindler Manuilov which is brought "to harm Our Friend." "Change Makarov." She has seen Dobrovolsky.

13. He "*entreats* you to be *firm*, to be the master, and we must give a strong country to Baby . . . I your wall am behind you . . . It is all getting calmer and better . . . Russia loves to feel the whip. . . . I am strong, but listen to me which means Our Friend."

14. "Be Peter the Great, John the Terrible, Emperor Paul, crush them all under you . . . now don't you laugh, naughty one . . . I could hang Trepov (the Premier) . . . Disperse the Duma at once. Milliukov, Guchkov,

and Polivanov also to Siberia.   My duty as wife and mother, and Russia's mother, blessed by Our Friend."

15. "Thanks so much for Manuilov."

16. "They touch all near me.   Sweep away the dust and dirt" (the Opposition majority in the very Conservative Council of State).

17. "Our Friend has disappeared.   Such utter anguish. Am calm and can't believe it."   (Rasputin had been assassinated.)

APPENDIX VII

Ivan the Terrible

In his first fit of rage, several great boyars, of the family of Rurik, were put to death by beheading, poisoning, or impaling; their wives and ch'ldren were driven, naked, into forests, where they expired under the scourge. In a second paroxysm, he marched as a conqueror against the subjugated Novgorod, and, imagining that he imitated, or perhaps surpassed, the victory of his grandfather, he butchered with his own hand a throng of the unfortunate inhabitants, whom he had heaped together in a vast enclosure; and when, at last, his strength failed to second his fury, he gave up the remainder to his select guard, to his slaves, to his dogs, and to the opened ice of the Volkof, in which, for more than a month, those hapless beings were daily engulphed by hundreds. Then, declaring that his justice was satisfied, he retired; seriously recommending himself to the prayers of the survivors, who took special care not to neglect obedience to the orders of their terrestrial deity.

Tver and Pskof, also, experienced his presence; Moscow, at length, saw him again, and on the same day the public square was covered by red hot brasiers, enormous cauldrons of brass, and eighty gibbets. Five hundred of the most illustrious nobles, already torn by tortures, were dragged thither; some were massacred amidst the joyful acclamations of his savage satellites; but the major part of them expired under the protracted agony of being slashed with knives by the courtiers of the Muscovite monster.

Neither were women spared any more than men; Ivan ordered them to be hanged at their own doors; and he prohibited their husbands from going out or in without passing under the corpses of their companions, till they rotted and dropped in pieces upon them. Elsewhere, husbands, or children, were fastened dead to the places which they had occupied at the domestic table, and their wives, or mothers, were compelled to sit, for days, opposite to the dear and lifeless remains.

To the dogs and the bears, which this raging madman delighted to let loose upon the people, was left the task of clearing the public square from the mutilated bodies wh'ch encumbered it.[1] Every day he invented new modes of punishment, which his tyranny, jaded by so many excesses, still looked upon as insufficient. Very soon, he required fratricides, parricides! Basmanoff was compelled to kill his father; Prozorovsky, his brother. The monster next drowned eight hundred women; and, rummaging with atrocious cupidity the abodes of his victims, he, by dint of shocking tortures, compelled their remaining relations to point out the places in which their wealth was hidden. These confiscations, joined to monopolies, taxes, and conquests, accumulated in his palace the riches of the empire and of the Tatars. To this he joined those of the Livonians, whom he plundered, though he could not conquer them.

In his long and fruitless wars against the Livonian knights, his transient successes were marked by frightful executions. The courageous resistance which the enemy opposed to him was, in his eyes, a revolt, and he ordered his prisoners to be thrown into boiling cauldrons, or spitted on lances, and roasted at fires which he himself stirred up.

Setting himself above all laws, this lustful being married seven wives; even his daughter-in-law was forced to fly from his death-bed, terrified by his lasciviousness. He was eager to procure an eighth wife from the court of his friend Elizabeth of England, and the daughter of the Earl of Huntington was offered to the inspection of the Russian ambassador at her own desire and the queen's. The daughter of Henry VIII was not shocked to hear at the same moment of the czar's wish to be married and of the birth of a prince borne to him by his seventh living wife; but before the English match was concluded Mary Hastings took fright, and begged Elizabeth to spare her the perilous honour. To complete Ivan's usurpation, he assumed the manner of one who was inspired, and all those external signs which our bounded imagination attributes to the Divinity; he made himself god in the minds of his people.

---

[1] According to the annals of Pskof, there were sixty thousand victims at Novgorod alone.

All that came from his hand, blows, wounds, even the most degrading treatment, was received with resignations — nay, with adoration. In the blind and servile submission of the Russian People God and the czar were identified; their proverbial sayings bear witness to this; and to the influence of things and men was joined that of words, the power of which is more durable than is commonly imagined.

Finally, in a humble supplication, which was addressed to him by the most faithful of his subjects, his frenzy again saw a conspiracy of the boyars, of which the eldest of his three sons, and the only one who was capable of succeeding him, was to be the leader; transported with rage, the madman felled to the earth, with a mortal blow from his ironbound staff, this hope of his race, to expire himself soon after (1584), consumed by regret without remorse, and giving orders for new executions.

From Kelly's *Compilation of Karamsin, Tooke, and Ségur* (London, 1854).

APPENDIX VIII

A BANQUET WITH PETER THE GREAT

*Being the description of an imperial feast in the days of Peter
the Great, and sent by a foreign ambassador as a
confidential report to his home government*

"THERE are twenty-four cooks belonging to the kitchen of the
Russian court, who are all Russians, and as people of that nation
use a great deal of onions, garlic, and train oil in dressing their
meat, and employ linseed and walnut oil for their provisions, there
is such an intolerable stink in their kitchen that no stranger is able
to bear it, especially the cooks being such nasty fellows, that the
very sight of them is enough to turn one's stomach; these are the
men who, on great festivals, dress about seventy or eighty or more
dishes. But the fowls which are for the czar's own eating are very
often dressed by his grand marshal, Alseffiof, who is running up and
down, with his ap on before him, among the other cooks till it is
time to take up dinner, when he puts on his fine clothes and full-
bottomed wig, and helps to serve up the dinner. The number of
persons invited is generally two or three hundred, though there is
room for no more than above a hundred at four or five tables; but
as there is no place assigned to anybody, and none of the Russians
are willing to go home with an empty stomach, everybody is
obliged to seize his chair and hold it with all his force, if he will
not have it snatched from him.

"The czar being come in, and having chosen a place for himself,
there is such scuffling and fighting for chairs, that nothing more
scandalous can be seen in any company, though the czar does not
mind it in the least, nor does he take care for putting a stop to such
disorder, pretending that a ceremony, and the formal regulations of
a marshal, make people sit uneasy and spoil the pleasure of conversation. Several foreign ministers have complained of this to the

czar, and refuse to dine any more at court, but all the answer they got was, that it was not the czar's business to turn master of the ceremonies, and please foreigners, nor was it his intention to abolish the freedom once introduced; this obliged strangers for the future to follow the Russian fashion, in defending the possession of their chairs, by cuffing and boxing their opposer. The company thus sitting down to table without any manner of grace, they all sit so crowded together, that they have much ado to lift their hands to their mouths, and if a stranger happens to sit between two Russians, which is commonly the case, he is sure of losing his stomach, though he should have happened to have eat nothing for two days before. Carpenters and shipwrights sit next to the czar; but senators, ministers, generals, priests, sailors, buffoons, of all kinds, sit pell-mell without any distinction. The first course consists of nothing but cold meats, among which are hams, dried tongues, and the like, which, not being liable to such tricks as shall be mentioned hereafter, strangers ordinarily make their whole meal of them, without tasting anything else, though generally speaking, every one takes his dinner beforehand at home.

"Soups and roasted meats make the second course, and pastry the third. As soon as one sits down, one is obliged to drink a cup of brandy, after which they ply you with great glasses of adulterated Tokay, and other vitiated wines, and between whiles, a bumper of the strongest English beer, by which mixture of liquors every one of the guests is fuddled before the soup is served up. The company being in this condition, make such a noise, racket, halloing, that it is impossible to hear one another, or even to hear the music, which is playing in the next room, consisting of a sort of trumpets and cornets, for the czar hates violins, and with this revelling noise and uproar the czar is extremely diverted, particularly if the guests fall to boxing and get bloody noses.

"Formerly the company had no napkin given them, but instead of it they had a piece of very coarse linen given them by a servant, who brought in the whole piece under his arm, and cut off half an ell for every person, which they are at liberty to carry home with them, for it had been observed that these pilfering guests used sometimes to pocket the napkins; but at present two or three Russians must make shift with but one napkin, which they pull

and haul for, like hungry dogs for a bone. Each person of the
company has but one plate during dinner, so if some Russian does
not care to mix the sauces of the different dishes together, he pours
the soup that is left in his plate either into the dish or into his
neighbour's plate, or even under the table, after which he licks his
plate clean with his finger, and, last of all, wipes it with the table-
cloth. The tables are each thirty or forty feet long, and ten and a
half broad; three or four messes of one and the same course are
served up to each table; the dessert consists of divers sorts of
pastry and fruits, but the czaritsa's table is furnished with sweetmeats; however, it is to be observed that these sweetmeats are
only set out on great festivals for a show, and that the Russians of
the best fashion have nothing for their dessert but the produce of
the kitchen-garden, as peas, beans, &c., all raw. At great entertainments it frequently happens that nobody is allowed to go out
of the room from noon till midnight, hence it is easy to imagine
what pickle a room must be in, that is full of people who drink like
beasts, and none of them escape being dead drunk.

"They often tie eight or ten young mice in a string, and hide
them under green peas, or in such soups as the Russians have the
greatest appetite to, which sets them a kicking and vomiting in a
most beastly manner, when they come to the bottom and discover
the trick; they often bake cats, wolves, ravens, and the like, in
their pastry, and when the company have eaten them up, they tell
them what they have in their guts.

"The present butler is one of the czar's buffoons, to whom he has
given the name of Wiaschi, with this privilege, that if any one
else calls him by that name, he has leave to drub him with his
wooden sword. If, therefore, anybody, by the czar's setting them
on, calls out Wiaschi, as the fellow does not know exactly who it
was, he falls a beating them all round, beginning with prince
Mentchikof and ending with the last of the company, without ex-
cepting even the ladies, whom he strips of their head clothes, as he
does the old Russians with their wigs, which he tramples upon, on
which occasion it is pleasant enough to see the variety of their
bald pates. Besides these employments or entertainments, the
said Wiaschi is also surveyor of the ice, and executioner for tor-
turing people, on which occasion he gives them the knout himself,

and his dexterity in the business has already procured him above thirty thousand thalers, the sixth part of the confiscated estates of the sufferer being his perquisite."

From Kelly's *Compilation of Karamsin, Tooke, and Ségur* (London, 1854).

APPENDIX IX

BEFORE we part with Peter I, it remains for us to complete our view of his personal character and habits by some further details, which could not well have found an earlier place on these pages without inconveniently breaking the course of the narrative.

A retail shopkeeper of St. Petersburg would hardly content himself at this day with the paltry wooden hut which Peter built for himself when he was laying the foundation of his capital. Its whole furniture consisted of a bed, a table, a chair, a lathe, and some books and papers. In the shortest days of winter, which are but seven hours long in that latitude, he always rose at four o'clock in the morning, and lighted his own fire; and at six he was to be found at the senate or the admiralty. When he went out it was generally on foot, or in a hackney sledge, and he sometimes borrowed of the first passer-by the money to pay the fare.

He dined at one o'clock. At his table, which was usually a frugal one, nothing came amiss to him except fish, which this naval monarch could never bear. His favourite food was such as was eaten by the people. He ate little, but often, wherever he might chance to be, and no matter with whom; and he drank to excess. The czars his predecessors admitted to their table only the ministers of foreign powers, the patriarch, and such of the grandees as they desired to honour by a distinguished mark of their favour; seated too on a throne, they ate at a separate table. Dutch and English skippers were Peter's favourite boon companions. With a clay pipe in his mouth and a mug of quass in his hand, he was "hail fellow" among them, and swore as roundly as any of them.

Peter's usual dress was as coarse as his domestic economy, and such as suited the manual occupations to which he was addicted. Many a time he was seen working with his own hands in the manufactories he had established. He often piloted the foreign vessels that came to Cronstadt, and he always received, like other pilots, the pay of a service which he was desirous to render honourable. On one occasion, having been compelled by the state of his health to stop at a foundry, he for some hours became a smith. On his return to Moscow, he went to the master of the foundry, and inquired what he paid his workmen. "Well, then," said he, "at that rate I have earned eight altins (about thirteen pence), and I am come for the money." Having received it, he said that "with this sum he would buy himself a new pair of shoes, of which he was in great want." This was very true; and he hastened to the market to make his purchase, which he afterwards felt a pleasure in wearing. "See what I earned by the sweat of my brow," said he to his courtiers, thus priding himself on the fruits of his labour, in the eyes of a nobility whom he wished to cure of the Oriental and haughty indolence with which they were imbued. The principle was a good one, but as usual he carried it to an extravagant excess.

With regard to the simplicity of his attire, the following is related in the manuscript memoirs of a diplomatic agent who resided a long time at his court. "On all the solemn festivals, he only wore the uniform of his preobajenskoi regiment of guards. I saw him in 1721 give a public audience to the ambassadors of Persia. He entered the hall of audience in nothing more than a surtout of coarse brown cloth. When he was seated on the throne, the attendants brought him a coat of blue gros-de-Naples, embroidered with silver, which he put on with great precipitation, because the ambassadors were waiting for admittance. During this time he turned his eyes towards the window where the czarita had placed herself to observe the ceremony. Catherine was heard repeatedly to burst out into fits of laughter, as the czar seemed to her to be astonished at seeing himself so finely dressed; and the czar laughed at himself, as also did all the spectators. As soon as the ambassadors were gone, Peter I threw off his embroidered coat, and put on his surtout."

It may well be conceived with what contempt Peter would treat the pompous etiquette observed by his predecessors in the first audience given to ambassadors. Peter received those sent to him without ceremony, wherever he chanced to be; for he said they were accredited to his person, and not to this or that hall or palace. He gave his first audience to the Austrian ambassador at five in the morning, amidst the confusion of setting to rights his cabinet of natural history. Printz, the Prussian minister, had to carry his credentials on board a ship. The czar was aloft, and bawled to him to climb up into the maintop. Printz pleaded his want of practice as an excuse for declining this aerial reception, and the czar came down to him on the quarter-deck.

The ministers of foreign courts, who were forced to accommodate themselves to Peter's humours, found that the honour of sharing his occupations and pleasures was not altogether free from danger. One day he invited some of them to a trip by water from Petersburg to Cronstadt. It took place on board a Dutch vessel, which was steered by the czar. About half-way an ugly squall came on. One of the ambassadors urged him to make for the shore. "We shall all be lost," said the terrified landsman, "and your majesty will have to answer for my life to the king my master." Peter laughed in his face, and replied, "Sir, if you are drowned, we shall all go to the bottom with you, and there will be nobody left to answer to your court for your excellency's life."

The Russians in Peter's time could no longer say: "God is on high, and the czar is far off," for such was the rapidity of his movements, that it seemed to them as if he was everywhere at the same time. The universal impulse which he gave to his subjects he everywhere kept up by his unexpected appearance. In all places and at all times each one looked for his arrival. They felt assured that nothing could escape his experienced eye, and that he would be certain to make himself obeyed. Service about the person of such a monarch could be no sinecure. Whoever happened to be nearest him had to put his hand to anything, no matter what, which the czar required to be done at the moment. His dentchik, or officer in attendance, had often to serve him in lieu of a pillow. He always slept an hour after dinner; when he was not at home, the deck of a ship, the floor of a hut, the bare ground, or now and then straw, when he could get it, served him as a bed. The dentchik had then to lie down, and support his master's head on his belly; and in that position it was his business to remain as mute and motionless as the bolster he represented. Woe to him if he coughed or sneezed, for the czar's waking was terrible when it was not spontaneous; kicks, thumps, a thrashing with a rope's end, or a stick awaited the unlucky man who troubled his repose.

One morning, the czar having come sooner than the senators to the hall where they assembled, he belaboured them all soundly as they entered, with the exception of the oldest among them. It is said, too, that having on some occasions, applied these brutal corrections by mistake, he thought it quite natural to tell the ministers whom he had beaten without a reason, that he would make an allowance for this error the next time that they deserved punishment; and he kept his word in all these instances. All this is but too well proved; and it is also true that he daily, and in public, cuffed or caned his principal officers, for slight faults as well as for serious cnes, almost without discontinuing his conversations with those great personages, and without conceiving that he had degraded them in their own eyes or in those of others! Yet such acts of boorish violence as these are susceptible of explanation; they admit even of excuse in a country which, for several centuries, had known no submission but that of slavery.

There chastisement, inflicted by the hand of the prince, seemed almost a distinction, a it implied a sort of intimacy, a vassalship immediately dependent on him; it was looked upon as a fatherly correction. So much did every one, when in the presence of the czar, consider himself as being in a state of minority, of childhood even; and so absolutely was there between him and his subjects not merely the distance between master and slave, but also that which exists between a man who has attained the age of reason and the beings who have not yet acquired the exercise of that faculty. In his presence all were divested of free-will; he was their living and irrevocable destiny.

From Kelly's *Compilation of Karamsim, Tooke, and Ségur* (London, 1854).

APPENDIX X

In a book published in the last century as the posthumous memoirs of the chevalier d'Eon de Beaumont, there appeared a very remarkable document purporting to be the will of Peter the Great. The notorious d'Eon is known to have gone to Russia in the disguise of a woman, as a secret envoy from France. It is said that his intimacy with the lascivious empress Elizabeth gave him extraordinary opportunities for making important discoveries, and that he transmitted this document to Louis XV, in 1757.

Doubts have been cast upon the authenticity both of the memoirs and of the so-called will; but we are not aware that the subject has ever undergone such a thorough inquiry as it certainly deserves. Independently, however, of its authenticity, the will possesses great intrinsic interest, as embodying principles of action which have been notoriously followed out by Russia during the last hundred years, with such modifications as time and circumstances, and the variations of the European equilibrium have rendered necessary.

The will begins thus:

"In the name of the holy and indivisible Trinity, We, Peter, Emperor and Autocrat of all the Russias, &c, &c, to all our successors on the throne and in the government of the Russian nation.

"Forasmuch as the Great God, who is the author and giver of our life and crown, has constantly illumined us with his light, and upheld us during his support," &c, &c.

Here Peter sets out in detail that, according to his view, which he takes to be also that of Providence, he regards the Russian nation as destined hereafter to exercise supreme dominion over Europe. He bases his opinion on the fact that the European nations have for the most part fallen into a condition of decrepitude, not far removed from collapse, whence he considers that they may easily be subjugated by a new and youthful race, as soon as the latter shall have attained its full vigour.

The Russian monarch looks upon the coming influx of the northerns into the east and west, as a periodical movement, which forms part of the scheme of Providence, which, in like manner, by the invasion of the barbarians, effected the regeneration of the Roman world. He compares these emigrations of the polar nations with the inundations of the Nile, which at certain seasons fertilise the arid soil of Egypt.

He adds, that Russia, which he found a brook, and should leave a river, must, under his successors, grow to a mighty sea, destined to fertilise worn-out Europe; and that its waves would advance over all obstacles, if his successors were only capable of guiding the stream. On this account he leaves behind him for their use the following rules, which he recommends to their attention and constant study, even as Moses consigned his tables of the law to the Jewish people.

Rules

" 1. The Russian nation must be constantly on a war footing to keep the soldiers warlike and in good condition. No rest must be allowed, except for the purpose of relieving the state finances, recruiting the army, or biding the favourable moment for attack. By this means peace is made subservient to war, and war to peace, in the interest of the aggrandisement and increasing prosperity of Russia.

" 2. Every possible means must be used to invite from the most cultivated European states commanders in war, and philosophers in peace: to enable the Russian nation to participate in the advantages of other countries, without losing any of its own.

" 3. No opportunity must be lost of taking part in the affairs and disputes of Europe, especially in those of Germany, which, from its vicinity, is of the most direct interest to us.

" 4. Poland must be divided, by keeping up constant jealousies and confusion there. The authorities must be gained over with money, and the assemblies corrupted so as to influence the election of the kings. We must get up a party of our own there, send Russian troops into the country, and let them sojourn there so long that they may ultimately find some pretext for remaining there for ever. Should the neighbouring states make difficulties, we must appease them for the moment, by allowing them a share of the territory, until we can safely resume what we have thus given away.

"5. We must take away as much territory as possible from Sweden, and contrive that they shall attack us first, so as to give us a pretext for their subjugation. With this object in view, we must keep Sweden in opposition to Denmark, and Denmark to Sweden, and sedulously foster their mutual jealousies.

"6. The consorts of the Russian princes must always be chosen from among the German princesses, in order to multiply our family alliances with the Germans, and to unite our interests with theirs; and thus, by consolidating our influence in Germany, to cause it to attach itself spontaneously to our policy.

"7. We must be careful to keep up our commercial alliance with England, for she is the power which has most need of our products for her navy, and at the same time may be of the greatest service to us in the development of our own. We must export wood and other articles in exchange for her gold, and establish permanent connexions between her merchants and seamen and our own.

"8. We must keep steadily extending our frontiers northward along the Baltic, and southwards along the shores of the Black Sea.

"9. We must progress as much as possible in the direction of Constantinople and India. He who can once get possession of these points is the real ruler of the world. With this view we must provoke constant quarrels — at one time with Turkey, and at another with Persia. We must establish wharves and docks in the Euxine, and by degrees make ourselves masters of that sea, as well as of the Baltic, which is a doubly important element in the success of our plan. We must hasten the downfall of Persia; push on to the Persian Gulf; if possible, re-establish the ancient commercial intercourse with the Levant through Syria; and force our way into the Indies, which are the storehouses of the world; once there, we can dispense with English gold.

"10. Moreover, we must take pains to establish and maintain an intimate union with Austria, apparently countenancing her schemes for future aggrandisement in Germany, and all the while secretly rousing the jealousy of the minor states against her. In this way we must bring it to pass that one or the other party shall seek aid from Russia; and thus we shall exercise a sort of protectorate over the country, which will pave the way for future supremacy.

"11. We must make the house of Austria interested in the expulsion of the Turks from Europe, and we must neutralise its jealousy at the capture of Constantinople, either by pre-occupying it with a war with the old European states, or by allowing it a share of the spoil, which we can afterwards resume at our leisure.

"12. We must collect around our house, as round a centre, all the detached sections of Greeks which are scattered abroad in Hungary, Turkey, and South Poland; we must make them look to us for support, and thus by establishing beforehand a sort of ecclesiastical supremacy, we shall pave the way for universal sovereignty.

"13. When Sweden is ours, Persia vanquished, Poland subjugated, Turkey conquered — when our armies are united, and the Euxine and the Baltic in the possession of our ships, then we must make separate and secret overtures, first to the court of Versailles, and then to that of Vienna, to share with them the dominion of the world. If either of them accepts our propositions, which is certain to happen if their ambition and self-interest is properly worked upon, we must make use of one to annihilate the other; this done, we have only to destroy the remaining one by finding a pretext for a quarrel, the issue of which cannot be doubtful, as Russia will then be already in the absolute possession of the east and of the best part of Europe.

"14. Should the improbable case happen of both rejecting the propositions of Russia, then our policy will be to set one against the other, and make them tear each other to pieces. Russia must then watch for and seize the favourable moment, and pour her already assembled hosts into Germany, while two immense fleets, laden with Asiatic hordes, and convoyed by the armed squadrons of the Euxine and the Baltic, set sail simultaneously from the Sea of Asof and the harbour of Archangel.

"Sweeping along the Mediterranean and the Atlantic they will overrun France on the one side while Germany is overpowered on the other. When these countries are fully conquered the rest of Europe must fall easily, and without a struggle, under our yoke. Thus Europe can and must be subjugated."

From Kelly's *Compilation of Karamsin, Tooke, and Ségur* (London, 1854).

APPENDIX XI

The Ashes of the Tzar

The story of an American consular agent who is said to have taken them from Ekaterinburg in Siberia to Harbin in China

To the Editor of The New York Times: —

"What happened to the ashes? Were they scattered? Or have they been preserved?"

Thus queries P. W. Wilson in his interesting article in the *Times* on the pathetic faith, still maintained by the former Empress of Russia, that Czar Nicholas and his family were not slain, but that they still live and will yet be set upon the throne of imperial Russia.

What really became of the last of the reigning Romanoffs? Where now are their ashes? These questions rightly engage the interest of the world — not only now, but almost from the very day that the curtain seemed to fall upon them at Ekaterinburg. Is there an answer? It may be that I can furnish it. Here are some facts:

I was in Russia (in Moscow and in Petrograd, making my home in Hôtel Métropole in the former city) in 1917 and 1918 — the most tragically important time in all the stirring history of that unhappy country, including, as it did, the closing weeks of the Romanoff dynasty, the revolution (accompanied by the downfall of the Czar), the Kerensky régime and the Bolshevist uprising, followed by the era of great disturbance and uncertainty that still persists.

While in Moscow I became intimately acquainted with an American gentleman who had formerly held important posts in our consular service but who was then connected with a large New York bank in its Russian department.

When the Bolshevists took possession this New York bank was compelled, like all other American financial and industrial enter-

prises in Russia, to close down its affairs and leave the country.
My friend, under these circumstances, cabled to the State Department in Washington, and, in view of his past well-known standing,
as given in official records on file, was made United States Consul
General to Siberia.

Owing to the strenuous conditions then prevailing it proved
impossible for this official to retain a permanent headquarters.
At first his office was in Omsk; but he was compelled to move
gradually eastward, until he found himself in Ekaterinburg — the
city to which the Russian Czar and his family had been removed
by the Bolsheviki from their first place of confinement in Tobolsk.
My friend kept on his slow way until he finally reached Vladivostok
— thence taking ship to this country, which he reached in the
summer of 1920, where he told me this story:

"I personally brought the bones of all members of the former
royal family of Russia out of Siberia in a trunk, together with the
ikons [sacred pictures] and minor articles of jewelry that were worn
by the victims at the time of their assassination. The bones and
personal belongings were delivered to me in Ekaterinburg, after
being removed from the disused mine shaft where the bodies were
flung after the event.

"Those who requested me to care for and remove the bones and
the articles indicated told me that they did so because I was an
American and they felt differently toward me for that reason
than they would toward any European. They added that their
action was not caused by any regret that the Romanoffs had met
what they declared to have been a just fate, but that, as Russians,
they still had sufficient regard for the 'old order' to wish that the
remains of their former rulers should find a more fitting burial place
than the disused mine shaft where they had been flung.

"I accepted the trust; and when I left Ekaterinburg, not long
thereafter, the trunk and its contents naturally formed part of my
consular baggage. As I was bound for Vladivostok, however, and
not to China, I turned over the trunk and contents to British officials
at Harbin, on the Mongolian frontier — taking their receipt —
who were then to forward them to Peking and deliver them to the
Russian Legation in that city. It is there, therefore [remember
that this was in 1920], that the bones and personal relics of the last

of the Romanoffs are at this moment awaiting such final disposal as may be thought fitting at a future time."

It is of dramatic interest that I should add in this connection that the gentleman whom I have quoted, though born in the Middle West, received an important part of his education in one of the great German universities. It was while in a German city, as a mere youthful student, that he, years ago, saw the Czar and his German bride pass through the principal streets, surrounded by a glittering suite.

"I little thought," said he to me, "as I witnessed the 'pomp and circumstance' of that event, that I should live to take the bones of that imperial couple, and those of their children yet unborn, out from the vast land of which they were the autocratic rulers, after their downfall from the very pinnacle of earthly greatness and power. Yet it was so to be."

And so passes the glory of this world!

ARTHUR ELLIOT SPROUL

NEW YORK, *March* 28, 1925

BIBLIOGRAPHY

The material and sources which the author has consulted fall into several categories. The personal testimony and descriptions of eyewitnesses furnished a living documentation which is unusually rich and detailed in its human revelations. Though each version will, naturally enough, bear the imprint of the narrator's personality and be colored by class and private motives, the fundamental issues and the outstanding events are beyond dispute. They have been set forth in the preceding pages in a sequence based partly on the notes gathered by the writer in Russia and elsewhere, and partly on the strength of the published statements of participants and critical observers. It would be impossible, in view of the rapidly increasing literature on Russia, to do more than regard them as the first spontaneous narratives of men and women reacting to the most stupendous emotional and political upheaval of modern times. But scientific evaluation of their intrinsic merits, though it may serve to rearrange or modify certain details, can hardly invalidate the accumulated force of admittedly common elements preserved even in divergent accounts.

For the period antedating the Revolution, recourse was had to standard Russian historians, among whom Klyuchevsky is *facile princeps*. Memoirs and monographs exist in abundance, many of them now assuming a prophetic character. Selected Russian novelists, dramatists, and poets are here included, not in their literary capacity, but as unrivaled portrayers of Russian psychology. Imagination, mysticism, and emotion have played as important a part in Russian history as the political realities. It has been said that Turgenev's *Sketches of a Sportsman* advanced the campaign for the liberation of the serfs more than all the political agitation of the parties. Similarly, Gogol's *Dead Souls* shocked the nation to its core.

Free use has been made of Russian newspapers and governmental publications, for example, the *Riech*, former organ of the Constitutional Democrats; the *Izvestia*, present official organ of the Soviet Government; and the Moscow *Pravda*, journal of the Communist Party. Remembering, however, that "Izvestia" in Russian means *news* and "Pravda" means *truth*, one must recognize the caution and restraint expressed in the warning whispered to foreigners in Moscow: "In *Izvestia* there is no *Pravda*, and in *Pravda* there is no *Izvestia*." These latter sources, however, together with the Red Archives and the publications of the Lenin Institute in Moscow, will find more proper place in a later volume which will deal specifically with the Bolshevist régime.

AKSAKOV, S., *Chronicles of a Russian Family* (New York, Dutton) *Russian Gentlemen; Years of Childhood*. Translated from the Russian by J. D. Duff (London, 1917)

ALZONA, ENCARNACIÓN, *Some French Contemporary Opinions of the Russian Revolution of 1905* (Columbia University, 1921)

ANDREYEV, L., *The Crushed Flower and Other Stories* (New York, Knopf, 1917) *The Seven Who Were Hanged*. Translated from the Russian by H. Bernstein (New York, 1909)

ANTHONY, C., *Catherine the Great* (New York, Knopf, 1925)

ARTSYBASHEV, M., *Tales of the Revolution*. Translated from the Russian by P. Pinkerton (London, 1917)

BADDELEY, *The Russian Conquest of the Caucasus* (New York, Longmans, Green, 1908)

BARING, M., *A Year in Russia* (New York, Dutton, 1907)

BAX, ERNEST BELFORT, *The Last Episode of the French Revolution* (London, Grant Richards, 1921)

BEATTY, B., *The Red Heart of Russia* (New York, Century, 1919)

BEAZLEY, R., BIRKETT, G. A., and FORBES, N., *Russia from the Varangians to the Bolsheviks* (Oxford, 1918)

BECHHOFER, C. E., *Russia at the Crossroads* (London, Keegan Paul, 1916)

BEHRS, C. A., *Recollections of Count Tolstoy* (London, Heineman, 1896)

BELLOC, HILAIRE, *Marie Antoinette* (New York, Putnam, 1925)
The Servile State (London, Foulis, 1912)

BENCKENDORFF, COUNT PAUL, *Last Days at Tsarskoë Selo* (London, Heineman, 1927)

BEVERIDGE, A. J., *The Russian Advance* (New York, Harper, 1904)

BOWMAN, I., *New World* (New York, 1922)

BRAILSFORD, H. N., *Russian Workers' Republic* (New York, 1921)

BRESHKOVSKAYA, C., *Reminiscences and Letters* (Boston, Little, Brown, 1919)

BRÜCKNER, A., *Geschichte Russlands bis zum Ende des 18 Jahrhunderts* (Gotha, 1896)

BUCHANAN, SIR GEORGE, *My Mission to Russia*, 2 vols. (Boston, Little, Brown, 1923)

BUKHARIN, N., *The Economic Theory of the Leisure Class* (New York, International Publishers, 1927)
Historical Materialism (New York, International Publishers, 1927)

BULLARD, A., *The Russian Pendulum* (New York, Macmillan, 1919)

BUNIN, IVAN, *The Village* (New York, Knopf, 1923)

Cambridge Modern History, Vols. IX, X, XI, XII (London)

CANTACUZENE, PRINCESS, *The Russian People* (New York, Scribner, 1920)
Revolutionary Days (Small, Maynard, 1919)

CATHERINE II, *Mémoires de l'impératrice Catherine II*, précédées d'une préface par A. Herzen (London, 1859)

CHEKHOV, ANTON, *Letters*. Translated by Constance Garnett (New York, Macmillan, 1920)
The Cherry Orchard and other plays

CHICHERIN, G. V., *Two Years of Foreign Policy: The Relations of the Russian Socialist Federal Soviet Republic with Foreign Nations from November 7, 1917 to November 7, 1919* (New York, 1920)

COLQUOUN, A. R., *Russia Against India* (New York, Harper, 1909)

CONRAD, JOSEPH, *Under Western Eyes* (New York, Doubleday, Page, 1924)

Constitution of the Union of Socialist Soviet Republics (Washington, Russian Information Bureau, 1924)

CRESSON, W. P., *The Cossacks* (New York, Brentano, 1919)

CROSLEY, P. S., *Intimate Letters from Petrograd* (New York, Dutton, 1920)

CUMMING, C. K., and PETTIT, W. W., *Russian-American Relations, 1917–1920* (New York, 1920)

CURTIN, J., *A Journey in Southern Siberia* (Boston, Little, Brown, 1909)

CUSTINE, THE MARQUIS OF, *Russia* (New York, Appleton, 1854)
La Russie en 1839 (Bruxelles, Wouters et Cie, 1843)

DAVIS, MALCOLM W., *Open Gates to Russia* (New York, Harper, 1920)

DENIKIN, GENERAL A. I., *The Russian Turmoil* (New York, Dutton)

DENNIS, A. L. P., *The Foreign Policies of Soviet Russia* (New York, Dutton, 1924)

DEUTSCH, LEO, *Sixteen Years in Siberia* (New York, Dutton, 1903)

DEUTSCH AND YARMOLINSKY, *Russian Poetry.* An Anthology (New York, International Publishers, 1927)

DILLON, E. J., *The Eclipse of Russia* (New York, Doran, 1918)

DOSTOIEVSKY, F., *The House of the Dead*
The Brothers Karamazov
Crime and Punishment. Translated from the Russian by C. Garnett (New York, 1919)
The Possessed. Translated from the Russian by C. Garnett (New York, 1913)

EASTMAN, MAX, *Leon Trotsky — A Portrait* (New York, Greenberg, 1925)
Since Lenin Died (New York, Boni & Liveright, 1925)

FARBMAN, M., *Bolshevism in Retreat* (London, Collins, 1923)

FIGNER, VERA, *Memoirs of a Revolutionist* (New York, International Publishers, 1927)

FLETCHER, GILES, *The Russe Commonwealth*

Fox, Ralph, *People of the Steppes* (Boston, Houghton, Mifflin, 1925)

Francis, D. R., *Russia from the American Embassy* (New York, Scribner, 1921)

Fraser, John Foster, *Red Russia* (London, Cassell, 1907)

Fülöp-Miller, René, *The Mind and Face of Bolshevism* (New York, Putnam, 1927)
Lenin and Gandhi (New York, Putnam, 1928)

Galitzin, le Prince, *La Russie au XVIII siècle* (Paris, Didier, 1865)

Ganz, Hugo, *The Land of Riddles* (New York, Harper, 1904)

Gerhardi, William, *Anton Chekhov, A Critical Study* (New York, Duffield, 1923)

Gide, André, *Dostoievsky* (Paris, Plon, Nourrit, 1927)

Gide, Charles, *Principles of Political Economy* (Boston, Heath, 1891)

Gilliard, Pierre, *Le tragique destin de Nicolas II et de sa famille* (Paris, Payot, 1922)

Gogol, Nicholas, *The Mantle and Other Stories*
Dead Souls
Taras Bulba

Golder, F. A., *Russian Expansion on the Pacific, 1641–1850* (Cleveland, 1914)
Documents of Russian History, 1914–1917 (New York, Century, 1927)

Goode, W. T., *Bolshevism at Work* (London, Allen & Unwin, 1920)

Gorky, Maxim, *Chelkash and Other Tales* (New York, Knopf, 1915)
Lower Depths. Translated from the Russian by L. Irving (New York, 1912)
My Childhood (London, Werner, Laurie)
Fragments from My Diary (New York, McBride, 1924)
In the World (London, Werner, Laurie)
Reminiscences of Tolstoy (New York, Huebsch, 1920)

Gourko, General Basil, *War and Revolution in Russia, 1914–1917* (New York, Macmillan, 1919)

Graf, H., *The Russian Navy in War and Revolution* (Munich, Oldenbourg, 1923)

GRAHAM, STEPHEN, *The Way of Martha and the Way of Mary*
(New York, Macmillan, 1917)
Undiscovered Russia (John Lane, 1912)
Russia and the World (New York, Macmillan, 1917)
The Dividing Line of Europe (New York, Appleton, 1925)
Through Russian Central Asia (New York, Macmillan, 1916)
GUEST, *The Struggle for Power in Europe* (New York, Doran, 1921)

HALLEZ, T., *Mémoires secrets — Pierre le Grand et Catherine I*
(Paris, Dentu, 1853)
HARD, W., *Raymond Robins' Own Story* (New York, 1920)
HARPER, S. N., *The New Electoral Law for the Russian Duma*
(Chicago, 1908)
HAYES, C. J. H., *A Political and Social History of Modern Europe*
(New York, Macmillan, 1924)
Brief History of the Great War (New York, Macmillan, 1920)
HERZEN, A., *Memoirs.* Parts I–IV, 2 vols. Translated from the
Russian by C. Garnett (New York, 1924)
Du développement des idées révolutionnaires en Russie (Paris, 1851)
HETTNER, A., *Das europäische Russland* (Leipsig, 1905)
HINDENBURG, VON, *Out of My Life* (London, Cassell, 1920)
Aus Meinem Leben
HINDUS, MAURICE, *Broken Earth* (New York, International Pub-
lishers, 1924)
The Russian Peasant and the Revolution (New York, Holt, 1920)
HOFFMAN, GENERAL VON, *The War of Lost Opportunities* (New
York, International Publishers, 1925)
HOWORTH, SIR H. H., *History of the Mongols from the Ninth to the
Nineteenth Century*, 2 vols.
HYNDMAN, H. M., *The Evolution of Revolution* (New York, Boni &
Liveright, 1921)

ISVOLSKY, ALEXANDER, *Recollections of a Foreign Minister* (New
York, Doubleday, Page, 1921)

KALPASCHNIKOV, A., *A Prisoner of Trotsky's* (New York, Doubleday, Page, 1920)
KAUTSKY, KARL, *Letters of Rosa Luxemburg* (New York, McBride,
1925)

KEHLER, HENNING, *The Red Garden* (New York, Knopf, 1922)

KELLY, WALTER K., *The History of Russia, Compiled from Karamsin, Tooke and Ségur* (London, Bohn, 1854)

KENNAN, GEORGE, *Siberia and the Exile System* (New York, Century, 1891)

KERENSKY, A. F., *The Prelude to Bolshevism* (New York, Dodd, Mead, 1919)

The Catastrophe (New York, Appleton, 1927)

KERNER, R. J., *Slavic Europe* (Harvard, 1918)

KLABUND, *Peter the Tzar* (New York, Putnam, 1925)

KLEINMICHEL, COUNTESS, *Memories of a Shipwrecked World* (London, Brentano, 1923)

KLYUCHEVSKY, V. O., *A History of Russia.* Translated by C. J. Hogarth (New York, Dutton, 1913)

KNOX, SIR ALFRED, *With the Russian Army, 1914-1917*, 2 vols. (New York, Dutton, 1921)

KORFF, S. A., *Autocracy and Revolution in Russia* (New York, Macmillan, 1923)

Russia's Foreign Relations during the Last Half Century (New York, Macmillan, 1922)

Die Geschichte des russischen Senats (Berlin, 1913)

KORNILOV, ALEXANDER, *Modern Russian History* (New York, Knopf, 1924)

KOROLENKO, V., *Makar's Dream and Other Stories* (New York, Duffield, 1916)

KOVALEVSKY, M. M., *Russian Political Institutions* (Chicago, 1902)

KRAUSSE, ALEXIS, *Russia in Asia* (New York, Holt, 1889)

KRAVCHINSKY, S. M. (Stepniak), *Underground Russia* (New York, Scribner, 1883)

The Russian Storm Cloud (London, Swan, Sonnenschein, 1886)

Russia under the Tzars (New York, Scribner, 1885)

Career of a Nihilist (New York, 1889)

KROPOTKIN, P., *Memoirs of a Revolutionist* (Boston, Houghton, Mifflin, 1899)

KUPRIN, ALEXANDER, *The River of Life* (Boston, Luce, 1916)

LAMB, HAROLD, *Genghis Khan* (New York, McBride, 1927)

LANIN, E. B., *Russian Traits and Terrors* (Boston, Tucker, 1891)

LASKI, H. J., *Communism* (London, Williams & Norgate, 1927)

LAWTON, LANCELOT, *The Russian Revolution, 1917–1926* (London, Macmillan, 1927)

LEITES, K., *Recent Economic Developments in Russia* (Oxford, 1922)

LENIN, N., "On Organization" (*Chicago Daily Worker*, 1926)
   Collected Works of, *Materialism and Empirio-Criticism* (New York, International Publishers, 1927)
   The State and Revolution (London, Allen & Unwin, 1919)
   Collected Writings of (The Lenin Institute, Moscow)

LENIN, N., and TROTSKY, L., *The Proletarian Revolution in Russia* (New York, Communist Press, 1918)

LEROY-BEAULIEU, ANATOLE, *L'Empire des Tsars*

Letters from Russian Prisons (Documents) (New York, A. & C. Boni, 1925)

Letters of the Tsaritsa (London, Duckworth, 1924)

LEVINE, ISAAC DON, *Letters from the Kaiser to the Tsar* (New York, Stokes, 1920)
   The Man Lenin (New York, Seltzer, 1924)

LORD, R. H., *The Second Partition of Poland* (Cambridge, Mass., 1915)

LUDENDORFF, GENERAL, *My War Memories*, 2 vols. (London, Hutchinson)

LUDWIG, EMIL, *Bismarck* (Boston, Little, Brown, 1927)
   Wilhelm Hohenzollern (New York, Putnam, 1927)

LUNACHARSKY, A. V., *Plays* (New York, Dutton)
   "Report on Educational Conditions" (Translated in part in *Current History*, April 1923)

McBAIN, H. L., and ROGERS, L., *New Constitutions of Europe* (New York, 1922)

McCULLAGH, FRANCIS, *A Prisoner of the Reds* (New York, Dutton, 1922)

MADELIN, LOUIS, *The French Revolution* (New York, Putnam, 1916)

MAISTRE, COUNT J. DE, *Correspondance diplomatique, 1811–1817*. Recueillie et publiée par A. Blanc, 2 vols. (Paris, 1860)

MARX, KARL. *Das Kapital*
   The Communist Manifesto
   Selected Essays

MASARYK, T., *The Spirit of Russia*, 2 vols. (London, Allen & Unwin, 1919)

MASSON, C. F. P., *Mémoires secrets sur la Russie pendant les règnes de Catherine II et de Paul I*, 2 vols. (Paris, 1800)

MAVOR, J., *An Economic History of Russia*, 2 vols. (London, 1914)

MELNIK, TATIANA, *Recollections of the Imperial Family* (in Russian) (Belgrade, 1921)

MEREZHKOVSKY, DMITRI, *Peter and Alexis* (New York, Putnam)
December the Fourteenth (New York, International Publishers, 1925)

MÉRIMÉE, PROSPER, *Demetrius the Imposter* (London, Bentley, 1853)

MILL, H. R., ed., *International Geography* (New York, 1919)

MILYUKOV, P., *Bolshevism, an International Danger* (London, 1920)
History of the Second Russian Revolution (in Russian) (Sophia, 1921)
Russia To-day and To-morrow (New York, Macmillan, 1921)
Essais sur l'histoire de la civilisation russe (Paris, 1901)
Russia and Its Crisis (London, 1912)

MIRSKY, PRINCE, *Contemporary Russian Literature* (New York, Knopf, 1926)

MOUCHANOW, MARIA, *My Emperor* (New York, Lane, 1918)

Nestor, The Chronicle of

NEVINSON, HENRY, *The Dawn in Russia* (New York, Harper, 1906)

Novgorod, The Chronicle of

O'HARA, VALENTINE, and MAKEEF, NICHOLAS, *Russia* (New York, Scribner, 1925)

OLGIN, MOISSAYE, *A Guide to Russian Literature* (New York, Harcourt, Brace, and Howe, 1920)
Soul of the Russian Revolution (New York, 1917)

OWEN, HONORABLE ROBERT L., *The Russian Imperial Conspiracy* (New York, A. & C. Boni, 1923)

PALÉOLOGUE, M., *La Russie des Tsars*, 3 vols. (Paris, Plon, Nourrit et cie, 1922)

PALEY, PRINCESSE, *Souvenirs de Russie* (Paris, Plon, Nourrit et cie, 1923)

PARES, SIR BERNARD, *Russia and Reform* (New York, Dutton, 1907)

A History of Russia (New York, Knopf, 1926)

Cambridge Modern History, Vol. XII, chapters 12 and 13

Reaction and Revolution in Russia, 1861-1909

PASVOLSKY, LEO, *Russia in the Far East* (New York, Macmillan, 1922)

PLATONOV, *A History of Russia* (New York, Macmillan, 1925)

POBYEDONOSTSEV, K. P., *Reflections of a Russian Statesman* (London, 1898)

POLIAKOV, V., *The Tragic Bride* (New York, Appleton, 1927)

POOLE, ERNEST, *The Village* (New York, Macmillan, 1918)

POSTGATE, R. W., *The Bolshevik Theory* (New York, Dodd, Mead, 1920)

PRESNIAKOV, A., "Historical Research in Russia during the Revolutionary Period" (*American Historical Review*, January 1923, pp. 248-257)

Pskov, The Chronicle of

PUSHKIN, A., *Le faux Pierre III* (Pugachev). Translated from the Russian by A. Galitzin (Paris, 1858)

PYPIN, A. N., *The Social Movement under Alexander I* (in Russian)

RADZIWILL, PRINCESS CATHERINE, *Rasputin* (New York, Lane, 1918)

RAMBAUD, ALFRED, *La Russie épique* (Paris, Maisonneuve et cie, 1876)

Histoire de Russia (Paris, Hachette)

RAPPOPORT, A. S., *Home Life in Russia* (New York, Macmillan, 1913)

The Curse of the Romanovs (London, Chatto & Windus, 1907)

REED, JOHN, *Ten Days that Shook the World* (New York, International Publishers, 1926)

RIVET, CHARLES, *The Last of the Romanovs* (New York, Dutton, 1918)

RIVIÈRE, C. DE LA, *Catherine II et la révolution française* (Paris, 1895)

RODZIANKO, M. V., *The Reign of Rasputin* (London, Philpot, 1927)

ROMANOV, NICHOLAS (Nicholas II), *Journal intime* (The Diary of the Tzar) (Paris, Payot, 1925)

ROSS, E. A., *Russia in Upheaval* (New York, Century, 1919)
The Russian Bolshevik Revolution (New York, Century, 1921)
The Russian Soviet Republic (New York, 1923)

RUSSELL, BERTRAND, *Bolshevism: Practice and Theory* (New York, Harcourt, Brace, and Howe, 1920)

SAMSON-HIMMELSTIERNA, VON, *Russia under Alexander III* (New York, Macmillan, 1893)

SCHUYLER, E., *Peter the Great*, 2 vols.

SÉGUR, PHILIPPE PAUL, COMTE DE, *Campagne de Russie*
Mémoires, souvenirs, et anecdotes, avec avant-propos et notes, par F. Barrière, 2 vols. (Paris, 1859)

SELIVANOVA, NINA, *Russia's Women* (New York, Dutton, 1923)

SHELLEY, GERARD, *The Speckled Domes* (New York, Scribner, 1925)

SIMPSON, J. Y., *The Self-Discovery of Russia* (New York, Doran)

SKRINE, F. H., *Expansion of Russia, 1815–1900*.

Slavonic Review (School of Slavonic Studies, University of London)

SNODGRASS, J. H., *Russia* (Washington, U. S. Government publication, 1913)

SOKOLOV, NICHOLAS, *Enquête judiciaire sur l'assassinat de la famille impériale russe.* From the original Russian text published by "Slovo," Berlin (Paris, Payot, 1924)

SOLOVIEV, *History of Russia* (in Russian)

SOLOVIEV, V., *La Russie et l'église universelle* (Paris, 1889)

SOROKIN, PITIRIM A., *The Sociology of Revolution* (Philadelphia, Lippincott, 1925)
Leaves from a Russian Diary (New York, Dutton, 1924)

SPARGO, JOHN, *The Psychology of Bolshevism* (New York, Harper, 1919)

SPENGLER, OSWALD, *Decline of the West* (New York, Knopf, 1926)

SPINKA, MATTHEW, *The Church and the Russian Revolution* (New York, Macmillan, 1927)

STEKLOV, G. N., *History of the First International* (New York, International Publishers, 1928)

STEPHENS, WINIFRED, *The Soul of Russia* (New York, Macmillan, 1916)

STRONG, ANNA LOUISE, *The First Time in History* (New York, Boni & Liveright, 1924)

"Symposium on N. Lenin, A" (*Current History*, March, 1924)

TELBERG, WILTON, *The Last Days of the Romanovs* (New York, Doran, 1920)

THOMPSON, DONALD C., *Donald Thompson in Russia* (New York, Century, 1918)

TOLSTOY, L. N., *Anna Karenina*. Translated from the Russian by L. and A. Maude, 2 vols. (London, 1918)

Resurrection. Translated from the Russian by L. Maude (New York, 1900)

TOOKE, WILLIAM, *View of the Russian Empire from Catherine II* (London, Longmans, Green, 1799)

TORMAY, CÉCILE, *An Outlaw's Diary: The Revolution and Commune in Hungary* (New York, McBride, 1924)

TROTSKY, LEON, *Literature and Revolution* (New York, International Publishers, 1925)

Whither England? (New York, International Publishers, 1925)

My Flight from Siberia. Translated by Malcolm Campbell (New York, American Library Service, 1925)

Lenin (Minton, Balch & Co., 1925)

Our Revolution (New York, 1918)

From October to Brest-Litovsk (New York, 1919)

TURGENEV, IVAN, *A Sportsman's Sketches and Other Tales*

Fathers and Children

TURGENEV, N. I., *La Russie et les Russes*, 3 vols. (Paris, 1847)

VANDERVELDE, EMIL, *Three Aspects of the Russian Revolution* (London, Allen & Unwin, 1918)

VASSILI, COUNT PAUL, *Behind the Veil at the Russian Court* (New York, Lane, 1914)

Confessions of the Czarina (New York, Harper, 1918)

VINOGRADOFF, P., *Outlines of Historic Jurisprudence* (Oxford, 1920)

Self-Government in Russia (London, 1915)

VIROUBOVA, ANNA, *Memories of the Russian Court* (New York, Macmillan, 1923)

VOGUË, VISCOUNT DE, *The Russian Novel* (New York, Doran, 1914)

Voices of Revolt: Robespierre; Lassalle; Marat; Liebknecht; Lenin, etc. (New York, International Publishers, 1927)

WALISZEWSKI, K., *Ivan the Terrible* (London, Heineman, 1904)
Le Roman d'une impératrice (Paris, Plon, Nourrit, 1893)
Le règne d'Alexandre I (Paris, Plon, Nourrit, 1924)
Peter the Great (1897)
WALLACE, MACKENZIE, *Russia* (London, Cassell, 1912)
WALLING, W., *Russia's Message* (New York, Doubleday, Page, 1908)
WALPOLE, HUGH, *The Dark Forest* (New York, Doran, 1916)
The Secret City (New York, Doran, 1919)
WEBSTER, NESTA H., *World Revolution* (Boston, Small, Maynard, 1921)
The French Revolution (New York, Dutton, 1919)
WIENER, LEO, *Anthology of Russian Literature from the Earliest Period to the Present Time*, 2 vols. (New York, 1902–03)
An Interpretation of the Russian People (London, McBride, Nast, 1915)
WILCOX, E. H., *Russia's Ruin* (New York, Scribner, 1919)
WILLIAMS, A. R., *Through the Russian Revolution* (New York, Boni & Liveright, 1921)
WILLIAMS, H. W., *Russia of the Russians* (New York, 1919)
WILTON, ROBERT, *Russia's Agony* (London, Arnold, 1918)
WINTER, NEVIN, *The Russian Empire of To-day and Yesterday* (Boston, L. C. Page, 1913)
WITTE, S. I., *Memoirs*. Translated by A. Yarmolinsky (New York, 1921)
WRANGEL, BARON N., *From Serfdom to Bolshevism* (Philadelphia, Lippincott, 1927)
WRIGHT, G. F., *Asiatic Russia*, 2 vols. (New York, McClure, Philip, 1902)
WRIGHT, RICHARDSON, *The Russians, An Interpretation* (New York, Stokes, 1917)

YOUSSOUPOFF, PRINCE FELIX, *Rasputin* (New York, The Dial Press, 1927)

ZILLIACUS, K., *Russian Revolutionary Movement* (London, 1905)

INDEX

Lightning Source UK Ltd.
Milton Keynes UK
UKOW02f2215030914

238038UK00001B/245/P